When
Descendants
Become
Ancestors

The Flip Side of Genealogy

DAVID A. KENDALL, PHD

BALBOA.
PRESS

A DIVISION OF HAY HOUSE

Balboa Press books may be ordered through booksellers or by contacting:

Balboa Press
A Division of Hay House
1663 Liberty Drive
Bloomington, IN 47403
www.balboapress.com
1 (877) 407-4847

Because of the dynamic nature of the Internet, any web addresses or links contained in this book may have changed since publication and may no longer be valid. The views expressed in this work are solely those of the author and do not necessarily reflect the views of the publisher, and the publisher hereby disclaims any responsibility for them.

The author of this book does not dispense medical advice or prescribe the use of any technique as a form of treatment for physical, emotional, or medical problems without the advice of a physician, either directly or indirectly. The intent of the author is only to offer information of a general nature to help you in your quest for emotional and spiritual well-being. In the event you use any of the information in this book for yourself, which is your constitutional right, the author and the publisher assume no responsibility for your actions.

Any people depicted in stock imagery provided by Thinkstock are models, and such images are being used for illustrative purposes only.
Certain stock imagery © Thinkstock.

Printed in the United States of America.

ISBN: 978-1-4525-2022-3 (sc)
ISBN: 978-1-4525-2024-7 (hc)
ISBN: 978-1-4525-2023-0 (e)

Library of Congress Control Number: 2014948587

Balboa Press rev. date: 08/29/2014

CONTENTS

Part 3

*To the "followers" in the world, whose collective
wisdom far exceeds that of their leaders*

and

*To the humble bridge builders whose life stories link the
generations and contribute to an ever-improving existence*

This inspirational poem addresses the contributions that we as future ancestors can make to our descendants. If the intent of my message could be limited to a short poem, the following one would be my choice.

The Bridge Builder

An old man going a lone highway,
Came, at the evening cold and gray,
To a chasm, vast and deep and wide,
Through which was flowing a sullen tide.
The old man crossed in the twilight dim,
The sullen stream had no fear for him;
But he turned when safe on the other side
And built a bridge to span the tide.

"Old man," said a fellow pilgrim near,
"You are wasting your strength with building here;
Your journey will end with the ending day,
You never again will pass this way.
You've crossed the chasm, deep and wide,
Why build this bridge at evening tide?"

The builder lifted his old gray head;
"Good friend, in the path I have come," he said,
"There followeth after me today
A youth whose feet must pass this way.
This chasm that has been as naught to me
To that fair-haired youth may a pitfall be.
He, too, must cross in the twilight dim;
Good friend, I am building this bridge for him!"

Will Allen Dromgoole
1860–1934

Cover Photo

Genealogy describes the passing of family information from ancestor to descendant, as each generation seeks answers to its heritage by combing through the histories of many previous generations. Information is usually sparse and scattered because, until recently, the world had neither widespread literacy nor relevant technology available to preserve the wisdom of the masses, but that world is changing rapidly, as is our longevity.

Today it is not uncommon for four or even five generations to exist simultaneously. We now have the capability to learn experientially from several at one time, as the cover photograph suggests. This is a family picture taken in 1958, showing a span of four generations. The child is the author's nephew, Keith, now a father and grandfather who emulates the loving attention he received in this picture; the older gentleman is Harry Kendall, the author's grandfather, and, of course, Keith's great-grandfather. At the time of this photo Harry was in his early seventies and semiretired but serving as the town and village of Clayton's (NY) justice of the peace. He died in 1973 in his eighty-seventh year.

Harry's birthparents are unknown; he was adopted into the Kendall family as an infant in 1886. His adoptive father, Eli, passed away when Harry was twelve; shortly thereafter, his adoptive mother remarried and inherited several small children who needed her care.

Perhaps unsettled by the influx, as a young teenager Harry left school and the family household and began life anew. He took whatever jobs were available and eventually became a nomadic sharecropper, a handyman, a construction worker, a boatman, and for many years the caretaker for a wealthy New York City family of an island in the Thousand Islands. His easy manner and personal popularity also earned him the endorsement of both political parties and the position of local tax collector during World War II, and later the aforementioned position of justice of the peace. His marriage lasted nearly sixty years until his wife's death in 1965. He was truly the very quiet but highly respected patriarch of his family.

Harry left behind nothing but memories, all of which will fade with the passing of each new generation. We know little of his essence, his internal makeup, that which defined him—except as we interpreted his behavior. Present and future generations must do better in preserving our legacies. In the cover photo Keith represents what we all are—descendants. Harry represents what we will all someday become—ancestors. It is the end inevitably reached but little appreciated and rarely coveted. In fact, that preordained movement into ancestry is often disregarded and usually feared; we seldom discuss it and frequently avoid such conversations. But it is a noble progression.

Keith and his father, Bob (my older brother who took the picture), consider this photo to be a classic image of intergenerational love and learning at its best—and rightly so. Observe the expressive faces of the young and the old, wistfully and joyfully engaging one another in the present moment, and the gnarled, arthritic hand of a departing past clasping the tiny fingers of a promising future.

More than any other, that picture describes this book!

PREFACE

I spent thirty years in academia but never considered myself an academic. I always felt like an outsider. Having been raised in a small humble village, I wanted to teach adults in a graduate school setting the relationship skills I had learned in my upbringing and in my quest for that essential PhD, but I could not identify with the research-oriented "publish or perish" mentality that led to promotions and salary increases, all too often at the expense of an emphasis on teaching. I wrote a few articles for professional journals—just enough to gain tenure and a moderate promotion—and even began a couple of books with colleagues but could not sustain the focus away from the classroom or my family that the effort seemed to require.

In my determination to help provide society with the best possible professional counselors, my mind kept wandering back to the small rural village in which I was raised and the wisdom of the people who nurtured my growth there. By today's standards they were minimally educated, but I saw them as very genuine and wonderfully caring, in stark contrast to the elite world of college academia, where long-winded rhetoric and competitive sniping were common occurrences, and the human ego was king. Anna Quindlen echoed my sentiments in her essay "Write for Your Life" (*Newsweek* January 22, 2007, 74). Her comment about the substance of corporate prose could just as well apply to much of academia: "Corporate prose conformed to an equation: information x polysyllabic words + tortured syntax = aren't you impressed?"

Retirement in 1998 provided the opportunity to return to my roots and once again engage the culture that I so admired. In my professional career I had rubbed shoulders with the most powerful and successful people in a number of occupations and professional settings, and most were only too willing to discuss their own ascendancy to prominence. Quite often their narcissism was exceeded only by their arrogance, and their wisdom was suspect at best. I longed to hear stories from the meek, the humble, and the ordinary—those whose genuineness was shown through daily behaviors of caring and kindness, but who were not necessarily prominent, even in their own local communities. I wanted to somehow convey to them my appreciation for the culture, wisdom, genuineness, and integrity that they showed in my formative years.

I was given space and support from the Thousand Island Museum in my hometown of Clayton, New York, to host a series of small group meetings where I could convey my message and encourage residents to write stories about their varied life experiences. My attempts failed miserably. While the few people who attended seemed genuinely interested, almost no one returned for follow-up sessions. I tried some outreach workshops in neighboring communities, but results were similar. I also tried both long and short newspaper articles to build interest in my ideas. Nothing seemed to work. My blueprint was flawed. Back to the drawing board!

After some extensive reexamination, I concluded that I needed some form of credibility, some way of conveying that I had an important message to bring to the average citizen in small-town, inner-city, and rural America, and to others who might feel that their life experiences are not worth sharing with descendants. I've spent the last ten years casually reading and gathering information about genealogy, and especially its counterpart, its natural extension, its flip side, where we are the ancestors, not the descendants. This book is the result of my efforts.

Upon return to my hometown, I found that the world of my youth had changed in the forty-plus years I had been away. Modern technology had ended the isolation that I remembered, and most of the adults that I so admired had long since passed on. When I would visit the local coffee shops and return home, my wife would often ask, "Did you see anybody you know?" to which my common response was "Probably, but I didn't recognize them."

Everyone had grown older, but among many there were slight facial and bodily resemblances to past generations that I had known, so I began routinely using the phrases "Are you a native of the area?" or "Did you grow up here?" or "Has your family been here a long time?" or "You look vaguely familiar; your name wouldn't be _____, would it?" These questions often began very fruitful and sometimes entertaining discussions, even when my curiosity was off-target.

Still, there were a number of residents near my age whom I recognized instantly, those whose features had not changed drastically since our childhood days. As I became reacquainted with the village population, and especially with the descendants of families I had known well, I began to realize that while much had changed, a whole lot hadn't! If you believe the well-known phrase "The acorn doesn't fall far from the tree," you will understand. While many new families had become permanent or summer residents in my forty years of absence, and some older families had left for numerous reasons, a core of long-time family residents remained and represented the culture I had remembered.

In my deliberations I have hoped to keep personal biases and opinions to a minimum because changing people's beliefs is antithetical to my message. Nevertheless, some preferences and even prejudices have undoubtedly slipped through on issues where I have been greatly affected in life, developed some expertise, or acquired some knowledge. As with every such book ever written, in many ways this book is about me, the author. It could not be otherwise. Therefore, some sense of my personal background may be very pertinent and is provided in chapter 1. For some who may feel intimidated to even get started on their own life stories, this account may also serve as an initial model.

For centuries famous people have been subjects of biographies and autobiographies, but personal stories written by ordinary, average, common citizens are relatively few. Does this mean that the latter are less capable? Maybe, or perhaps life conditions and circumstances prevented them from showing latent talents and wisdom. Or could it be that those in the public eye have opportunities to show their capabilities on a more regular basis, while most private citizens may have a lot to contribute but are bogged down with the personal details of day-to-day living?

Stand aside for a moment and consider the state of the world today. How well have our political, social, and cultural leaders governed us over past centuries? Might this country and the entire world be better served if we knew the thoughts and feelings of those ordinary citizens who keep them bottled up on a daily basis?

Pulling levers or marking ballots in a voting booth every couple of years is not the same; nor are thoughtless, emotional public protests designed to show power and intimidate those with opposing beliefs. Such behaviors draw attention to problems but rarely offer substantive solutions.

For over twenty years I have begun stories of my life, only to put them aside "temporarily" while I tended to more immediate tasks. I never got back to most of them. Others have told of similar experiences. It is obvious that we need one another's assistance to provide the encouragement and incentives to keep going. Ongoing community support groups are often essential to both initial and continued motivation and are strongly recommended. It is very difficult to stay enthused and focused on transmitting life experiences without the interest, feedback, questions, and reactions of others.

A wise old saying tells us that thousands of libraries are burning down worldwide, every few seconds of every day, with all their contents lost forever. We read about them online and in the newspapers. They're called obituaries! They give us a few facts about the accomplishments and family circumstances of the deceased, but very little about their inner lives, the real essence of their existence. As with an iceberg, that which is exposed to others is but a fraction of the total substance, and each person who dies without leaving records of personal stories of life as she/he has experienced it is a library burning down, full of practical books that could be invaluable, but will never be read.

Of course, new libraries are being built every few seconds as well, and most will soon be filled with thousands of untitled manuscripts. They're called births, and they provide us with hope and energy as we help these new descendants write their own personal history books. Their stories will be different from ours, but no more nor less valuable. Still, those too will be lost unless we as their mentors provide incentives and examples for them to follow.

I want to save my library—and help you to save and preserve yours! I don't know how many ears will be open to these words, but ancient wisdom says that if we sow enough seeds, some will fall on fertile ground. Only time will tell if you, as you're reading this, represent fertile ground or barren rock. The only certainty is that every person and every community has a rich history, much of which will die without everyone's involvement.

David A. Kendall

Acknowledgments

The process of writing life stories is easily duplicated. All it requires is literacy, dedication, and discipline. But contents can never be copied, for they are unique to the writer.

This book is about me. It could not be otherwise. Therefore, I must take full responsibility for its presentation, its flaws, and its ultimate value. I developed, organized, revised, and edited the contents with little outside help, and I did it intentionally. Only my wife read the ongoing saga, making occasional comments that might enhance clarification. The entire process took parts of about ten years and will likely be the only book I'll ever write. But such a project never could have been completed without the support and encouragement of family and friends—and of many acquaintances who probably didn't even know they were helping. There is a danger in naming such people, for there are always some who in hindsight should have been mentioned. Nevertheless, I must take that risk in order to thank those who have been most prominent in their influence or support.

My nuclear family provided me with a set of values that has formed the foundation for my beliefs. Mom and Dad—wherever you are in your deceased ventures—thank you! You taught and modeled respect, empathy, equality, commitment, and especially the best form of self-love, all of which have shaped the core of this book. You also emphasized the importance of strong family ties, and your children have followed suit. My older brother, Bob, and younger sister, Mary, while in different parts of the country and engrossed in their own extended families, have always been supportive of me, as I have tried to be of them. A special thanks goes to Bob for permission to use his prize photograph on the cover, and to his eldest son, Keith, for portraying as a child the symbol of a new generation of descendants. And let me not forget the generations of family ancestors who came before me and prepared my path; someday I hope to meet them in another world. I especially owe a debt of gratitude to my maternal great-grandmother, Dorliska Dean Vincent, whose 1865 diary stimulated my thinking about the flip side of genealogy, about our responsibility to future generations and not just our curiosity about past ones.

Eventually, I had to leave the warm and cozy nest, test my wings, and create a nuclear family of my own. Fifty-two years later, I can still smile and laugh with two wonderful middle-age daughters, Shari and Lori, and a wife, Cynie, all of whom have offered encouragement along the way. I cannot imagine a better soulmate—a wife and mother who taught school, nurtured the girls, and ran the household for over thirty years while I was busy acquiring academic degrees, then teaching college at night, and finally establishing a private practice in personal and relationship counseling. In our retirement, she has remained dependably by my side, managing the household chores as always and encouraging the completion of this book. Cynie, my admiration and gratitude is surpassed only by my undying love for your continuing presence in my life.

Important as family is, life is incomplete without the companionship of close friends. None is closer than Gene and Joyce Moffitt, a relationship covering the past fifty years. Whether skiing, hiking, canoeing, golfing, or just enjoying a game of cards and each other's company around a roaring winter fireplace in your mountain retreat, Cynie and I count the two of you as among our greatest blessings. You have always been there for us whenever we needed support—helping in a household move or educational journey, joining in a stress-reducing recreational activity, or connecting for a casual dinner replete with wonderful conversation. Amid some serious discussions, whenever we meet, we joke and laugh in ways that both reflect and confirm our interminable friendship. I'm most relaxed when in your company, and I cherish you both more than you can ever know.

I find it easiest to write while enjoying quiet noise, and much of my writing has been done in local diners, libraries, parks, and museums. Owners, staff, and patrons have put up with my presence for hours at a time, providing me with space and a pleasant environment, while silently encouraging my efforts. All have been an integral part of this book and deserve recognition: Kathy Danielson at her Lyric Bistro; Lori Durand and her staff at the Koffee Kove; Melissa Hardy, owner of Bella's Restaurant; and Mary Zavitoski, proprietor at The Scoop—all in my hometown of Clayton, New York; the Panera Bread establishment and its engaging manager, John Dillenback, in Watertown, New York; the Hawn Memorial Library in Clayton; the McSherry Library in Alexandria Bay, New York; and the Flower Memorial Library in Watertown; and special attention must be given to the Thousand Island Museum in Clayton, and especially to Sharon Bourquin, head volunteer extraordinaire, whose help and friendship cannot be measured.

Norm Wagner, town and village historian in Clayton, who succeeded my dad in that position, has provided a wealth of knowledge about the area that I had either forgotten or never known. Norm was a boyhood friend with a lifelong devotion to the local residents and has always been available to answer my questions.

In the last section of chapter 3, I have given much-deserved praise to Debbie Dermady, a fifth-grade teacher in the Thousand Island school district. My wife and I have served this year (2013–14) as adoptive grandparents to her class, meeting with them irregularly to share memories of our past and to help them create memories of their own. As retired educators, we have served with and observed teachers of varying abilities and styles. Debbie is without doubt one of the very best, and is truly a master teacher who loves and understands her students. We need more like her!

Two groups that deserve special attention are the Jefferson County (NY) Genealogical Society and Poets and Writers', INK—local associations whose monthly meetings have helped keep me focused. The membership of these groups is composed primarily of dynamic retirees and seniors whose energy and dedication to research, writing, and self-improvement is unmatched and very contagious.

Finally, my thanks to Stephanie Cornwaithe at Balboa Press for her gracious understanding of my situation when I didn't meet self-imposed deadlines. She kept in contact with me every month, accepting my explanations and apologies with a minimum of pressure and a maximum of professionalism. I always knew I could count on her to give me guidance and answer questions promptly.

Most recently, Donovan Gerken at Balboa has answered many queries and shown me how professional line editing could enhance the quality of this book. My initial belief that I could do it myself proved to be naïve. Donovan's low-key and very personable approach conveyed a sense of trust that inspired my confidence, and line editor Larry Dale's comments and suggestions were invaluable in cleaning up the manuscript without attempting to alter the content.

As I'm writing this, I know that there is still much to do with other members of the Balboa staff as this book nears completion. I'm confident that our contacts in the next few weeks, prior to final publication, will be as profitable.

INTRODUCTION

Valuing Our Personal Histories

Congratulations—you're going to be an ancestor (someday). You cannot escape it. Nor can I. Nor can anyone else. That's not necessarily a bad thing, depending on your beliefs about an afterlife, but each body ultimately ceases to exist. We all know that. From the moment of birth each of us begins a journey that must ultimately conclude with our entrance into ancestry. What we don't know (intentional self-destruction notwithstanding) is how or when that journey will end, but the horizontal dash that is commonly placed between birth and death dates on gravestones depicts that journey.

That dash represents innumerable stories about a life that has been lived but tells us nothing about the substance of those stories or the life that created and influenced them. What's more, no one but the deceased individual could ever give an accurate and truthful account of the meanings that life events had for him or her. So, unless the departed person has deliberately preserved some of those stories in her or his own voice or handwriting, they will cease to exist, as will the potential value that such stories might contain for future generations.

What happens at death to our intangible components (soul, spirit, essence, inner nature, core, etc.), if indeed there *are* such components, is purely speculative; we can guess, imagine, pretend, theorize, and believe, but the only scientific certainty is uncertainty! It was rumored that the greatest magician of all time, Houdini, vowed to return to earth with the ultimate truth about afterlife, if at all possible. But if he did return, it certainly hasn't been publicized.

The closest we can come to immortality is through a legacy, stories about our lives that we produce and leave to descendants. It's the most important do-it-myself project that each of us will ever encounter. To ensure accuracy, we must take personal responsibility. If we assign that task to others, surely it will be neglected, misrepresented, or distorted by those who may mean well but could not possibly retrieve our minds or hearts.

Recently I was listening to a news program discussing details of the Boston Marathon bombing during which the younger suspect was portrayed by some acquaintances as an all-American boy who never showed or voiced destructive tendencies, but who must have harbored some such beliefs or ideas not publicly shown. His alleged behavior seemed shocking to many who knew him. But then don't we all keep hidden some opinions, beliefs, ideas, or concepts that we're reluctant to share publicly? The recent demand for "political correctness" has only intensified such reluctance, as harsh social punishment awaits those who refuse to heed this new requirement of democracy.

Even history is undergoing change. Just a few decades ago there was little controversy about the details of history. History was history, dull and boring for most. Today textbook authors are putting many different "spins" on the same historical event, and verbal sparring occurs over the accuracy of various accounts. Even the reported "facts" of current events are suspect, as political forces foist their agendas on a highly informed but often naïve or disinterested public. Questions seldom before considered are now under constant scrutiny.

Who was responsible for which event? How old is the world, and how was it created? When does life begin—at conception, in the womb, at birth? Did the Holocaust actually happen? Was 9/11 a plot of the United States government to justify invasion of the Middle East? Who's responsible for economic disasters and recoveries? Is climate change happening, and what's causing it? There appears to be no end to the topics, interpretations and subsequent controversies. While the questioning of past, present, and future events and their causes and effects can be very healthy and point us in more accurate directions, it has also caused great confusion and frustration. In most cases, truth and accuracy are matters of interpretation and ideology, based on attitudes, beliefs, and concepts already firmly established by subcultural values. Too often the disagreements that result unleash much polarizing heat but very little synthesizing light.

Lost in the morass of such daunting national and worldly issues is the importance of each individual's contributions to the future of humanity. Regardless of political, religious, or cultural affiliations, everyone shares a common denominator. For some unknown or uncertain reason or purpose, by accident or design, we have all been born and raised on this planet. Each of us must decide how we wish to use our remaining existence. For those with a religious outlook, the phrase "God don't make junk" may be personally meaningful as you contemplate the significance of your life activities. For avowed atheists, you may consider yourself an extension of some natural or accidental phenomenon, but your life has still mattered in some way. You are still a link in the continuity of humanity and can decide how you wish to use that power. Whatever you believe about creation, your existence is unique. Fingerprints and DNA attest to that, and that uniqueness is a prelude to your importance and a testament to your legacy! Still, as significant as each individual is, it is precisely our uniqueness that creates a whole lot of problems when it clashes with the uniqueness of our neighbors.

Institutions Are Limited

Ancient civilizations developed institutions and associations to help them cope with these complications accompanying community living. Down through the centuries we have modified those institutions to meet ever-changing needs, but we have not eliminated them. Indeed, we have strengthened or weakened their influence according to cultural dictates. In most of the democratic nations, we have formed governments to protect us, religions to direct us, and schools to teach us. We have then chosen leaders to manage those institutions in ways that provide the greatest good for the greatest number. While many are constantly trying to keep education, religion, and government separate, it is too often a losing battle, as political and philosophical ideologies seem to blend them in ways that precipitate emotional furor and unrelenting opposition.

As you look at our world today and ask yourself, "How well is that working out?" do you like what you see? Did your personal ancestors, the forerunners of our generation, like what they saw? What! You don't know? Why not? Could it be because they didn't leave many clues? They probably lived life aimlessly, as many of us do today, content to exist day-to-day as long as our expectations and demands are reasonably well met by these schools, churches, organizations, and governing units. This perspective needs some adjustment.

With the world teetering on the brink of nuclear disaster, we must think more deeply and broadly about the survival of our planet and humanity. Clearly, the wielders of power in the world have been unable to settle differences among nations peacefully. While the vast majority of people in every culture yearn for nonviolent solutions, governments attack and defend with increasing intensity and terrifying weaponry; but most are paralyzed or tunnel-visioned in their perspectives and need the help of ordinary citizens, even while resisting it. Deadly riots and protests in nearly every country in the world attest to the failures of our institutions to solve the major issues of the day.

Politicians write memoirs in order to preserve their own historical interpretations of these issues and perhaps to show future generations how to avoid their mistakes and capitalize on their successes. Can't we all do likewise? Serious autobiographers may have additional reasons—not all altruistic, of course—for recording their stories. Most can be put into a few categories, however. Egotism, profit, and desires for immortality probably head the list. While initial motives may not matter, internal honesty does if we're trying to be helpful to future generations. There is certainly a place for fictional writing, but deliberately portraying false stories about one's life is dishonest, possibly harmful, and potentially confusing. Only an angry or vengeful person would want to intentionally leave such a false portrayal. Should you then be painfully honest about every aspect of your life? There is no definitive answer to that question. If there are issues you choose not to include (due to embarrassment, privacy, fear, or social inappropriateness), bear in mind that each of us can decide which topics to include in our stories and which ones to avoid.

Some would say, "Why can't we just leave all that to historians?" Keep in mind that most history books only discuss major events, people, and places. They cannot be relied upon to convey the essence of any given community or its inhabitants. If any genealogical history is to be written about small, lesser-known communities and about local contributions to these communities, it will have to come from those of us who are currently living in them. We can do this by reporting on the facts of our life events and by creating our life stories through the avenues of interpretation and perspective. We can make of our lives whatever we wish, because each of us alone determines the meanings of our individual experiences, and many of those meanings change and evolve over time.

Why Should I?

There are basically five reasons why all people should be recording their life experiences and interpretations. The most common and obvious is to provide a path of continuity for family descendants. Up to now, genealogy has been like a hobby for most, pursued for curiosity, family identity, and self-interest. Perhaps of equal importance, but not as obvious, are the other reasons, one of which has been briefly identified in the preceding paragraphs—the education of future generations beyond what our leaders can provide. Other reasons will be mentioned in this introduction and then periodically examined throughout the book.

Models are scarce. There are painfully few recorded legacies that describe in detail the internal lives of our ancestors. Even the few old family diaries that exist are usually filled with vague generalities and boring weather reports. As we read some of these, unanswered questions flood our minds. Where did you go? How did you get there? What did you do? Who did you go with? Where did you live? What did you think? How did you feel? What can I learn from you? How did you experience life? What were your values and religious beliefs? How much schooling did you have? What was your family like? Did you have rules/philosophies to guide you through life? What were your politics? How did you recreate? How would you describe your work life? How much money did you make? How did you spend it? What were your daily routines? And for each "what," "where," and "how" question, there is an underlying "why" that could even be more helpful. We need to answer some of these same questions for our descendants.

As I and many others throughout my own and other communities have become passionate about researching our ancestry, it has become obvious just how little we really know, outside of: names and locations; birth, death and marriage dates; occupations; and occasional stories passed down verbally from generation to generation (the accuracy of which becomes increasingly distorted with each version). But what do we really know about our ancestors as people—their personalities, their beliefs, their likes and dislikes, their friends, their stresses and anxieties, their philosophies and outlooks on life, their hopes and fears, their daily activities, and other attributes that are parts of all lives but rarely discussed? As suggested earlier, an occasional diary or newspaper obituary may have survived, but most likely it was sketchy or written by others.

So we're left with a host of unanswered questions. One hundred, five hundred, one thousand years from now, our descendants will have those same questions and probably even fewer answers—about us—unless we start anticipating their questions and providing and preserving our responses now! We can excuse our ancestors because they didn't have the modern technological, preservation, and research capabilities of today—computers, CDs, DVDs, smartphones, digital cameras, iPads, copiers, and who knows what other phenomena are on the horizon! Even though these conveniences and luxuries have become essentials and necessities in some minds, leading to and resulting in time-consuming complications and complexities of life previously unimagined, we still have much discretionary time to use for activities beyond mere survival! We have everything we need in order to record and preserve our personal, cultural, and community histories. What we have lacked is the awareness, the encouragement, the inspiration, the determination, the support, and perhaps even the caring with which to begin! It's as if we have been programmed to disregard our own importance and to devalue our descendants. Perhaps we have.

Because older generations have longer memories of the past, their involvement is crucial but not sufficient. Support, participation, and encouragement must also come from younger generations—children, grandchildren, and great-grandchildren. Young people may show little interest in the preservation of individual and community histories, but adults know that this will change for many as they age. Therefore, it is imperative that we provide opportunities and conditions that will help them understand and appreciate the ancestral cultures and historical accounts that we as descendants have longed for or absorbed from our ancestors, and are continuing for them—ones that they will inherit and hopefully pass on to their descendants. Only then will this process be replicated for, and by, future generations.

Those of us who have survived the twentieth century and are continuing to live in the twenty-first century represent a gigantic, crucial link between the limited thinking of past eras and the limitless possibilities of an infinite future—whatever form that future eventually takes. We can't leave such an important task in the hands of a few dominant individuals and groups—politicians, historians, academics, celebrities, and industrialists (how many of these do each of us contact on a daily basis?)—while the rest of us, those upon whose backs the rich and famous have always prospered, remain silent and thereby encourage descendants to assume that our lives can be easily understood and transmitted by those who've never walked in our shoes.

A third reason for writing life stories is the help it affords in making sense of our personal existence. Most of us go through life quite haphazardly—day to day, month to month, and year to year—without really connecting the dots. We live in a survival mode. If there is a grand plan for the universe, as most of us apparently believe, we remain unaware or unconvinced of our own niche in that plan. Too many believe that our lives don't really count unless we've done something publicly significant or spectacular. We become members of the "just a" club (a concept to be further discussed in a later chapter), as in "I'm just a housewife" or "just a teacher," or "just a mechanic," or "just a waitress," or "just a felon" or "just a bum," or "just a _____" (you fill in the blank). But if a free and compassionate world for all is ever to develop on this planet, there can be no such label as "just a" applied to any individual; and if there is a loving Creator who rules the universe, as most also seem to believe, the concept of "just a" makes no sense. We all have had—and still have—a significant role to play. Wouldn't it be beneficial and comforting to better understand that role before we pass on?

Life examination can help us with that understanding. But few of us can do this without some assistance. We frequently need encouragement and memory joggers—words, events, objects, comments—contributed by others, which often lead to, "Now I remember; I had forgotten all about that" or "I didn't think anyone would want to know my feelings about that experience." As each of us gains greater access to our memories, we also discover insights with which to make greater sense of our lives. Perspective is a great teacher. It gives us the vision and objectivity with which to put the past in order, and it helps to make sense of experiences that may have seemed like "non-sense" at the time.

The other two reasons for recording our stories are related to creation and earthly accomplishments and will be discussed further in a later chapter. For now, just let us remember that, whatever our life conditions and circumstances, our lives have mattered far more than we might think.

Complications and Challenges

The intent of genealogy is to discover and better understand ancestral connections to our present generation (how they have mattered to us). My vision is for us to expand those connections to future generations by further exploring and discovering ourselves, and by revealing that which we discover to those generations, most yet unborn. It can seem a difficult and elusive task until we understand and engage the process.

It's virtually impossible to write in the here and now of time because our lives are dynamic and ever-changing. As soon as a thought is transferred to paper, it becomes part of our history and is subject to reinterpretation. Memory of an event is similar. While the event is recalled in the present, accurate reflection can never be pure because time, energy, and psychological and emotional distance have intervened, causing alterations in perception and interpretation, however slight they may appear to be. We are continually reframing our experiences because each new one contains remnants of relevant older ones that must now be accommodated. So the memories we leave to descendants are really up-to-date modifications of aspects of our past, and represent only current conclusions, which then rapidly become past ones as new insights and perceptions become available.

Others who then read our stories do so within the framework of their own pasts, a process that adds a further dimension of interpretation. It could not be otherwise, for experiences are always ongoing and dynamic, subject to reexamination at every turn of life. It matters not whether we are participants or observers. Either way, we absorb information and learn anew—behaviorally, intellectually, emotionally, and spiritually. In many cases, these activities overlap and infringe on one another, causing a great deal of confusion on the journey!

Then why bother? The answer to this and similar questions is the primary focus of this book, which emphasizes "why to" rather than the usual "what to" and "how to"—other common considerations when communicating our legacies. Without thorough commitment and dedicated determination, however, what and how will never emerge. Nevertheless, some attention will be paid to the process of finding appropriate topics, and to considerations when expressing their contents. "Who to," "Where to," "When to," and "How much to" are more obvious and can be easily discussed and dismissed in this introduction.

The "who" is everyone who is living and is yet to live in our universe. There are no exceptions for age, location, or living conditions! We can ill afford to eliminate the contributions of anyone. The "where" is everywhere. There are no longer safe havens in our shrinking globe. We're all involved, vulnerable, and responsible. Wherever we are, we must contribute.

The answer to "when" is clear—*now!* Procrastination is a recipe for potential disaster. Danger surrounds us and is closing in. Governments worldwide are fraught with corruption and struggles for personal and political power. Can we really wait, and expect them to clean up the messes that they caused in the first place? Everyone's experiences, ideas, and stories are needed. There can never be too much, for who knows what will be the keys to survival and continued progress? With few exceptions, leaders worldwide and for generations have tried and failed with their grandiose schemes. It's time for the grass roots to take charge! But first we must overcome our reluctance.

We're experts at rationalization, at creating "acceptable" reasons for our behaviors after we've decided what those behaviors are going to be. And how do we decide what those behaviors will be? Usually by the pain/pleasure principle (avoid pain; pursue pleasure), sometimes by the pragmatism principle (whatever works to meet a goal is okay), and often by the "What's in it for me?" principle ("me first"). In spite of our rhetoric about social values, morality, and ethics, except in crisis situations, we often behave selfishly. The "me" generation of the 1960s has not receded; it has multiplied. And in that self-serving here-and-now mode, we also tend to *verbally* denigrate the past ("it's old-fashioned"), worship the present ("whatever feels good, baby"), and ignore the future ("live for today"). Paradoxically, in our *behavior* we also seem controlled by the past that we malign, confused by the present that we adore, and enamored by the future that we ignore. Certainly an unpleasant and bewildering picture for our descendants to view and learn from!

We're Good in a Crisis

But is that who we really are? At our core aren't we much more than consumers, survivors, competitors, and egotists? We may lose our way from time to time when our caring natures give ground to the greed and hostility of our egos, but when the family, tribe, or nation faces attack from beyond that inner circle, compassion and even heroism erupt with tsunamic force.

History is peppered with examples, which may even rival exceptions in significance. Our own national independence, solidarity, and growth stemmed from crises of enormous magnitude. The American Revolution, the Alamo, the Civil War, the Maine, Pearl Harbor, and 9/11 are obvious examples. But so are times of economic hardships, such as the Great Depression; and natural disasters, including earthquakes, hurricanes, and tornados; and national mourning following the unconscionable assassinations of the 1960s.

If exceptions to cooperation and unity do indeed prove the rule, we have plenty of more recent examples to fit that category as well, as the United States today appears to be polarizing on many fronts. Debates about responsibility for the economic downfall and stock market collapse in the fall of 2008, political fights about border and immigration issues, religious and ideological differences over gay marriage, abortion, debt ceilings, gun control, drug legalization, and affordable health care may all serve that purpose. But aren't most of these divisive issues primarily institutional; that is, related to the governmental, educational, social, and theological structures and organizations we've created to help us live together in peace and prosperity? Aren't these mainly issues of social living unrelated to our core essences? Perhaps these contentious glitches remain unresolved because they haven't reached epic proportions in the minds of most citizens. Perhaps we're not yet dysfunctional enough to be concerned. Need we worry? Is it just a matter of time before we reach the point of social explosion?

Teachers and mental health professionals are very aware of the loyalties that exist in even the most dysfunctional families. The victims living there can furiously defend homes that are constantly in a state of disruption, chaos, and violence. Does that also describe our nation today?

Conversely, anguish may be equally intense in families that appear to outsiders to be calm and stable, as witnessed by Edwin Arlington Robinson's poem about Richard Cory (see appendix A). Perhaps this explains our country's status even better. It's often hard to discern internal truth from outward appearances!

Indeed, in both family and country, it is often during relatively peaceful times, when we have no imminent external enemy from which to defend ourselves, that we are most deviously self-defeating in our relationships, thus laying the groundwork for future problems. At such times we can turn our aggression toward friends and family, thereby fostering future resentment and delayed vengeance. In spite of our inconsistency and unpredictability, we are nevertheless resilient, and when we gather together as one body for the sake of emotional, economic, social, and/or physical survival, there is clear evidence that banding and bonding are as powerful ingredients in humans as in pack animals.

If, as suggested, we work quite well together in crisis situations but not so well in peaceful ones, then the obvious solution is to always remain in crisis. Some might say that's exactly what's happening, but it hardly seems a constructive solution for stable and happy lives. A better alternative might be to first recognize that tendency and then to intentionally pursue changes in our thought and behavior patterns. It's a sad commentary on our world that we have to concentrate so intensely on reestablishing caring relationships and human connections that may well be inborn but have been swept away by feeble attempts to use our institutions to improve that which already exists. A song in the musical *South Pacific* recognizes that exact theme. In the midst of the ravages of World War II, Lieutenant Cable passionately describes how, "You have to be taught to hate and fear; you have to be taught from year to year; you have to be carefully taught!"

A few recent findings that seem to substantiate our helpful and caring natures and seek to remedy teachings of hate and fear were mentioned in the *New York Times* on 12/01/09 in an article by Nicholas Wade entitled "We May Be Born With an Urge to Help." In this article he cites recently published studies and books by a developmental psychologist, two anthropologists, a primatologist, and three biologists, all of whom have considered this issue. While many questions still remain, there may be a general consensus that humans are not as bellicose as our actions would often suggest. In his review, Wade concludes,: "Indeed, it is in our biological nature, not our political institutions, that we should put our trust … Our empathy is innate and cannot be changed or long suppressed." Then, quoting Dr. Frans de Waal from his book *The Age of Empathy*, Wade emphasizes our innate cooperative tendencies: "I'd argue that biology constitutes our greatest hope. One can only shudder at the thought that the humaneness of our societies would depend on the whims of politics, culture, or religion."

In a somewhat paradoxical manner, anthropologist Lawrence Keeley, Wade continues, "writes in his book, 'War Before Civilization,' that, 'Warfare is ultimately not a denial of the human capacity for cooperation, but merely the most destructive expression of it.'" In other words, we quite naturally band together for protection, socialization, and sustenance (Isn't that why we create social, political, educational, and religious institutions?), but sometimes it gets out of hand, and we go too far!

The antidote, then, means "unlearning" many personal and social attitudes that divide us by class, race, religion, gender, culture, and material possessions. But it also means broadening our horizons to include betterment of the species. Parents naturally want their children to have happy, productive lives—as good as or better than what they've experienced. Is it too great a mental jump to include in those desires all future generations in all countries and all cultures? Is it asking too much to include the children and descendants of neighbors in our hamlets, villages, towns, and cities? Is it too taxing a burden to act now, in order to take an active part in human progress long after our deaths? Is our response to these questions, "How can I help?" or "I can't be bothered." The answer to these questions may be found in how we view ourselves.

Plan of the Book

Part 1, which follows, provides a foundation of inspiration and motivation upon which all else is built. Without knowing why each of us can and should contribute to our descendants and our culture, country, and planet by recording stories of our lives, and how we're equipped to do so, few will even begin. Somehow, we seem to have overlooked that fundamental question of why, or to have assumed that the answers were self-evident. But the main obstacle to writing our life stories is that we don't know why this might help or be useful, and if we don't have a "why" for what we do, there is little likelihood that we will commit our time, efforts, and resources to such tasks. If we do have a passionate why for doing something, however, there is very little that can hold us back!

In chapter 1, I have provided a summary of many of the influences that have led me to write this book, including some of the contributions and limitations of traditional education. Chapter 2 describes why the input of every citizen matters and why life-story writing is not that difficult. Chapter 3 asks you to examine the nature of your life stories and contributions in order to maximize your efforts with the least amount of personal discomfort and the most amount of pride and success, including why our institutions of government, religion, and education cannot tell our stories, and why we need a do-it-ourselves mentality. Chapter 3 also describes specific roles that each of us "ordinary" people can assume.

Chapter 4 explains some of the problems inherent in the communication and preservation of oral history and the usefulness of putting stories in writing, while Chapter 5 describes the obstacles to be overcome by those involved in this endeavor. Chapter 6 suggests guidelines for discovering topics to write about, and chapter 7 concentrates on ways to write stories that will be most helpful to our descendants.

Chapter 8 challenges readers to access their own potential by looking at the origins of our attitudes, beliefs, and concepts, and questions the viability of some of our most cherished institutions. Chapter 9 delves into the basic philosophies of life that earthlings have developed and encourages readers to consider how those philosophies may impact interpretations and resulting stories. Finally, Chapter 10 looks at the broader picture of our universe and how this knowledge might influence the accuracy of stories we leave for posterity.

Part 2 contains examples of stories from my own life that correspond to the ideas and suggestions that have been imparted in earlier chapters, while Part 3 challenges each of us to redefine real love as connecting and sharing with one another and with future generations via our inner essence and being. Emphasis is on our innate goodness and how the unproven concept of original sin has become a self-fulfilling prophecy, causing us to fight needlessly both among and within ourselves.

Thoughts/Activities to Consider

1. Someday you're going to be an ancestor. Beyond the obvious, what does that certainty mean to you?

2. How much do you know about your personal ancestry? What more would you like to know? What motivates (or not) your interest in it?

3. Which of the reasons mentioned for recording your life experiences makes most sense to you? How do you account for your answer?

PART 1

CHAPTER 1

Connecting Means Sharing

Descendants Become Ancestors

While the search for family roots may be somewhat ingrained, the intense interest in genealogy that has developed and multiplied in recent years is largely due to explosions in both technology and research. The influx of personal computers on American society has spurred an unprecedented market for historical research. This demand for knowledge about family ancestors has led to the development of numerous websites, with researchers scurrying about to provide bits and pieces of data to continually satisfy all levels of genealogists.

What is often forgotten in this flurry of activity for ancestral knowledge is our own responsibility for keeping it going! Excited about the prospect of learning more about deceased relatives, we fail to plan for the day that we too will be added to that list.

Of course, this neglect is not universal. I have seen some marvelous life story accounts, numbering one hundred or more pages, carefully bound or placed in protective notebooks and intended primarily for family viewing and reading. In contrast, many consciously consider such endeavors to be frivolous, sentimental nonsense and a complete waste of their time.

Though the former group may profit from further encouragement and from some of the background material in this book, they have already "paid forward" their dues as the ancestors to coming generations. Their task is now expanded and modified. Above and beyond continuing to write their own ongoing stories, they can act as inspirers and mentors to all those who have not yet told their stories but silently might wish to do so. Perhaps they could even influence those skeptics who might never initiate story writing but might respond to the urging and nagging of friends and relatives.

However, this book is intended primarily for the huge majority of citizens in between these two extremes—those who value telling their stories but have not done so, those who have thought about it but are yet to begin, and those who have started and stopped, perhaps several times. While some of these may yet remain unwilling to actually write anything, they might be persuaded to verbally record their stories, if convinced of the importance.

My parents fit into this in-between group, so my brother and I videotaped nearly four hours of their life stories in the mid-1990s, a few years before their deaths at ages eighty-six and ninety-two. We have since transferred those four hours onto DVDs, which have been copied and made available to relatives for safekeeping. This procedure represents but one example of overcoming an initial reluctance to share life stories. Such stories can then be kept within the family or shared publicly at a later date, perhaps as a gift to a local museum.

Though older adults have perspectives on life not available to younger generations, children and teenagers should also be encouraged to contribute their ongoing experiences. Wouldn't most of us love to read the journals and diaries of our great-great-grandparents when they were in their youth? What a treasure that would be—not only to view the substance but also to have access to their thought processes, styles of communication, educational levels, daily activities, health issues, career aspirations, and so on! We adults can encourage new generations toward these activities, both by our enthusiasm and our modeling behavior.

Getting to Know My Initial World

It would be hypocritical of me to encourage readers to record life stories, while remaining silent about mine. Like everyone else, I am a product of genetics, education, life experiences, environmental influences, personal interpretations, and acquired beliefs—all of which have combined to shape my ongoing aspirations, behaviors, and attitudes. These are what make you and me different from one another and yet intrigued to discover not only our differences but also our similarities. **Sharing lives and stories is the essence of existence. It's what makes life meaningful. It's what connects us. It's how we learn from one another.**

Born during the Great Depression and growing up during the 1940s in a small village in a rural, economically depressed summer resort on the Canadian border in northern New York State, I was both protected and insulated from the massive post-World War II changes occurring in the big cities.

One hundred miles to the south was the nearest sizable city—its two TV stations unable to transmit clear images to our few well-to-do citizens, despite their oversized roof antennas and state-of-the-art seventeen-inch monitors. I never saw a TV set until I became a teenager, and then there was as much snow on the screen as there was on the ground outside. We got our news primarily from three sources: the regional newspapers to which nearly everyone subscribed, the radio newscasts of reporters such as Eric Severeid, Douglas Edwards, and Edward R. Murrow, and the Movietone and RKO Pathe news clips at the local movie theater prior to the showing of the feature film. Some of the news, of course, was weeks old by the time it got to us.

New technology was virtually nonexistent in our village. Phone calls were still patched in by live operators in a small building on the village waterfront, and many times I would have a short conversation with one of them, the mother of a friend, after I heard her familiar voice, "Number, please." Nor was it unusual to lift the receiver and listen in on conversations of others on the party line. Today such eavesdropping would be considered a terrible infringement of privacy, but back then it was merely an accepted nuisance and inconvenience. Of course, there were no computers, copiers, tapes, CDs, DVDs, video games, cell phones, digital cameras, iPads, iPods, or other conveniences we now take for granted.

Few families had automobiles, and none had more than one. Doors were left unlocked at night because crime was rare. Our tiny village jail in the middle of town, when in occasional use, housed mostly weekend drunks "sleeping it off" until they could be driven home by the community's lone policeman. Saturday nights might occasion a few raucous parties, but pews in the village's four churches were generally filled on Sunday mornings with repentant sinners.

By the accounts of many big city folk, we were backward and primitive. But that's not what I perceived. I saw a simple but caring community where people looked out for one another. I saw intact families where marital commitment was far more than a ceremony or piece of paper. I saw (and experienced) kids being kids, where we made up our own games and rules—with adult knowledge and permission but without adult interference.

Yes, there was a subtle pecking order in the community, especially between the haves and have-nots, though there were few of either in the extreme. Some bullying did exist in the schools. There was a distinct, yet vague, intolerance among the churches, especially between Roman Catholics and Protestants, but that was at the adult level; we children seldom knew the difference, or cared.

In spite of these underlying dynamics, most of us thrived in that environment. Yes, the school dropout rate was high as the culture and economy forced many students to help feed their families, and fewer than 20 percent of graduates went on to college. Most stayed in the area, married, worked, and raised families, many of whose descendants are still solid contributors to the community.

As early as elementary school, as I began reading about the violent horrors of ancient worlds and the ravages of World War II (I was eight years old when that war ended), I daydreamed about becoming president of a United World and ending all the senseless sparring and killing. While I engaged in a few harmless childhood tussles myself, I only remember one short-lived fight. Certainly my size helped, as I was physically larger than most of my male classmates. Still, I never wanted to fight and usually found a way to avoid that means of settling arguments.

Academics came easily to me in our small K-12 centralized school, and I did well in all subjects, though my favorites were social studies and English. While I was more interested in athletics than academics, my occupational goal of somehow promoting peace in the world kept gnawing at me behind the scenes. Though the Great Depression of the 1930s, among other family tragedies, had denied both my parents a desired first-generation college education, further schooling was an unspoken expectation for their children. My continuing interest in history and government influenced my college major, and my specialization quite naturally was international relations.

So I went to college—not just any college, but a huge Ivy League university jammed with great scholars from large city high schools. I felt lost and misplaced. I knew I didn't belong; I just didn't fit in. Athletics had always been my fallback activity, but I had broken my leg in senior year football, and it was still painful, so I couldn't compete. I tried baseball, but my skills in that sport were marginal at best. I had no money, and I was clearly overmatched—academically, socially, athletically, and economically. So I isolated myself and studied—and studied—and studied! By sheer perseverance I managed to last four years and graduate, albeit in the bottom quarter of the class.

I still had dreams, but reality now dominated desire. Upon graduation, I had no money, no permanent job, no prospects, and lots of debt. I had been accepted at the American Institute of Foreign Trade in Arizona for graduate study but could not even afford travel costs, much less tuition and living expenses.

I was not at all interested in teaching, but teachers were in demand and, through a series of circumstances in late summer, I was offered a last-minute job in the same K-12 school from which I had graduated four years earlier. Even though I had not been trained as a teacher, I grasped the opportunity to make some money and begin a life of relative independence. To my surprise, I actually enjoyed the experience, and my future was altered forever.

My Vision Expands

I began to realize that each of us is a teacher, whether professionally trained or not. We cannot escape that role. Like it or not, we are all role models. Others learn from our behavior whether or not we desire that outcome. And not only do we teach our contemporaries, but we are also links between our past and our future. We are the genealogy of our offspring. We are the lineage and roots of the yet unborn.

As we research our own ancestors and mourn the lack of information available to us, we forget that we are the future ancestors of our descendants. And if we don't leave to them the kinds of information about our lives that we crave to know about our own forefathers, then we are merely perpetuating the problem. The only solution is to begin recording our experiences, to show the world how our lives have unfolded, and to do it with intention.

We cannot accurately accomplish this goal without understanding our own past influences, present circumstances, and future desires. We cannot adequately comprehend our own existence or proclaim to coming generations life's processes and our conclusions without examining our own life experiences. In simpler terms, understanding our personal journey—whatever it may uncover—is essential to fully understanding ourselves and to teaching our descendants about life. We must remember that our stories and experiences become part of their heritage.

I had only been teaching for six months and was just starting to settle into a comfort level when I received a mandated invitation from Uncle Sam asking me to serve him, so I immediately joined the Army Reserves in order to limit my initial active duty to six months rather than two years. Though upon termination of active duty it meant attending weekly meetings and two weeks of summer training for the next five and a half years, at the time that option seemed more attractive, or perhaps less invasive. In retrospect, my vague dreams were becoming a bit clearer, but I had developed absolutely no plans to implement any of them. I remained lost.

My eight weeks of basic training began in late June at Fort Dix, New Jersey, and continued on to Fort Gordon, Georgia, where I received my first cultural jolt. Upon arrival at the stopover Atlanta airport (my first airplane ride) in September 1960, I found myself staring at signs I'd never seen before—signs of racial separation and discrimination.

Prior to that time I'd been exposed to only a few African Americans (none in my home village, and only a few at the university), except during the basic training I'd just encountered at Fort Dix. I'd never seen forced separation of seating areas, dining areas, restrooms, or drinking fountains—and I cringed at what I saw. As a history student, I knew all about the Civil War and its remnants, but knowledge is far different from experience.

Both at Fort Dix and Fort Gordon, most of my classroom instructors were white and college-educated, while my field trainers were African American and noncollegians. Yet, in many cases, I found the integrity and wisdom of the latter group to be far superior. As I reflected on my small-town roots and on the many relatively uneducated people who had shaped my environment and prepared my path, I saw that same integrity and wisdom.

For over fifty years that incongruence has gnawed at me. So many "ordinary" people, with so much to offer present and future generations, and so few writing down and preserving their stories! And elsewhere, so many highly educated, powerfully positioned people making decisions from lofty pedestals for a populace they could never know and whose lives were totally different.

Ironically, I would come to join that elite group, though I never identified with them in my heart. I always felt like an outsider in academia. While certainly motivated to improve my life circumstances, I remained inspired by those who had nurtured my growth, those who had so much to contribute but were largely silent, those ignored by the outside world.

Worse yet, too many of these villagers seemed to believe that they were indeed insignificant or trivial, with little influence outside their immediate locale. Convinced of their relative unimportance, congruent behaviors usually followed. Experience taught me that my observations were not isolated instances, that such were the results whenever and wherever affluence and other indications of success were absent, and in some cases where they were present.

Since I was also afflicted with some of the same thought processes, I first had to heal myself. As I improved in my own mental and emotional strength, it fostered my desire to teach others about recognizing their own value and about relating more productively both to one another and to the outside world—issues I had observed in both adults and children and struggled with many times in my own development. But the entry-level education for my eventual goal was a PhD.

I finished my active army obligation in December 1960, and decided to use the following semester to attend graduate school and finish my master's degree, which I had begun during my one year of teaching. During that unsettled time, I recall a conversation with a friend who advised me that I could get my educational master's degree in one of three areas—classroom teaching, administration, or guidance counseling. The prospect of spending a lifetime in a public school classroom was not appealing, nor was sitting behind a desk dealing with budgets, discipline, PTAs, boards of education, and the like. I knew nothing about school counseling, as it had been virtually nonexistent in my educational experience, so I chose that track by eliminating the other two.

Frankly, most of my courses in that curriculum were dull and boring, but a summer program at a distant university provided a new and exciting perspective as to what school counseling could become. In 1964, for the last two courses in my program, I attended an NDEA (National Defense Education Act) Counseling Institute at Rutgers University, and was mentored in a more personal, developmental type of counseling that transcended the traditional advice-giving, standardized testing, career-oriented, and informational guidance activities common in most schools.

As my enthusiasm grew, I looked for other innovative counseling programs to attend and found a full-year post-master's degree institute at Portland State College in Oregon. So my wife and I (we had been married in 1962) trekked across the country for the school year 1965–66 where I had a marvelous hands-on experience in family group counseling—learning how schools could facilitate domestic communication in an era of increasing family turmoil and disruption. Only later in life did I begin to realize that my childhood dreams of promoting peaceful solutions to world problems were indeed to be implemented on a smaller scale, within the school, family, and community.

Disillusioned but Determined

Armed with a vibrant new sense of direction I returned to the public school counseling position that I had acquired in western New York State following my active military service, determined to put my new skills to work. Unfortunately, most of my fellow educators were not so inclined, and my ideas met with great suspicion and resistance from classroom teachers, administrators, and especially other counselors who had been educated in more traditional ways. Parents and students were far more receptive, but school personnel seemed to view this extension of services as unnecessary, frightening, and dangerously intrusive to family and community life. Without the internal cooperation and approval of the schools, I could do little to implement significant change. After three years of increased resistance, I decided that I needed to move in a different direction— toward teaching new counselors that they could have a far greater impact on student lives than just steering them toward jobs and colleges.

Call it fate, luck, destiny, or Creator intervention, a nearby college was just about to begin a new master's degree program in counseling and asked for my help. This led to a full doctoral scholarship to a major university and a verbal commitment to hire me full time at the new program upon completion of my degree. The next thirty years were spent with a few like-minded colleagues implementing an innovative, nationally recognized program that turned out hundreds of counselors, not only for schools but also for agencies, community centers, colleges, and private practice. In addition, I was able to establish my own part-time private practice working with families, marriages, and groups to help them reconcile their differences in more productive, nonviolent ways.

In each of these venues, I always found myself believing more in the abilities of students and clients than they believed in themselves. I pushed hard to get their best and in my academic classes was often referred to as the "iceman" because of my tenacious and sometimes dispassionate efforts at getting results, at instilling a sense of competence and influence among those who too often seemed to consider themselves "average" or below.

Today I am still enchanted with the wisdom of the masses and disenchanted with the collective efforts of our state and national leaders to resolve major issues. As author Jim Wallis and others have written, almost all of the greatest achievements in history have come from an uprising of the masses, which eventually get fed up with political incompetence. If future generations are to survive and thrive, we need the accumulated wisdom of those masses to be recorded and preserved. As these pages will detail, everyone should be involved. There is no one whose voice is unimportant, but there are many who cannot accept their own significance in a world that seems not to believe in them, or not to care.

To the extent that we create and absorb the belief that we must leave the transmission of our lives and culture to the academics and professional experts, we demean and discredit our own lives and those of our neighbors. Certainly, advanced knowledge in any field of endeavor can be useful and is sometimes essential. But it should be noted that public education emphasizes knowledge, not necessarily wisdom, ethics, morality, or common sense, all of which are essential to the appropriate application of knowledge. In addition, educational institutions at every level have become more political lately, too often using the classroom as a subtle propaganda venue and sometimes promoting ideologies and behaviors alien to parental and student values.

However, in a world as educated as ours, basic knowledge such as reading, writing, math, science, and history can usually be taught at home as the significant rise in home schooling can attest. Peripheral studies such as art, music, home studies, industrial arts, physical fitness, and social skills can also be learned at home—sometimes more effectively—through spontaneous field trips, collaboration with other families, online instruction, and the use of public and private agencies. In addition, education can be more flexible and ongoing at home without the usual 8-4, Monday-Friday, September-June rigidities of an institution.

Perhaps most important, children in their formative years can learn the educational values of their parents, while parents need be less concerned about their children being taught by poorly trained, insensitive, or incompetent teachers—tenured for life and supported by powerful unions with political agendas—over which they have little control. Few would argue the premise that all schools (not unlike businesses, industries, and governments) make mistakes in hiring practices, and the recent trend toward better evaluation processes is long overdue, though in its infancy. Nevertheless, dire concerns about public education remain—concerns that an increase in spending will never eliminate!

Schools, of course, do offer a standardized and convenient means for society to educate its children without much parental involvement and so serve a purpose for overburdened or uninformed parents. Time is the critical variable for most parents, though, not ability. Through our tax dollars we pay others to educate our children just as we privately pay others to repair our houses, build our autos, grow our food, and service our appliances. In past decades and centuries, our ancestors were multitaskers in their daily activities and were far more self-reliant than we are today. But many were uneducated or illiterate and so could not teach their children basic academic skills.

Today these roles are reversed. Thanks to universal education, most of us are now more capable of educating our children in basic curricula but less competent in repairing and installing items around the house. We use our brains more and our brawn less. Yet we still hand over the transmission of our lives and culture to those who have sheepskins or social prestige.

We Are All Wiser Than Our Minds

The heading for this section is actually a quote from the works of psychologist, therapist, teacher, and author Carl Rogers. Because I was often quoting his philosophy in the graduate classes I taught, many years ago one of these classes had the saying framed and presented to me at semester's end, and now, in retirement, it hangs on my home office wall—a reminder to anyone who carefully analyzes it that we learn far more than we're taught, and we know far more than we think. Yet we live in a put-down society where academics are emphasized, dropouts are degraded, and folk wisdom is ignored. Somehow that's supposed to motivate us toward greater academic learning, but it doesn't. Too often it just reinforces the doubts about our competence that most of us secretly harbor, anyway.

But who of us could not—if we had to—teach our children basic academic skills? Who of us could not teach our children to read? In fact, many of us do. Not as efficiently or even as effectively perhaps as college-trained teachers. But definitely—and without as many of the aforementioned troublesome side effects that have accompanied traditional education: values alien to parental wishes, bullying, social difficulties, gang development, harmful comparative strategies, self-confidence issues, political bias, substandard teachers, and propaganda unrelated to basic education. Most recently, even childhood safety has become a major issue, highlighted by the tragic deaths at the Sandy Hook elementary school in Connecticut. Meanwhile, our national Congress and various state legislatures trade arguments and pass laws that deal primarily with the means of social violence but rarely with its causes.

That being said, this is not a treatise against traditional education. That is not my purpose. Institutional education is what it is and will continue to develop and change according to our desires and mandates as we vote on the decision makers in the democratic process. My point is that we've purchased a bill of goods about ourselves and about education—a pack of lies or half-truths at best—that we have then generalized into believing that only highly educated academics, high-ranking politicians, famous people, or professional experts are capable of providing cultural contributions of historical significance to future generations.

What we really need is the wisdom and common sense to apply learning appropriately, attributes often missing in educators and legislators who are primarily dispensers of knowledge and creators of laws—much of which is suspect at best. As Gregg Braden has recently written in his book *Deep Truth*, much of what is being taught in the name of science is inaccurate anyway. Citing an eight- to ten-year gap between key scientific discoveries of the last several decades and their use in the classroom, he concludes: "This means that we're placing the hopes, trust, and promise of our future in the hands of young people who are learning science based upon obsolete beliefs" (Braden 2011, 13).

The premise that only the most highly educated or successful among us can contribute significance has unfortunate implications for the lives and legacies of every member of society and for those of our descendants, as will be explained in these pages.

I am both amused and awed as I review the developments in my life. I have not saved the world as I had hoped in my childhood. In fact, the world has probably gotten worse. Certainly it has become more dangerous and less predictable. Like many naive youth I had grandiose ideas and solutions, but along the path of life most were derailed or obliterated, and I had to adjust my goals. Nevertheless, without my conscious intent the theme remained intact. I wanted to bring nations together in peace, but settled for more attainable outcomes. My overall impact may not have been as far-reaching, but it's been valuable to a few. My life has mattered to some, and I have stories that need to be told, for those stories may well matter to future generations.

What Really Matters?

Recently I was reminded of the story about a couple walking along the shore sidestepping a quantity of shellfish that had been beached. As they walked, one picked up an occasional shell and tossed it back into the ocean. Observing this behavior, the companion commented, "You're wasting your time. There are too many of them to matter." The Good Samaritan smiled as he picked up another one and tossed it into the water. "Mattered to that one," he said.

Likewise, each of us has stories to tell, and we cannot know which ones we toss out into the ocean of life will matter the most to those who hear them. But if we leave them on the shore to die, they surely will. Stories contributed by the least of us may matter the most to future descendants and generations. I am continually inspired when I read news stories about the wonderful accomplishments of the children and grandchildren of maligned villagers and subsistence farmers I remember in my youth—people who were poor economically, academically, socially, and culturally. We just don't know how the life stories of us "commoners" are going to impact the future. Our task is only to provide them.

Perhaps due to my Christian upbringing, I have always had a strong sense of right and wrong and a dominating moral conscience. To be completely accurate, my sense of wrong has been far stronger than my sense of right. I usually know if a thought or action is wrong, but I have much less certainty of what is right, except that it is seldom the opposite of wrong. Examining Christian philosophy more thoroughly than ever before has certainly helped, but translating two-thousand-year-old spiritual wisdom into modern culture, where "feel good" and "anything goes" seems to trump "be good" and "obey God's commandments," creates many internal and social conflicts in a free society such as ours. And all too often I have compared myself to other people's behaviors, rather than to higher standards. In the former comparison, my ego considers me a giant, while in the latter my conscience convinces me that I'm only a fledging. I have such a long way to go in self-discipline, spiritual understanding, and initiative taking. And while my heart feels very patient, compassionate, and open to others, too often warmth, friendship, and love are not communicated—even to those who know me best.

I was blessed at birth with many assets—a loving and stable family, a competent mind, a sound body, and a moral upbringing. As I developed, though, I acquired many of the unfortunate liabilities associated with social interaction—fear, confusion, lack of confidence, and hidden anger. These assets and liabilities traded places of dominance from time to time, but eventually I learned to lean on my strengths—academics and athletics—and to retreat from my weaknesses—socialization and intimate relationships. I began to rely on myself more and to trust others less and, consequently, became quite withdrawn.

But there was also a good side, because the challenges I faced opened up opportunities that I might not otherwise have considered. Only in hindsight have these dynamics become clear. Relying primarily on average brainpower and reasoning ability, common sense, intuition, and human instincts (all gifts from the Creator), I developed above-average listening, writing, and observation skills;

attitudes of respect, empathy, acceptance, and compassion; sensitivity toward mental, emotional, and physical pain in all living things; an ability to see beauty in both life and death where others do not; and subtle insights into the consequences of behavior—all attributes that led me ultimately into a career of teaching and counseling.

But, as I have explained, the route was neither a straight one nor an easy one. Still, as with every other person who has ever lived, it left me with lots of stories about life to tell to future generations.

Thoughts/Activities to Consider

- What about life do you think your descendants could learn from you?
- If you were to write a synopsis of your life under the heading "Getting to know my Internal World," what would you emphasize?
- Considering where and when you were raised, and the person you've become today, how would you connect the dots?
- What was your biggest early cultural jolt?
- If you (could) home-school your children today, what part of your curriculum (would/do) you emphasize most? Why?
- How are you "wiser than your mind?" Explain.
- What about life matters most to you? Write a story about it.

CHAPTER 2

Why Bother?

Finding a Purpose

Most of us are intimidated when asked to write a life story. Images of famous people writing full-length autobiographies conjure up self-doubt, skepticism, and fear—and a whole lot of work. What do I have to offer? Who cares about my life? Where would I find the time? How would I get started? What would I write about? How would I write it? Who would read it? What would I do with it?

These and similar questions provide stumbling blocks to the gathering and dissemination of valuable information about life that could be useful to future generations, if not also to ourselves and our contemporaries. Underlying each of these questions is still another one, deeper and more profound, though implicit and rarely scrutinized. *Why?* Why would I want to do this? What purpose would it serve? What meaning could it possibly have? For me? For others? While all of those aforementioned questions will be touched upon in succeeding pages, emphasis will be on answering this most vital but ignored question of "why?" because once we understand and passionately desire a goal, increased efforts to attain it usually follow. Some call this fuel for the mind "motivation," and some call it "inspiration." There is a difference, which will be discussed later. For now we need only realize that either one can provide the energy needed for action.

As noted in the bibliography, several books are available that describe the details and logistics of recording life events and their meanings. Some are very useful, but most seem intended for those who already know why they wish to leave a legacy. For the most part these are people who are well known or famous or who believe they have contributed something significant to mankind and want the world to remember who they are. A few, with strong family or ethnic ties and desiring to follow in the footsteps of ancestors, feel an obligation to continue a tradition already begun. Fewer still, perhaps stimulated by the genealogy craze or by the excitement created decades ago by Alex Haley's *Roots*, are attempting to launch a new custom that they hope will be carried on by descendants. Always on the periphery are those who wish to attain recognition and profit from the insatiable desire of readers for the shock, drama, and sensationalism that some writers' lives offer.

Most of us, however, beset by daily struggles of cultural survival that impinge on our time and resources, have neither the inspiration nor the motivation to convey the essence of life as we have experienced it. Without a strong why, the task seems like an exercise in waste and futility, perhaps thousands of hours of thinking, remembering, examining, concluding, and transmitting information that may never be appreciated or used and may even be painful to consider. Who needs the grief?

Well, here's the good news. It doesn't have to be that difficult. It's easier than it appears—and potentially far more valuable than any of us might realize. It can even be meaningful and fun. Consider this: *recording stories about life is decidedly different from writing life's story*. The latter suggests entirety, completeness, comprehensiveness, totality, and even conclusion—enough to scare the most enthusiastic story writer. But the image of documenting stories about life is much different because it approaches the task with the assumption that the totality of life is made up of many, many stories, each of which can be considered and transmitted separately.

It's perhaps startling to think that stories of our own simple lives are unique, but of course they are. Though we can certainly identify with common themes, no two people have lived those themes in the same way. That's why—given a supportive and accepting environment—we love to swap tales.

Picture the scene where campers are roasting marshmallows over a roaring fire in a park-like setting. In such an atmosphere, the storyteller comes out in most of us, amidst 100 percent attention from our companions. And when one story ends, another begins. Everyone contributes, from the youngest to the eldest, and the listeners are not only captivated but also stimulated to be next in line with another story. No one tells a life story, but everyone tells life stories. And no two stories are ever the same.

I recall fondly the many times my dad and I, as adults, sat for hours deep in conversation at the dinner table long after the dishes had been cleared. It didn't matter what topic or issue we started with; eventually we touched upon most issues of the day—economics, politics, education, religion, ethics, sports, and social needs are only examples—and we shared our thoughts and feelings about each issue. The stories we shared characterized our ongoing lives—our perceptions, experiences, and conclusions. And one topical discussion led into another, without either of us realizing what was happening. At the end of the evening, which was often beyond midnight, we sometimes had to be reminded by our wives that bedtime was approaching. Our simultaneous response was usually a resounding "What? It can't be that late. Have we been talking that long?"

The value of sharing stories cannot be overemphasized. It's how we learn from one another. Each individual story shared is complete within itself, and yet ongoing at the same time. Such is the reality and also the paradox of life. The end of one story can also be the beginning of another. What goes around also comes around. Much of life is made up of defined experiences with a beginning and an end but also with the potential to be revisited later, sometimes in bizarre ways. Nevertheless, we can usually compartmentalize events in ways that allow us to share "short stories" or shortened versions of longer stories.

Like each day, which officially closes at midnight, "time" also allows similar closures for weekly, monthly, yearly, and even hourly occurrences. As with sleep, the passage of time provides a dividing point, a hiatus in which consciousness takes a breather. There is always another day. Life continues anew the next morning, though often with a slightly different perspective as we "sleep on it." We can rarely experience 100 percent closure because so many of our experiences involve ongoing relationships and circumstances.

Over time, we may even discover that events in our lives are connected in ways we don't initially or completely understand. Some say there are no coincidences in life, that even the most remote incidents are somehow related. Whatever our thoughts on that issue, there are natural breaks in our unfolding life experience that allow us temporary endings, and as we share seemingly unrelated stories, a kind of life examination often results, culminating in a deeper appreciation of the development and purpose of our unique existence.

My Hero Dorliska

When my mother casually introduced me some thirty years ago to the 1865 diary of my great-grandmother that had been handed down to her, I had only passing interest. But, as the years have unfolded, so has my excitement and passion. What a gift! She was not an extraordinary person. History books will not record her accomplishments. But for my efforts, her very existence fades into oblivion.

Yet that one small diary has had an impact that she, Dorliska Dean Vincent, could hardly have imagined. (See appendix B for selected contents of the diary.) She wrote only a few short comments each day, nearly always beginning with the weather, and her words lay dormant and ineffectual for over 130 years. But when I decided in 1996 to transfer those words, exactly as written, to a new and more permanent record by typing them into a word processor rather than have the words remain only on pages whose ink would eventually fade away, I opened up a whole new venture for myself and became the link through which her life experiences and her wisdom could be communicated to future generations.

Through that single small diary, spanning one year in the life of a then struggling twenty-two-year-old mother who would live for eighty-one years, I began to understand and, most significantly, appreciate some of the heritage into which I was born, thirteen years after her passing. My mother could convey little about this grandmother of hers, as she was only eleven years old when Dorliska died. Her only clear remembrance was of a stern, serious, and somewhat aloof, nongrandmotherly woman who withheld the outward affection given by her other grandmother.

This description both intrigued and frustrated me because I saw nothing in her diary that would suggest such an assessment.

Of course, a very young woman wrote the diary, and my mother's recollections were of a rather old woman. So what life experiences would cause the changes in her that apparently occurred between youth and old age? This and similar questions I found fascinating and compelling. As I researched the sparse and fragmented information I could find about events in her life development, I began to piece together some possible cause-and-effect items and to find some of the answers I sought.

For example, I found that she buried five of the six children born to her and that her husband, captain of a three-masted, cargo-carrying sailing schooner on the Great Lakes, was absent from her life two-thirds of each year for the first forty years of their marriage. I developed a new appreciation for her strength and courage and a greater understanding of the detached behavior remembered by my mother. As a link in the chain of our family history, it is now my responsibility to convey the essence of her life to other family members, both present and future.

All of this has occurred because of one small diary, written during an historic year, with mostly mundane entries, the meaning of which has had to be pieced together and interpreted according to logic and psychological knowledge as we presently understand it. But what if Dorliska had recorded many stories, over many years of her life, with the deliberate intent of informing and influencing future generations? How valuable would that have been? And what can we learn about our own dates with immortality from this story?

One lesson could be that our lives are far more valuable than we might think. Perhaps we are so caught up in our own day-to-day survival and TV reality shows that we forget that our greater purpose may be as links between past and future, between those who have discarded their physical bodies and those who will be acquiring them. Our descendants will wonder about how and where we fit into their mental and emotional pictures of themselves. Of that we can be certain, just as we wonder how our ancestors have influenced our lives. Such curiosity is one of the attributes with which we are all born. We can choose to become consultants to their quests, providing them with vital information from our life experiences, or we can choose to ignore such curiosity and become another weak, obscure link in family history.

Why Indeed?

We will never know why Dorliska wrote her diary in 1865, or if she ever wrote another one. We can only speculate. Certainly she could not have known on January 1 how significant that year would become in her own personal life and in American history—the end of the Civil War, Lincoln's assassination, and the deaths of her beloved mother-in-law and four-year-old son.

Perhaps diary-writing was a fad of the times, and she was simply copying the activities of other young mothers in the village, though I am unaware of the preservation of many other diaries in the village during that era. Or perhaps she just wanted to pass the time while her husband was away for those several months every year. If so, why did she not continue the activity into other years? Or perhaps the diary was a form of catharsis motivated by the isolation and loneliness of the times, though she appeared to have daily contact with family, friends, and visitors.

Though we can't be certain, it's most likely that she wished to preserve memories to be examined later by herself and her children, a combination of self-exploration and family heritage. Considering that the year was filled with multiple tragedies and that she never missed a day of entries, she certainly was disciplined in the task. Whether consciously or not, she definitely had a "why" that was pushing her to continue. At the same time, it may have been those depressing tragedies that influenced her to discontinue such potentially painful entries in succeeding years.

The issue of self-examination as a motivating force is so vital that it will be visited later in this chapter and occasionally throughout the book. For now, let it be noted as a valuable reason for recording life stories. Today diary writing is often referred to by its companion activity of journaling. While there may be some differences in the two activities, for the purpose of story writing their similarities are far more significant.

For many life story writers, connecting family generations is a primary motivator. Many ethnic groups put great value in preserving family and tribal histories, as a means both of honoring ancestors and educating descendants. The Native American culture is a well-known example in which stories of the past have been preserved in an effort to enlighten future generations, who may encounter similar situations and circumstances. Religious groups worldwide also share stories—often written in ancient sacred books—that are assumed to be somehow relevant to each new generation.

The recording of individual family histories can lead to valuable outcomes, as each new generation is provided with a series of blueprints detailing numerous experiences of personal ancestors. Each generation learns horizontally from one another, so why not vertically from past lives into future ones? By preserving our stories, we are eliminating obstacles and clearing pathways. Do we not recognize the circular and repeating nature of our universe and everything in it? Do we not realize that each life experience arises from previous ones and influences future ones?

Beyond providing a means to self-exploration, which can affect our very personal day-to-day choices, activities, and experiences, and besides beginning or enhancing the education of our own family descendants, our life stories may be instrumental to the continuation of our species as a whole. Scientific knowledge of Earth's history reveals "ages" of ice, fire, and floods in which many species of living organisms became extinct because they could not adapt to change.

Some will argue that the current changes to our planet are being caused by our own stupidity and ignorance, as we continually deplete Earth's resources and carelessly pollute its air and water. No doubt there is truth to that argument. But scientific history and common sense mandate that we differentiate between changes that we cannot (yet?) control and therefore to which we must adapt, and those that we have caused by our collective choices. The colossal error that our current culture tends to be making is that we can (or should be able to) control virtually everything we encounter. This leads to blame, uncompromising political ideologies, hot and cold wars, and innumerable power struggles.

The aspect of global warming is the most obvious example. Science aside, why would we not expect an occasional return (every few thousand years or so) to conditions that the Earth, prior to industrial development, has endured before? And won't such recurring conditions require adaptation and specie cooperation rather than political bickering? Are we destined to destroy ourselves, to "extinctify" our species because of a desire to compete, compare, and control rather than adapt? As long as winning and losing are looked upon as our only options, we will certainly all lose. However, history tells us that few leaders or opportunists will give up their obsessions with power, ideology, or profit, so it's up to the rest of us to leave our stories, our wisdom, to future generations, if only to show that we're not all insane!

If you still lack the "why" for recording your own stories, consider your creation. It makes no difference what religion you embrace or if you're an atheist. Fact is, you're here! Like it or not, you were created, perhaps through the hand of some intelligent force, or perhaps by some accident of the natural universe. However you view your existence, you have thousands of ancestors, and your family (or species) will likely have thousands of descendants. Are you not grateful for the opportunity to be a link in the chain of human development? Bear in mind that you cannot escape being a link. The only question remaining is this: Will you be a weak link or a strong one?

No matter what life has afforded you, or what choices you have made, or what outcomes you have encountered, you can still contribute. Cultural "success" is not a criterion, nor should it be. As we shall see, all human progress has been made through trial and error. If you have made many errors, you have conducted many trials. Therefore, you have been on the right path. You may not have reached your desired destination yet, and you may never do so. But that doesn't mean that your experiences on the path should go unnoticed. Quite the contrary. Those stories of trying and failing, perhaps succeeding in some areas and not in others—those stories need to be told so that others can hear and learn. Otherwise, we all lose out.

There is a natural bond between parents and their children and grandchildren. Sometimes that glue is tenuous and severely tested but, given the right circumstances and conditions, seldom is it absent. It is rare for parents and grandparents to deliberately wish poor fortune upon their offspring. More likely, a much better life is desired. Nearly every species shares that goal, whether through the instinct of the animal kingdom or the mental awareness, companionship, love, and acuity of the human mind and heart.

Due to circumstances beyond their conscious control, my parents were unable to attend college. Married at the beginning of the Great Depression of the 1930s, Dad had suffered a near-fatal car accident during high school, which left him with a lifelong crippled leg, and Mom had lost her dad through an occupational disease, also while in high school. Though college had been a dream of both in the decade of the roaring '20s, economic and emotional survival became the goal of the '30s. Still, their educational dreams lived on and were brought to fruition in their three children, two of whom acquired PhDs and the other a master's degree. This desire to contribute to a better life for our children and later descendants is not unusual. It is a goal of all but the most callous parents. We are long on caring and good intentions, though sometimes short on awareness and follow-through.

"Mattering" Matters

One of our most beloved movies, *It's a Wonderful Life*, is shown yearly during the holidays. After a series of tremendous misfortunes, banker George Bailey wishes he had never been born and contemplates suicide. But an angel takes him back through life events in which he played a favorable part and which never would have happened if he had not been born. The recognition that his existence unknowingly played a very positive role in the lives of many people significantly changed his attitude toward himself and toward life. Only through this heavenly reexamination of his life was he able to reframe his existence from despair to joy.

Several years ago I witnessed a similar phenomenon with a former teacher of mine. At our twenty-fifth high school reunion in 1980, I took time to reminisce with my former social studies teacher, Clarence Katzmayer, a man whom I greatly admired and a major influence on my decision to major in the social sciences in college. Retired, and in the latter stages of life, this reserved and humble man had impressed me as much with his character as with his knowledge.

During our conversation I told him in some detail how appreciative I was for his substantial contribution to my life. He listened carefully and then sat silently for a moment before mumbling through misty eyes, "Thank you." Nothing further was said for several minutes, as we both observed the festivities going on around us. I assumed that our conversation had ended and got up to leave when I felt his hand touch my forearm. He turned slowly toward me, looked warmly into my eyes, and added, "You know, I've often wondered if I ever made any real difference to anyone I taught. You've just answered that question."

It's a sad commentary that so few ever express gratitude for the impact of others on our growth. With so little positive feedback, it's no wonder that our efforts often seem trivial and unrewarding. Mr. Katzmayer taught hundreds of students over the course of more than three decades, and his name was often recalled with great affection when former students gathered together in years following graduation. Yet he apparently never knew how much he mattered until long after his retirement.

Is there anything more devastating than believing that our lives have not mattered, that our existence has had no meaning, that our time in this physical body has been wasted? Older people are sometimes accused of being "set in their ways," unwilling to change, enamored with perceptions of the "good old days." But the foundation of such behaviors may well be a passion to view one's life as useful and meaningful. Admitting that we have been on the wrong path or have added little or nothing significant to mankind for several decades, and that life will soon be over, may be too much for some to bear. The way to avoid such despair may be to revel in the past, to belittle the present, and to ignore the future.

As with individual lives, species development is a process, and each life and generation is a vital part of that process. Rarely do people succeed at their first effort in acquiring a new skill. Human progress is no different. Each person in each generation adds a little bit more, and no one has the ultimate answer to our destiny. But we all contribute, knowingly or not. Wouldn't it be better for all of us—the living and the yet to be born—if we examined those contributions and deliberately passed them on?

In the previous chapter I asked, "What really matters?" The answer is clear: "mattering" matters, and it makes no difference who we are, what our age, how little we've accomplished, or how many horrendous mistakes we've made. We have lived, we are still living, and our lives have mattered! Furthermore, we can use our understanding of those lives to benefit our descendants. We must tell them how our lives have played out, so that we can become the foundations on which they can build their own. Making our lives count for something, making a difference, knowing that our lives have meant more than mere existence, believing that we have had, or are having, a positive impact on our little corner of the world—this proves to all that our time on earth has been fruitful.

Even if we have not received such feedback, or cannot accept that we have made important contributions to our world without such feedback, the opportunity still exists. Each of us has accumulated a lifetime of pragmatic wisdom, and no one has interpreted life in exactly our way. Every person—no matter how rich or how poor, how white collar or how blue collar, how social or how reclusive, how moral or how immoral, how (you add the category)—has important stories to tell and important contributions to make to the lives of future generations.

Why is it, then, that autobiographies seem to be published only by famous people—politicians, entertainers, inventors, industrialists, athletes, academics, and celebrities? Beyond what has already been noted, commercialism has to be a primary reason. Publishers sell books, and bookstores market books in order to make a profit. Their families, their neighbors, and even their local communities may admire Jane and John Doe, but that will not sell the thousands of books needed to cover publishing costs and produce profits. In fact, residents in small communities may well expect books written by local citizens to be donated, thereby eliminating potential revenues. Sadly, this is more a commentary on public perception and corporate gain than on author contributions. As Jesus once pointed out, it's hard to be famous and effective in your own community.

The current population, however, has an alternative with the advent of self-publishing. We can write and publish our own books, without the editing that publishing houses must do in order to ensure book sales. We can cost-effectively ensure that future generations will know us as we wish to be known through our writings. For those who prefer vocal and vision legacies, technology has provided CDs and DVDs, with other forms of recording undoubtedly on the horizon. Making multiple copies for distribution has arrived with the touch of a few buttons. Aside from the economics involved, most obstacles to leaving our legacies have been eliminated, and as costs diminish relative to personal income, as usually happens with time, each of us will have access to leaving our marks. No excuses!

All we really need in order to ponder and provide our stories is the inspiration and motivation to begin. At the very least, we can write journals or diaries in our own handwriting for others to examine upon our deaths.

Unfortunately, as potential authors of our life stories, we unwittingly contribute to our own failure. When we consider ourselves marginally important or unimportant, we also tend to believe that we couldn't possibly know significant people. Therefore, if I know an author, s/he can't be very good; and if I am an author, only insignificant people will patronize my work. So why try? Comedian Groucho Marx once commented that he wouldn't think of belonging to an organization that would accept him as a member. Our thoughts often mimic his humor, but the results are far from humorous.

It Makes No Difference

It makes no difference whether our lives have been uneventful or filled with luxury or tragedy. All lives include each of these, anyway, and all assessments and conclusions are matters of interpretation and personal appraisal. A recent news report claimed that some of the world's happiest people live in Africa, while the far more prosperous US population ranked far down the list. Anecdotal evidence within our own country shows similar results, as some of the most joyful individuals, groups, and families live in conditions far less comfortable than most of us would consciously choose.

It makes no difference whether our family has remained intact or split in many directions, whether we have been adopted into a family or raised by the one that birthed us, whether our development was pleasant and steady or unpleasant and disjointed, or whether we have children born to us. What we do with the hand we've been

35

dealt is all that matters in the long run. And what we can convey to descendants is our current understanding about this experience and, ultimately, about the meaning of life. We can tell it like we think it is, like we believe it has been, like we wanted it to be, like we hope it will be. We can reframe our experiences, our interpretations, and our conclusions in any ways we wish. The resistance of our minds is the only obstacle.

Beyond the issue of making our lives immortal through our legacy recordings is the related issue of making sense of our lives. Not only can we contribute to future lives, but we can also gain a more complete understanding of our own lives. Paradoxically, making sense of our lives, a mental process, begins with attention to our feelings, an emotional process. Whether we write ongoing stories or retrace our steps at a later time, it is mentally impossible to do either without some kind of reexamination. The mere process of recording our stories demands investigation into the conditions and circumstances that created them. Our attention to these stories cannot help but bring back emotions that accompanied them. While many of us try to ignore, hide, suppress, or circumvent these emotions, due to fear, habit, pain, or misunderstanding of their purpose, few would deny the impact of feelings on our behaviors.

In 1995 Daniel Goleman published a groundbreaking book that redefined what it means to be smart. Similar to Carl Rogers's belief that we are all wiser than our minds, Goleman broadened our thinking with his research into emotional intelligence, attributes that take into account unheralded intangibles such as self-awareness, self-motivation, self-discipline, character, compassion, empathy, and social appropriateness—the lack of which has ruined the careers and relationships of academics, politicians, celebrities, and corporate leaders whom society otherwise edifies and depends upon to transmit current data to future generations. Furthermore, the possession of a high degree of emotional intelligence does not require any formal education at all and is often the basis of success in many life endeavors, being related more to wisdom and common sense than to the mental knowledge that is emphasized in academia.

It has even been suggested that emotions form the foundation of an inborn universal guidance system, the purpose of which is to focus our attention on unique inner goals of which we may not even be conscious. That is, when we feel "good," it's because there is basic congruence between our inner desires and outward behaviors (we act in ways which feel satisfying to our ego or spirit) and when we feel "bad," there is a formidable incongruence (we act in ways that are disturbing to our ego or spirit). Thereby we are continuously being pointed in the direction of internal satisfaction by an awareness of our feelings. What a simple, yet profound, perspective. Those who prefer to be victims and skeptics undoubtedly can uncover flaws and disadvantages to such musings, but perhaps life is not quite as complicated as some have made it.

Because we have placed so much emphasis on intellectual development and so little on emotional development in our society, we exhibit little control over the latter. And with limited control comes fear, in a self-perpetuating cycle. We fear and avoid what we cannot control because it makes us feel powerless, and we cannot control what we fear and avoid, thus reinforcing powerlessness. Rather than accepting unpleasant feelings as part of a self-correcting guidance system, we perceive such emotions as conditions to be ignored, rationalized, blamed, or overcome—a surefire way to subconsciously maintain and increase their power.

If we really believe there is a purpose to our lives, and that each of us matters, we need next to consider how we can contribute to our world in the most productive sense. The next chapter will discuss how the nature of our unique contributions depends on our personalities and ambitions, including a look at some of the institutional intrusions which have influenced our development and which are still impacting children today.

Thoughts/Activities to Consider

1. Why have/haven't you written stories about your life?
2. Consider a condition, event, or situation experienced as a preteen. How might your interpretation of it be different at age eighty? How do you account for the difference?
3. How can you become a stronger link between past generations and future ones?
4. How has your life mattered?

CHAPTER 3

What Kind of Person Are You?

Can You Identify Yourself?

Mary Kay Ash, founder of the enormously successful Mary Kay line of cosmetics, is reputed to have described three people types in terms of their impact on society. Though related to business success, they could just as well apply to life in general; my assessment of (and additions to) those categories as applied to life story writing follows.

The top of the list is reserved for those who *make things happen.* These are often the people who rise to the pinnacle of economic and social prominence, the ones who make the newspapers, who usually live in the best neighborhoods, and who often command huge sums of money as speakers. These are the entrepreneurs, the explorers, the risk takers, the inventors, the creators, the organizers, the opportunists, and the otherwise talented leaders in our population. These are the models of success who give hope and promise to the rest of us, but who are hardly representative of the lives we actually lead.

Are you one of these who have made things happen? If you so describe yourself, you know that you have added much value to the world. You know that your descendants will thrive because of your contributions. And you will probably want future generations to know of your accomplishments. And so it should be! Just don't wait too long to record your stories. And not just the results you've attained, but the hardships you've encountered along the way, the obstacles you've overcome, and the resources you've called upon to jump over, go around, or push through those barriers. And don't forget to include your conclusions about life, your interpretation of events, and your mistakes and regrets—all of the experiences that have made you the person that you have been, that you are, and that you may yet become.

Those who *watch things happen* represent a second category. In their life experiences these individuals are often regarded as more timid and cautious, unwilling to take chances on which the first group thrives, unable to capitalize on opportunities that they often recognize but seldom embrace. These are the worker bees that show up every day, who seldom question outwardly the instructions given to them by the first group, who wait patiently and calmly for the right time to react to situations, and who opt more for safety and obedience than adventure.

They may be no less brilliant than the first group initiators but are less likely to be spontaneous and daring. They are implementers, not inventors. They stand back and assess the landscape before setting foot on unknown soil. They are human calculators who make important but not life-altering decisions. In military, political, corporate, social, athletic, and business nomenclature, they are captains, not generals; advisers, not leaders; junior executives, not CEOs; managers, not owners; agents, not producers.

In these roles, they are the watchdogs of society and are enormously valuable in determining its future. Because they usually have less ego involvement in specific outcomes, they possess perspectives unavailable to those engrossed in making things happen.

As observers, interpreters, and evaluators, they can play a prominent role in conveying opinions and conclusions to future populations. What a great contribution this could be toward eliminating some of the errors and mistakes that leaders of each new generation commit! The greatest hurdle to fulfilling this task rests in their lack of belief in its significance. In the fulfillment of their functions seems to be the implicit but false belief that a participant-observer is a second-class citizen to the entrepreneurial adventurer.

Still, there is even a lower-appearing classification, the group that *wonders what happened.* These individuals might be depicted by society as oblivious bystanders, caught up in the events of the world but with no comprehension of what's really going on around them. They're aware of movement but not of significance. They land wherever the wind blows them, then get up, dust themselves off, and continue on their repetitive journeys. They cannot make things happen; they cannot even evaluate or understand what's happened; they merely survive and react. Like the puppet Mortimer Snerd of ventriloquist Edgar Bergen days, they are sometimes considered mentally asleep, accepting without reflecting, and conscious but unaware.

I had the dubious honor of acquiring the nickname "Mort" at age five, during radio's heyday. My slow comprehension of events and even slower reaction time accompanied a reserved but obedient personality to remind those around me of Charlie McCarthy's sidekick in the Bergen household. Mortimer's hollow-headed response to Bergen's repetitive question, "Mortimer, how can you be so stupid?" always resulted in a drawn-out, drawled response that had listeners howling with laughter. "Well, you see, Mr. Bergen, it's like this. I work at it."

So how can such people possibly be useful to future generations? The answer lies in the word "wonder." As long as we are wondering what happened, we have an important role to play. Uninvolved as these individuals may be in making or watching things happen, they represent a large group affected by the outcomes. To the extent that those in this group enter voting booths, they are enormously influential in determining our leaders and, thereby, the direction of our culture. Therefore, they are potentially very beneficial, for they offer another perspective on their generation's activities. In politics most citizens probably fit into this category. They leave the bickering to the elected officials, voting every two or four years to keep them in or vote them out of office, usually on insufficient information. To their credit, they do not get mired in the abysmal day-to-day rhetoric of the career politicians. But they pay a price for this privilege of remaining uninvolved. While their collective influence may be substantial, their individual influence is marginal, and they may feel the greatest impact from decisions in which they do not directly participate.

An additional category might be reserved for those who *aren't aware that anything has happened.* Prior to the twentieth century this category fit far more people, with today's decrease primarily due to the rapid changes in the field of global communication. Auto and air travel, radio, television, cell phones, and the Internet have combined to virtually eliminate the hermit-types, those who can remain ignorant of both local and world events. Still, some do exist, as evidenced by talk-show hosts who occasionally wander the streets randomly interviewing unsuspecting (but often very well educated) citizens unable to identify even the most noteworthy among national and world figures and events. Still, these same people can often identify and describe people in the fields of entertainment and athletics, or in other fields of personal interest. Social and cultural information from this population could provide significant enlightenment about today's world to future generations, data that is unlikely to be reported in textbooks. In addition, these individuals could also provide valuable insights about what caused their lack of interest in, or focus on, mainstream events.

This category may also include those who wish to avoid concentration on the preponderance of negativity in today's society. Wishing to escape inundation with news reports that invariably emphasize the horrors and tragedies of modern life, these people may consciously choose to remain uninformed. Our culture has created images of the laboratory scientist, cooped up in his little area of the world as far away as possible from everyday happenings. Other brilliant individuals, such as monks, philosophers, entrepreneurs, and visionaries, may elect to remain outside the mainstream of society in order to avoid contamination with their life purposes. And, of course, many are just too busy trying to survive their own daily economic and social crises to care much about ongoing military and political games that rarely affect them directly. Their perspectives on the world of today could be enormously helpful to those who will live in the worlds of tomorrow and may face similar circumstances and conditions.

There is a fifth category that I would suggest and that overlaps all of those mentioned above. It's an attitude category, best described as *"those who don't care."* Those who make things happen may not care to give the benefits of their perspectives to future generations. The same could be said for those who watch things happen, who wonder what happened, and even to those who aren't aware that anything has happened. Those who don't care about leaving a legacy, who don't care about contributing to the betterment of the unborn, who don't care about the advancement of our species and our planet, come in all categories. Not caring is an aspect of feeling unimportant, depressed, insignificant, and victimized, on the one hand, or selfish, narcissistic, superior, and predatory, on the other. But if only we could corral their input and insights! Why don't they care? Did they ever care? If so, when and how did their attitudes change?

Compared to What and Whom?

Beyond merely identifying ourselves according to behavior and personality, at some point in our lives most of us become preoccupied with trying to figure out how we came to be this way. Was it nature or nurture? Inbred or acquired? Cause or effect? Caught or taught? Internal or social?

The answers we receive from experts and researchers are hardly satisfying, for they are usually inconsistent and inconclusive. "All of the above" seems to be their ultimate response, and we are left to our own investigations. In the end, perhaps who we are is more "nature," and what we become is more "nurture." The former may be permanent but the latter is most certainly variable and attributable to conditions over which we have some control—those involving families, schools, churches, organizations, financial institutions, and workplaces.

Since who we are, what we've become, and our future development are all basic to how we live and the stories we potentially write, some discussion of the customs and institutions we've developed and our thoughts about creation must be addressed.

Perhaps the most common yet devastating by-product of our social and educational systems involves the use of *comparison* as a tool for the evaluation and motivation of people. Since it is often confused with the economic or sports-oriented term "competition," and thereby mistakenly accepted as an aspect of capitalism, its harm is barely recognized. Perhaps initially considered an innocent and expedient sorting tool by family members and teachers, adults in general have become very adept at applying this tool for their own benefits, at the expense of gullible and unsuspecting children.

I recall my early career days as a school counselor when I argued for students who achieved well but whose standardized test scores did not measure up to those of their friends with whom they wished to take classes. Those were the days of "ability grouping," where actual results were often deemed secondary to "tested intelligence." Academic standards were applied across the board, and children were psychologically both stretched and shrunk in the adult efforts to make them fit the right compartments. Local, state, and national paper-and-pencil tests were used to determine interest, aptitude, achievement, and ability, and both professionals and amateurs too often interpreted the results in ways that were detrimental to the development of social and emotional health. People skills became subordinate to academic and technical scores.

Not much has changed. Emphasis on these artificial standards of excellence continues, and blue-collar work is still frowned upon. Furthermore, when job skills are cited for hiring, an academic degree and the ability to manage computer technology programs seems to far outweigh the value of appropriately interacting and intermingling with people. Who has not encountered on the phone, online, and in person, a plethora of rude and mindless bureaucrats and customer service personnel? Not surprisingly, social skills are deteriorating and social conflicts are escalating. Meanwhile, even with increased attention, test results have changed little, and the US ranking in the world of education continues to plummet.

Moreover, some educators have been obsessively concerned with the negative effects that over-achievement might have on the psyche of developing children and adolescents, as though it were possible, aside from chance or cheating, to achieve results of which one is incapable. In attempts to protect the mental health of children, crimes far worse are being committed, as motivations and incentives are eliminated and the joys of learning accompanied by friends extinguished. Trying to avoid too much academic pressure, educators contribute to low self-confidence by conveying that good results produced by hard work with enjoyable surroundings are a waste of time if you don't "test well." Instead of improving mental health, such messages—such comparisons—destroy it.

Given this scenario, is it any wonder that hard work has given way to today's cynicism, laziness, and expectations of entitlement? Is it any wonder that millions of our citizens compare themselves to others and come up short when reinforced by self-doubts, the results themselves of prior comparisons? Is it any wonder that ordinary citizens, the backbone of our society, see little value in writing stories of their lives and leaving them to succeeding generations?

Even first-born infants cannot escape the curse. "I wonder if he'll be as smart as his cousins." "Will she be as good an athlete as her mother?" "She doesn't seem as energetic as my friend's baby." "Do you think he'll be as good-looking as his father?" We never run out of comparisons because it's the avenue by which we view our own and our family's worth. If our baby is "as good as" or "better than" the object of comparison, then that result transfers to the entire adult family as well. Already there is evidence of the return to selective breeding among some, a throwback to the days of royalty from which our forefathers fled. Commonly accompanying this elitist attitude is the elimination of compassion for those less fortunate.

Of course, those who come out "on top" in any comparison would seem to fare quite well, but that can be a hollow victory. When an entire family's reputation is at stake, sometimes for many generations, the pressure upon the identified "good child" can be monstrous and can lead to a compulsion for perfection and the potential for psychological damage. Even if other siblings are high achievers as well, that pressure may not be lessened, for who wants to be "the odd one out?" Taking that first step at eleven months can label a child as "a bit slower" if older siblings have started walking at ten months. Being merely well coordinated may not "make it" in a family of otherwise outstanding athletes.

But if those who end up high on the ladder of comparison suffer from the lack of oxygen, how much worse is the burden of those holding the ladder at the bottom? Born into an atmosphere of economic, educational, spiritual, emotional, and/or social deprivation, for most there is little hope of a legitimate climb up the ladder. They can see those at the top; they just can't get there themselves. Our culture edifies and rewards those who are well educated, well mannered, and well heeled. In comparison, the bottom-feeders get the crumbs and leftovers. History, of course, verifies such outcomes. If precedent has any value, that's the way it will always be. According to many evolutionists, physical "survival of the fittest" has ruled much of nature from the beginning (see discussion of "Spontaneous Evolution" in chapter 10). Humankind has followed suit, tragically ignoring an intelligence that could enable it to overrule the killing aspects of nature. The plant and animal kingdoms instinctively obey laws that are optional for us. Yet we seem to believe we have no other choice than to compare ourselves to one another—and we act accordingly.

Jesus was born into a highly comparative society and shocked the population continuously by collaborating with the poor, the sick, and the humble. The beatitudes are but one example of how he addressed the plight of the downtrodden—those who had no hope for themselves and seemed marginally valued by others. Chapter 7 of the gospel of Mark indicates how Jesus accepted the comparative culture of his time and yet recognized the worthiness and hopes of a despised and underprivileged segment of the population. When begged by a Gentile woman to heal her daughter, a compassionate Jesus told her "First, I should help my own family—the Jews. It isn't right to take the children's food and throw it to the dogs" (verse 27).

This was evidently a comparative statement, but in response to the woman's humble reply that even puppies are given scraps from the children's plates, an empathic Jesus was obviously pleased and told her that she had answered well and that he would indeed heal her daughter—perhaps an attempt to give "a nobody" some status and prestige after all. Still, the woman seemed to accept her social ranking as a lower-class citizen, hopeless and undeserving, much like many in today's society who consider themselves unworthy of being significantly remembered by their descendants.

Though perhaps in a class of his own, Jesus both followed and preceded other great humanitarians, not all professing a Christian philosophy but all who saw potential greatness in every human being. Albert Schweitzer, Mahatma Gandhi, Nelson Mandela, Mother Teresa, the Dalai Lama, and Martin Luther King Jr. are but a few of the most recent examples that might be noted, but all religious, cultural, national, and ethnic groups have their own heroes.

Then, of course, there is always the rhetoric that professes to value the masses but behaves hypocritically. Our own national history is proof enough. The Declaration of Independence begins with the concept of equality for all—except, of course, for nonwhites, nonlandowners, and nonmen. Over time many of these flaws have been recognized and corrected, but new and less recognizable ones have surfaced. Considering the recent political debates on class warfare, how can we expect the real and true stories of our own generation and future ones to ever be told accurately? The players have changed and the rules have been modernized, but the same hypocritical games go on.

Examples of individual, corporate, union, organizational, institutional, bureaucratic, and governmental greed and dishonesty, in addition to corruption, abuse, exploitation, and discrimination are reported daily by news media all over the world. Distrust and cynicism have replaced the confidence, dependability, and credibility in our neighbors that many once hoped for and that some took for granted. A recent AP poll (Newsmax 11/30/13) reported that the majority of Americans now have significant distrust toward their fellow citizens, a perception that both reflects and forecasts the state of our nation.

As surely as if by legislative mandate, our aloofness and indifference has socially and emotionally disenfranchised the future ancestry of the masses and left the portrayal of our history in the hands of the least competent to describe it—those at the top of the pyramid. As if by premeditated cunning, we have designed a system of living whereby the most power-hungry, the wealthiest, the most out-of-touch, and, correspondingly, the most ignorant elitists will transmit the essence of our culture.

Through the silence of the masses, our descendants will ingest a distorted image of our lives. Through the processes of comparison and self-elimination, most of us will quietly defer to the fantasies of the rich and famous, thereby thrusting the final knife into our hearts and into the hearts of our descendants. But does it really matter?

What Would Real Change Require?

Perhaps it matters not to historians and writers of history texts, for their job is to convey a larger, more global, sense of the present and past. And while a basic and reasonable understanding of such events may be part of the makeup of an educated person, it does little to inspire the average citizen in small-town, inner-city, and rural America.

As a young history teacher fresh out of college, I taught the curriculum in much the same way as I had been taught—from the outside in; that is, there was a focus on the European world's global pursuit of riches, leading to the eventual colonization of the Americas. Explorations, politics, wars, economics, and the interminable balance of power, as various cultures and nations sought advantages in all of these areas, formed the content of history classes. Long ago and far away from the lives of young students!

But what if history reversed its focus and concentrated first on the family scene, then on neighborhood and local history, branching out eventually to regional, state, national, and international dynamics? What if we put every student at the center of his or her curriculum? What if we began the teaching of history with circumstances surrounding the birth of each learner? Yes, given the emotional and social state of the family in today's culture, with its disrupted, dissolved, divorced, and disillusioned dimensions, some rather sensitive issues would likely emerge and would require the hiring of perceptive teachers, especially in the elementary grades. Of course, that's where our most patient and compassionate teachers should be anyway—and usually are—in the initial training of young minds.

We would need considerable revamping of our teacher training programs, but the models for such awareness training (minus the political agendas that have recently corrupted such training) have been available for decades. All that's needed is the will to implement them and the desire to withhold judgmental comparisons of students. Comparisons themselves, of course, are quite natural and not inherently damaging to children. Rather, it's the conclusions and comments we make about those comparisons that lead to difficulty.

Educators must learn to assume and think "different" rather than "pass/fail," "better/worse," or "more/less valuable," with an emphasis on teaching students to think and to question rather than influencing them to ingest and comply. As soon as we make a comparison between individuals or intact groups and follow it up with the word "therefore," we are usually asking for trouble.

Young learners could be introduced to family heritage and encouraged to initiate and explore family discussions at a time when their enthusiasm for learning is at its peak, in their preteen years, before the distractions and hormones of adolescence dominate their existence and the responsibilities of young and middle adulthood consume their thoughts and behaviors. If family heritage is presented in a positive framework—and it always can be, as demonstrated by Alex Haley in the portrayal of his family roots—boys and girls can avoid the shame or adulation of comparison that too often accompanies family knowledge.

Collectively, such changes could have an enormously productive influence on every aspect of society. But, of course, learners need resources to pull from. And if we don't provide our descendants with stories from our own lives, how will they ever understand the efforts that went into their inheritance? How will they ever truly understand themselves?

Helped to interpret family history in positive terms by compassionate teachers, students would enter adulthood with stronger identities and more uplifting self-images with which to face their worlds. Then they can feel positive about the stories that define their own lives. It's all a matter of interpretation. In the past our culture has thrived on comparison, separation, and negativism. Where there is none, we seem to manufacture it. The media both fosters our appetite for the bad and the bizarre, and responds to our insatiable demand for it. When that's what we see and hear about, it's all too easy to assume that it's an accurate portrayal of the world.

But it's not! Negativism sells because it's different and often exciting, and therefore gets our attention; adults get bored with sameness and emotional distance, in the same manner as young students. Negativism also helps us feel better about ourselves in comparison with the rest of our world. We can choose to identify with difficult and tragic events and people, and thus decrease our sense of isolation and alienation, or we can compare our circumstances with those much worse off and thereby feel a sense of superiority. Either way, our egos gain something! But such negativism is of questionable value in the long run because it creates and sustains separation and animosity and presents a false image of reality.

In the way current news reports work, we may really need to worry when they become primarily positive; because that will indicate that the positive is unusual. When the network news begins to report the number of airplanes that landed safely today, the number of automobiles that arrived at their destination without incident, the number of people that did not contract a certain disease, the number of marriages that did not dissolve this week, the number of children who were not abused this month, those reports will indicate the normality of crises. For now, the positives far outweigh the negatives and so get little attention. It's all a matter of how we interpret the news and what we wish to emphasize.

Unfortunately, citizens too often interpret the bombardment of negativism as the norm, thus instilling moods of frustration, stress, and hopelessness. Why would anyone want to write such stories as these and leave them for descendants? The media could change all of this but prefers to capitalize on the public's "desire for blood." We need a new network that would focus only on the positive aspects of the news, reframing and reporting human events that show only our innate goodness. There would be lots of such news, but would there be an audience? Each of us needs to seriously ponder that question, for without a committed audience there will be no change! Truth is we blame the networks for displaying the trash that we enthusiastically devour! As the saying goes, we have met the enemy and it's in the mirror!

By the time a child enters school, the meaning of comparison is usually well established, albeit unconsciously. As mentioned briefly in chapter 1 and reemphasized here, the educational system then pours and hardens the cement through traditional attempts at efficiency and effectiveness—segregation by age, gender, and/or ability, as well-meaning parents and educators slot each child into statistical categories that seem reasonable and logical to the facilitation of teaching, though not necessarily to that of learning. The publications of academic honor rolls represent one such method of comparison— showing all who view them who's "smart" and who's not. When not well thought out, good intentions can easily lead to unplanned and hurtful results.

Again, my intent here is not to disparage the educational system but to demonstrate that those who do not fare well in such endeavors are inclined to think poorly of themselves, perhaps an unintended consequence but a potentially devastating one, nevertheless. These are the people who grow up to be ordinary, average citizens—the backbone of every nation, without which all cultures would collapse. Yet these are the same people who are rarely encouraged to tell their stories, unless they defy the odds and rise to the top in some category or are somehow involved in some spectacular event, such as winning the lottery.

Ironically, even winning the lottery rarely changes the "I'm Just a Nobody" theme mentioned earlier. Conditions in the winner's life may change, but the inner feelings remain untouched by monetary prosperity, as behavioral results have often shown. Unless by design and intention we deliberately embark on a mission to change our thinking, the old ways will continue unabated. We must modify our obsession—most evident in the winning and losing of sports and politics—with the concept of comparison that demoralizes a large segment of our society, thereby reinforcing this "I'm not important" mentality.

Even those who do well in our world of comparisons can suffer enormous blows to their self-confidence, as indicated by my own story from elementary school (see part 2, "The Perfect Curse"). Pressure to excel or stay on top can produce significant stress, which can be very self-defeating and lead to "giving up," often considered by an individual as a better solution than meeting the very high expectations of significant others. After all, many convince themselves, how can I fail if I don't try? To avoid the stigma of *deliberate* failure, however, we publicly resort to the phrase, "I'll try," a gimmick for similarly avoiding action but allowing us to "fail with honor"—for who can argue with promising to make an effort? To be accused of not trying, though, is the equivalent of failing with dishonor—behavior that invites criticism, further lowers self-esteem, leads to underachievement, reinforces one's feelings of insignificance, and ultimately discourages written legacies. Either way, the results are similar. We can attempt to fool others by *pretending* to try, but the truth lies within us.

Educators rationalize that students need to be challenged by competition, and often they do, but not by comparison and not always in the same manner! Readiness is a major factor in meeting challenges, and the timing of readiness varies greatly within and between individuals.

What often seems like common sense is too often common fallacy. Potential consequences must be carefully considered. Bestselling author John Maxwell stressed the importance of our approach to life and work in *Thinking for a Change*. This title provides a powerful double message depending on whether we emphasize the first word or the last. Either way, the message is that productive thinking is not all that common but is necessary for positive change to occur. For example, is not a solution possible between the supposedly opposing concepts of "Everybody wins" and "Being #1 is all that matters"?

Communicating Our Inner Essence

There is a tendency, especially among younger generations, to dismiss the value of sharing experiences in any form from one generation to another. We're told that much technology is obsolete almost as soon as it is invented and that we live in a technological and informational age. In a new world of such rapid change, where old traditions, cultures, and subcultures are quickly and effectively dismantled and new ones are far from stabilized, present generations may feel lost and confused in the ensuing vacuum. In the process, that which divides us is exaggerated, that which unites us is minimized, and that which defines us is all but obliterated. One need only analyze the current political situation for evidence of this occurrence.

When we continually emphasize those "isms" of modern society—consumerism, materialism, institutionalism, capitalism, conservatism, liberalism, Catholicism, Protestantism, socialism, racism, sexism, fundamentalism, regionalism, nationalism, and all of the other "isms" that impact our worldly existence—these human creations dominate our attention. While these isms represent the idols and devils of our community struggles for survival and power by providing convenient labels, they are not the essence of who we are. There is an inner core, a spiritual core perhaps, that links each generation unto itself and also unto past and future generations.

People of every culture and generation experience the ability to think and reason, to alter courses of behavior, and above all, to choose. Unlike the animal kingdom, we're not limited by instinct. We can work with, or against, our environment. According to the Bible, we have dominion over all the earth and its inhabitants—an awesome power but also an obligation of stewardship. We have the intelligence and wherewithal to both destroy and preserve that with which we are entrusted: we can continue with tradition or break from it; we can educate ourselves or remain ignorant, and we can choose the topics for each category; we can behave and think habitually, or we can leave our comfort zones, challenge old ways, and venture into new patterns; we can even try to avoid all patterns and live each day anew. Very little is beyond our reach and power.

Still, estimates indicate that we use less than one-tenth of our mind's potential, and to the extent that we keep personal perceptions to ourselves, our accomplishments are even further limited. Though perhaps made in the image of God, we are not godlike. We are neither omniscient nor omnipotent. Our ability to learn is truly extraordinary but our capacity to retain is far less potent, and our inclination to interpret what we see and hear according to preconceived notions leads to suspect conclusions at best. We build, own, and depend on computers, which we then allow to dictate our directions in life. We use lifeless statistics to determine social policies and even individual behaviors, though power seekers with intentions to spin or distort the truth for their own benefit can easily manipulate those statistics.

We depend on powerful governmental and nongovernmental agencies to furnish honest and timely information and to protect us from unscrupulous corporations and scams, while at the same time eagerly inviting into our homes TV ads that feast on both child and adult ignorance in order to market their products and control our buying decisions. And then, when we're unhappy with the results, we complain with phrases like, "I wish I'd have known that before; somebody should've told me." So we go to the polls and put a new political party into office. But the more things change, the more they stay the same. Two or four years later, we repeat this yo-yo, revolving door process, and our dizzying, pendulum-swinging existence continues undiminished.

However, this isn't a book about politics or punishment. It's a book about life, about history, about our personal histories, and about teaching future generations so they can learn from our successes, mistakes, perceptions, visions, and conclusions. Paraphrasing a well-known bit of advice, those who deny, ignore, or forget the lessons of history are bound to repeat them. But who would intentionally wish to repeat the twentieth century—the wars, the economic struggles, the social problems, the religious bickering, and the destructive policies of powerful interests around the globe? And world terrorism and economic failures beginning the twenty-first century merely exacerbate the problems and offer little hope.

Nevertheless, we have made substantial progress in other arenas, and may somehow be laying the foundation for peace, mutual respect, and prosperity on which future populations can build. The unplanned and often horrific sacrifices of twentieth century generations may yet propel us to victory over ourselves, in the same ways that our parental sacrifices are intended to make life more pleasant and meaningful for our children and grandchildren. This emphasis is also consistent with many religious beliefs that stress the importance of personal sacrifice for the sake of loftier goals.

Whether or not you as a reader believe in intelligent design, whether or not you are an advocate of evolution or some big bang theory, whether or not you have found some way of integrating aspects of all three, or whether you just don't care, the only overriding fact is that you and I have received the gift of life. Judging from the past several thousand years, unless we annihilate one another in the meantime, present generations will be followed ad infinitum by future ones, and they will need our stories to build on, much like we have built on ancient historical knowledge and projections.

To Each Her/His Own

Regardless of our political, ideological, or spiritual beliefs, we can all contribute stories for the future of the planet and to those who will monitor it. As mentioned earlier, some will say we should leave that to the historians, the politicians, the academics, and the wealthy who have the time and money to engage in such luxuries. But that would be a false picture. How can a rich penthouse owner in a big city, or a powerful politician in Washington or elsewhere, or a history professor in an Ivy League university possibly write about, or even know about, what life has been like for me, or for you? Generations from now, if God's grace allows me to observe the world from afar, I don't want my descendants to have a distorted view of my life, or to base their lives on historical perspectives that were far from accurate or universal.

As explained in chapter 1, I was born and raised in a very small village in the far reaches of northern New York State, in a summer resort area known as the Thousand Islands. Except for tourism in the summer, it has been an economically depressed area for decades, far from the seats of political power, but with some of the most wonderful, down-to-earth people imaginable. Recently I examined a textbook being used to study the history of the state. Only one-half page was devoted to the Thousand Islands, and that was in a section about the geography and topography of the entire state. Nothing was mentioned about the local people who live there or the original settlers—our ancestors who helped clear the land, build the towns, service the people, and raise their families. A poorly funded and sparsely staffed local museum makes a yeoman-like effort to collect, organize, and categorize bits and pieces of historical documents, anecdotal information, and newspaper clippings about local families as they have developed over the years, but few personally written stories exist.

This neglect is being repeated in villages, hamlets, and rural and inner-city areas all over the world. If we don't give our ancestors (and ourselves) the credibility and respect they (we) deserve in developing our world, who will? Naysayers will argue that textbooks can only relate the highlights of history; they couldn't possibly detail the lives of people in every small community. And they're correct, of course, which is why we all must contribute to that task, in every part of the world. Each community must urge its citizens to provide personal stories, and then show outward appreciation to those who accept that challenge and choose to record and contribute those stories to local libraries and museums.

Every day that we delay, we lose valuable information. I began this book by comparing each human death to the loss of a library. That was my mother's influence. As she grew older and gained additional perspective on life, she would occasionally paraphrase an old proverb: *Whenever a person dies without having left a record of his or her existence, it's like a library burning down with all its contents lost forever.* Such an outcome is not just unfortunate. It's tragic! Libraries are burning down daily all around us, and we seem oblivious. Someday my library, and yours, will also cease to exist, and our gift of life demands that we leave a record behind. Isn't that the least we can do for our descendants? Postponement is too risky. Lives are being snuffed out daily, through aging, accidents, weather, starvation, addictions, murders, diseases, and neglect, and we are losing precious information about both past and present.

But, as we can't leave the transmission of society to its "pillars," neither can we leave the burden of legacy to the elderly, as many are prone to do. The young die also. Death seems not to discriminate by age. So we need the legacies of our young and middle-aged as well. To get these, we must enlist the cooperation of entire communities, especially parents and teachers.

Children Can Lead the Way

Toward that end, one teacher in particular in the Thousand Islands Central School District has been an inspiration to me. Working primarily with ten- and eleven-year-olds, Debbie Dermady a few years ago initiated a program that required her students to create stories about their developing lives, complete with pictures taken with disposable cameras furnished by the school. The yearlong project culminated with the presentation of their stories to parents and other interested adults. But such programs have been severely modified, curtailed or abolished by time and priority constraints, wavering interest, and limited funds, as statewide curricular demands and the insistence of using robotic-like methodologies continue to create additional burdens on the efforts of such imaginative teachers.

According to Mrs. Dermady, many of her students have initially resisted such assignments. After all, it seems like a lot of work, and it is. After the completion of the project, however, in the required written evaluations about those projects and the work entailed, a nearly unanimous sense of pride and accomplishment has been evident. As is the case in most public schools, not all students write well. But self-critiquing and class teamwork emphasized throughout the year help to ensure that all students are able to communicate stories about their lives quite capably. In addition, the positive side effects of such assignments are far-reaching. Increased self-esteem, improved writing skills, practice in public speaking and teamwork, appreciation for life, insight into themselves and their families, leadership training, and the possibility of establishing lifelong habits of concern for the future are just some of the potential rewards of such projects.

And there is another advantage that cannot be overlooked—the influence that their efforts may have on other members of their families. With a project of this magnitude, it is almost imperative that students will enlist the help of both nuclear and extended family members. In the process, conversations will take place that may intrigue older generations and encourage their further participation. Students may question parents and grandparents about the latters' lives as children and youth, thereby strengthening important generational linkages.

As noted earlier, one of the greatest obstacles adults face in communicating stories of their lives is the indifference and disdain shown by youth, who often ridicule and trivialize their elders' experiences. Yet there is an underlying affinity that also bonds the young and the old and upon which society can capitalize. With more projects of the kind demonstrated by Mrs. Dermady, young students can be lured naturally into generational discussions, which they enthusiastically initiate as they complete their assignments—quite a change from the lectures, dictates, and demands many of them are accustomed to experiencing from teachers and adult family members.

The doors of dialogue swing open as children seek answers to questions they would otherwise rarely consider. In this way, schools could actually be catalysts in improving family communication and ancestral appreciation, providing educators with opportunities to become more positively involved in family affairs.

Children, parents, grandparents, and teachers—all working in harmony to link the past and present for the benefit of the future. It sounds so wonderful, so productive, and so logical. So what's stopping us? Certainty! Absolutism! Permanence! Righteousness!

These similar concepts lead to beliefs and attitudes that divide rather than unite us, and stifle rather than free us. Our obsession with being "right"—certain, absolute, and permanent—in our examination of politics, religion, education, economics, and numerous social issues is obstructing our efforts to actually find solutions, and is the theme of chapters 8 and 9. But first, for those who are ready to face the challenge sooner, eager to get started with their own stories, chapters

4 through 7 will discuss some of the logistics involved in writing them, beginning with suggestions for content and the numerous challenges to be faced, and then progressing to the processes to be considered.

Thoughts/Activities to Consider

1. How do you personally respond to the question that forms the title of this chapter?

2. How are you contributing to the future of our species? Which of the five person types mentioned do you most resemble?

3. How often, to what degree, and under what conditions do you compare yourself or your family members to others? How does this help you?

4. Take the worst-case scenario of a personal or family situation and interpret it in a positive way with a short story.

5. Write about a time when you said, "I'll try," knowing full well that it was a way to escape criticism but that you really had no intention of following through.

6. How much do you rely on other people or institutions to define you, to convey to the world the essence of your being? (Examples might be a church, a relative, a political party, an academic degree, an occupation, a dwelling, etc.)

7. How many books in your internal library will never be written or distributed for the benefit of future generations? What chapters of your life do you wish to keep hidden, even after your death? What might the titles of those chapters be?

CHAPTER 4

Is an Oral Legacy Good Enough?

StoryCorps—A Good Beginning

Due to individual circumstances related to literacy, timing, illness, conditions of living, and other variables, providing oral stories may be the only viable option for some. Certainly we want those stories and encourage the use of modern technology. To see and/or hear those whose lives ended decades or even centuries ago will likely be thrilling for our descendants, and to use such technology is an addition that can only be exciting for future investigators. Seeing and hearing ancestors convey stories on CDs and DVDs could add significantly to our descendants' understanding of us and our experiences. But it is seldom a substitute for the many benefits of written stories. Of course, oral stories can be readily transcribed into written ones for those who have access to the technology and will take the time, money, and inconvenience to pursue that end.

One of the most promising developments for oral histories is StoryCorps, a decade-old organization that has provided a wonderful model and incentive for those who wish to vocalize a tiny portion of their legacies. A publicly funded, nonprofit group with permanent stations (as of this writing) in New York City, San Francisco, and Atlanta, and a mobile presence on both sides of the Mississippi River, it offers ordinary Americans opportunities to share personal stories on CDs and provides copies to both the participants and the Library of Congress.

Shortly after its inception, I heard about this program on a chance meeting with an acquaintance with whom I was sharing my ideas. On their website I discovered that one of their mobile units was moving up the East Coast, following the better weather as summer approached. To my astonishment (I thought they would stop only in the largest cities) they scheduled several days in northern New York State, not far from my rural summer residence. My wife and I immediately scheduled the normal half-hour session, set up in a beautiful soundproof trailer with an outstanding audio system. It was truly an inspiring experience.

Another exciting development was recently reported in the AARP Bulletin (September 2013). A project called the People's Library has been initiated at the Richmond, Virginia, public library. Memoir-writing classes are offered, and participants are encouraged to produce their stories and contribute them, in their own handwriting, to a section in the library where visitors can check them out as they would other books.

However, considering the enormity of both the US and world populations, these programs are microscopic. They can accommodate hundreds and thousands of precious stories over time, but millions and billions will never be heard. Still, it's a beginning! We need to start somewhere. Yes, a few stories are being preserved on CDs and bookshelves, but the main contribution of such programs, to the extent that their availability becomes known and utilized, may be consciousness-raising. We cannot depend on StoryCorps driving its trailers to every village, farm, and hamlet in the country or world and collecting our stories; and the Richmond Library serves only a small regional clientele. We must recognize this as a do-it-ourselves, wherever-we-are, project.

Why Not Just "Show and Tell?"

As with the campfire example in chapter 2, being in the same location physically and then verbally sharing stories may seem preferable to other possibilities and work against written versions, but verbal stories have their limitations. The messages we wish to convey verbally and spontaneously are not always the ones received, even when recorded on discs. Decades ago, research confirmed what most of us know intuitively, that how we communicate and how we look when we communicate trump the words we actually say. This may be unimportant when all messages are congruent. But when our facial expressions, mannerisms, and voice modulations appear contradictory to our spoken words, those words have little impact. (Of course, when actual behavior differs substantially from our rhetoric, credibility all but vanishes, as with the public perception of politicians.) Despite its usefulness in conveying information, oral communication can also be quite inaccurate and undependable.

Consider this common example. Imagine the typical family conflict when one member makes what he or she considers a relatively innocuous statement but which nevertheless receives a venomous response. Stunned by the reaction, the first member pleads, "All I said was ..." to which comes the further reply, "It wasn't what you said, it was how you looked when you said it." Or, alternatively, "It was the tone of voice you used when you said it." Parents of young teenagers are especially cognizant of this type of silent or indirect rebellion.

From childhood onward, our survival instinct—physical, social, emotional, and mental—dictates that we seek safety in times of extreme discomfort. Biblical scholars might point to Adam and Eve as initially responsible for that human attribute by first denying possession of the apple and hiding from God and then, upon being caught with the goods, putting the blame elsewhere. Mental health professionals might use other explanations, but the end result is the same. Some of our earliest learning is to lie, deny, deflect, exaggerate, blame, and distort, because we find that these strategies work to keep us safe, at least momentarily.

By the time we enter adulthood, most of us are already experts at manipulating words for the perceived benefits of safety. We justify and rationalize our maneuvers by inventing terms such as "little white lies," which we define as harmless and differentiated from those more insidious "bad lies" that we attribute to others. We use sarcasm and social humor to ridicule our victims and then put the blame on them ("Can't you take a joke?") when they react with pain or anger. Politicians and the media count on our naïveté and gullibility by inundating us with their illogical logic. And we accept their contradictions, inconsistencies, and hypocrisies because we've learned that we live in a world of words, and though we continue to hope for accuracy and honesty, few of us really expect it. Rather, we tend to accept the rhetoric, propaganda, and outright lies as part of the price we pay for freedom.

Estimates suggest that half of our face-to-face communication is transmitted nonverbally; that is, by such variables as facial expression, eye contact, limb movements, and other forms of subtle body language. Para linguistics (perhaps best described as language byproducts) account for most of the other half; that is, voice inflections and word emphases, slowness or rapidity of speech, loudness or softness, excessive silence or verbosity, intensity or calmness, and other such speech patterns. That leaves only about 10 percent of credibility devoted to the actual meanings of the words. This is a well-known, but poorly understood or often forgotten, aspect of human communication.

Most of our conversational interpretations are learned but seem intuitive, based as they often are on vague and ambiguous observations and verbal deliveries; we don't think about them and we're not immediately aware of them. But our unconscious abilities in this regard have been practiced and improved since early childhood when we first tried to figure out our parents' communications and inconsistencies. We then used this knowledge to develop strategies to ensure our emotional and physical survival within the family and elsewhere. Such needs and deeds rarely occur in the animal world because they operate primarily on instinct. It is indeed our human ability to think, reason, and choose that separates us from this animal kingdom. The following example reflects a simplified version of another typical human communication.

Suppose you were to say something to me, whereupon my face turned a bright red. You know what that means; you've learned it through many years of socialization! Armed with that understanding, suppose further that you said, "Oh, I didn't mean to embarrass you." Having learned early in life to protect my ego, my face-saving response might be "Oh, I'm not embarrassed." What would you believe, what you saw or what I said? And what if I glared expressionless at you after you joked about some aspect of my behavior? Seeing my staring response you might say, "Look, I didn't mean to offend you." Upon my next face-saving response, "You didn't," would you believe my words or your eyes?

Of course, interpretations of verbal discourse involve all parts and parties to a communication. Depending on our past association and relationship, in the above examples I might well interpret your words differently from what you meant—even if in fact you were being truthful and authentic. I might not at all believe you when you say you didn't mean to embarrass or offend me. I might interpret your tone as slightly sarcastic or your countenance as a bit too gleeful. So much for the infallibility of face-to-face discourse!

This isn't to say that written communication will solve all these problems associated with verbal sharing, only that the latter has its own set of issues and is often overblown as a favored mode of communication. There are times and places where written documents are far more useful and far less problematic, and sometimes life story delivery is one of these.

Weapons of Mass Protection

While we may instantly recognize in other people some of the flaws just described, we don't do nearly so well with recognizing the impact of our own facial expressions, bodily mannerisms, and vocal tendencies, though they may also account for upward of 90 percent of the messages we deliver in daily relationships. Unaware as we are, that's why they do us in. Since verbal deception seems easy and rewarding, to escape perceived danger we don't practice modes of honest communication nearly as much, and without practice we cannot perfect them. Instead, we watch and listen for the vulnerabilities of others, then defend ourselves with rationalizations and deflections. In the unlikely event that such behaviors are exposed and confronted, instead of seeking forgiveness we double down our protection.

Regardless of what parents may say, children have only to look at them to know how they really feel and what they are likely to do next. Then they can plan their next strategy. It's usually the only means of gaining power and protection that children have, so it's practically their full-time job. They concentrate on knowledge that we adults once knew as children but have since dismissed as we have matured and become "educated."

When children need an additional source of power, as when they're told to do something they'd rather not do right away, they also rely on the voice tone of the adult as their guide. They learn quickly that the first demand is seldom serious and that they still have "time to kill." They studiously listen for voice inflections, word emphases, rates of speech, and other paralinguistic attributes in order to determine adult levels of seriousness and truth. Their ongoing interpretations and conclusions about what they've just heard and seen determine their resulting behavior.

Children are very pragmatic and gauge the appropriate time to take action based on what they have learned about that adult's patience quotient, earlier determined by their assessment of the adult's behavioral consistency. Children internalize this social education as they develop, and apply it daily and habitually as they progress into adult relationships. The point is, the actual words spoken in the presence of others may well be the least reliable form of communication. Need we say more than "political campaigns"?

As suggested, the receiver of the verbal message can also be an unreliable variable, because every message is filtered by the past memories and present interpretations of the listener. Every spouse and parent understands the concept of "selective hearing." We may hear what we want to hear or what we thought we heard, according to our intellectual biases, past influences, and present state of concentration, rather than to what the speaker is actually intending.

A simple experiment is all that's needed to communicate this. Line up several people and whisper a short story to the first one, who in turn is told to convey the same story in the same way to the next person in line, who then whispers to the next person, and so on. Then compare the original story to the one being told by the last person. The difference is often enormous as each person filters what is most and least meaningful to him/her down the line.

Finally, there is the problem of spontaneity—immediate "off-the-cuff" remarks that rarely entail deep thinking, philosophical thinking, or visionary thinking. Spontaneity instead is often accompanied by temporary emotion, shallowness, and exaggeration. When telling stories, we forget important details and background information and are often tempted to engage in one-upmanship, thereby distorting such stories in order to make them more colorful and exciting for the listeners or more advantageous to the goals of the storyteller.

In addition, the more that needs and emotions of the moment come into play, the less honest and truthful our stories tend to be. We become entertainers and wishful thinkers, but our stories become tainted. There is certainly a place for entertainment and imagination in our documented legacies, but if our goal is to convey accurate time-and-place events for the benefit of future generations, some degree of caution should be exercised.

Much of our history has been obtained through verbal storytelling, so it is not to be underestimated. But consider how much more accurate and beneficial these ancestral stories might have been if they had been written down, after deep and thoughtful reflection, with a goal of providing perceptions and conclusions about life drawn from the experiences of those who have lived before us. Not many such writings exist, aside from those left by a few famous, wealthy, or powerful people who desired immortality of some sort. Most of us, like our ancestors, have instead developed a passive resistance to leaving written legacies.

The World Has Changed

Experts in social communication understand our tendencies to talk too much about ourselves and the subsequent problems narcissism can cause in relationships. Yes, we all seem self-centered (though not necessarily "selfish"), and there is often a fine line between narcissism and the positive sharing of our persona. But future generations will make no such distinctions or judgments. Trust me, they will never have enough information, and they will always have more unanswered questions. We can never satisfy the unquenchable thirst for knowledge of the past that many of the yet unborn will request. But we can do our part in preserving our own history by sharing with them stories about our lives.

Since the beginning of human time, our ancestors have sought to communicate stories. When language did not exist beyond grunts, they drew pictures on the walls of caves. As the power of language was uncovered, primitive attempts at using different sounds provided symbols that enhanced communication. Gradually, these symbolic sounds became words understood throughout their limited worlds. As hundreds and thousands of these worlds developed on the planet, refinements took place, according to the needs of each region and culture, resulting today in a hodgepodge of languages, dialects, and accents. Because of this, oral communication can still be difficult between countries and regions of countries, but written communication is becoming increasingly standardized within each language, and technology is being produced to provide nearly instant translations between languages. Beyond this, there are other important advantages to providing our stories in written form.

We have been brainwashed into believing that face-to-face communication is preferable to that which can be put into writing. Whoever perpetrated that hoax did us all a disservice. Certainly, our daily functions would be held to a crawl if all communication had to be written down. No one would advocate that because much communication is relatively noninvasive and routine.

But when important, significant, and vital information is at stake, "Put it in writing" is a commonly used phrase. Retail transactions, business messages, and legal contracts are put in writing, not only because of the convenience of exact copying and duplication but also because written words can be scrutinized for clarity and appropriateness before being released.

One can only imagine the anger and chaos that would be produced if such communication were orally transmitted to thousands and millions of people. Even with the protection of the written word, messages are often unclear and misconstrued. The term "read the fine print" has become a joke, sometimes a cruel one for those who do not pay heed. For the average citizen, legal jargon can be impossible to translate and understand. Yet courts make decisions according to the fine print. Difficult and inconvenient as this may be, businesses know that the dangers and problems inherent in oral communication can be far worse. Years ago a promise and a handshake would consummate a contract, but in our present world of distrust and immorality, only the foolish would bypass legal means.

It is common that many television ads provide verbal disclaimers about possible dangers or side effects when using their products, while other disclaimers are written on the bottom of the screen, though in such small print that they are impossible to read, even if they stayed within sight long enough to actually scan the words. What is my point? How does all of this relate to conveying stories about our lives?

When significant information is to be conveyed, it is preferable to put it in writing. Yes, oral communication is light years ahead of none at all, but so is drawing pictures on the walls! When possible, preserving stories in written form may be the most useful mode to the yet unborn. An even better possibility is to combine oral and written accounts as is frequently done today with books and discs. Giving future genealogists access to both visual and auditory enlightenment can only enhance their investigations.

Beyond legalities and business functions, writing may have advantages over face-to-face dialogue in some of our social relationships. "If you have anything (nasty?) to say to me, say it to my face" is an oft-heard expression. Combined with tone of voice and facial expression, this communication is often received as challenging and intimidating—hardly conducive to problem solving. If both (or all) parties are well meaning, well intentioned, deeply caring, and open-minded throughout a difficult interaction, the chance of a decent resolution to interpersonal conflict is possible. But how often is this the case? My nearly forty years of experience as a teacher and as a relationship counselor to many families and friendships has convinced me that this is indeed a rarity, even when accompanied by professional intervention.

On the other hand, when an emotionally charged interpersonal dialogue is called for, written communication can convey a clear message while de-escalating a potentially volatile situation. Both sender and receiver can in isolation read and reread several times the content of a letter or e-mail. The sender can write as many drafts and revisions as necessary—adding, subtracting, and modifying words and phrases in the process until satisfied with meaning and intent. Sometimes it even becomes unnecessary to send the message at all, as the mere act of putting it on paper may calm the emotions or provide insights that were previously absent.

The receiver also benefits from the lack of what might have developed as a hostile, relationship-ending verbal encounter. Not only can the message be privately revisited as necessary, leading to reframing and reinterpretation according to the total background relationship, but further internal reflection and examination over time may also change the dynamics of a response, if one is desired at all. Moreover, it is very difficult not to respond immediately to a face-to-face confrontation, often with spontaneity that worsens the relationship in a way that neither party would desire if there were time for additional contemplation.

When writing our own personal stories for future generations, similar dynamics apply. Each of us is a sender, and our descendants will be the receivers. Spontaneous recordings on DVDs or CDs are subject to the same difficulties as face-to-face encounters in the present. We may say things without thinking clearly—messages we don't really wish to convey or stories from our egos that contain only partial truths—or we may leave out or forget material that we later believe would have been helpful. In addition, the future misuse of verbal editing techniques could result in harmful and misleading outcomes, as political clips have for decades demonstrated.

What Now?

So, as with many activities, there are pros and cons to our choices. We have the opportunity to do for our descendants—our children and grandchildren for many future generations—what our ancestors could not do for us. We can excuse prior generations because they didn't have the technology, literacy, and know-how to leave us either written or orally recorded legacies. Their lone option was unrecorded oral stories, often fascinating but also inconsistent, ever-changing over time, and subject to mistaken interpretations and cultural expectations of future relatives and historians.

Of course, these problems are also common with written history as well, but the likelihood and magnitude of inaccuracies are usually far greater when passed down in a vocal manner. Consider the New Testament of the Christian Bible, written from the memories of disciples or observers. Controversies erupted over whose memories were most accurate in the portrayal of Jesus, and many were left out of the final revisions because they didn't exactly fit the desires of the most influential.

We have long acknowledged such concerns with little criticism, for how can people be blamed for nonuse or misuse of skills and technology not available to them? But our generation and those that follow cannot be excused so readily. Illiteracy is becoming nonexistent in developed countries and will become so in Third World countries with increasing rapidity as universal education and access to global communication gain speed.

Most of us have the means to leave written stories of our lives as legacies, but do we have the internal motivation to do so? Will we allow ourselves to be inspired by those unseen external forces in which surveys indicate most of us believe, but whose power is so often ignored?

Thoughts/Activities to Consider

1. Record orally some story about an event or activity in your life. Wait a few days, and then put the same story in writing. Now compare the two versions. What differences do you note? Which version is most accurate and complete? How do you account for the differences?

2. For a few days, pay special attention to your many daily conversations. Notice how your own and others' messages are strengthened, weakened, and modified by how they are conveyed and by how the actual senders look as they furnish them. How congruent are the looks, the deliveries, and the actual words?

CHAPTER 5

Challenging Our Obstacle Courses

What's Your Excuse?

Over the past few years I've conducted many spontaneous, informal surveys to help determine the sources and characteristics of resistance I've found to writing stories about one's life. Occasionally I have also used more formal surveys during times when I have spoken to groups about this possibility. I prefer the more spontaneous kind, often given in the midst of sharing general information at a social or recreational function because, in that way, I catch people "off guard," without time to formulate a rational or socially acceptable response.

By far the most common initial response is, "I haven't really thought about it." This lack of awareness about the value of sharing one's life with others in the present and future has provided the foundation for this book. Considering the difficulties associated with the lack of mass printing technology for thousands of years, this deficiency may also be an outgrowth of a collective unconscious made permanent by inertia. Even after such technology became available nearly six hundred years ago, the idea that common, ordinary people could influence the present and future direction of our descendants by recording life stories was still incredulous. And even if such thoughts did occur among some, many commoners were illiterate and poor or had no means to reproduce their perceptions.

More recently there have been grave concerns about privacy issues. The computer age and the ingenious, though illegal and unethical, practice of hacking and stealing private information and identities has fostered suspicion and fear among the most trusting of us. Even the US government has admitted to monitoring phone calls and e-mails of millions of citizens, though officials have denied accessing any specific content.

When the purpose of a small gathering is known to be helpful in its intent, under the leadership of competent professionals (as in group therapy or family counseling), there is still a reluctance to share deeply personal thoughts and feelings. Along with our own guilt and the pain involved in verbalizing our inner selves, we are very concerned about how others in the group will use our revelations. We fear social, legal, and political repercussions—and with good reason.

Putting these stories into print only intensifies those fears because it makes retractions more difficult. Our cultural reliance on legal documents has influenced us to rationalize "seeing" as more powerful than "hearing." All of these issues can come into play when writing personal stories. Though we always retain initial control over what and how we write and who reads it, our suspicions continue.

No matter what our lives accord us by comparative standards, nearly all of us live healthier, more luxurious lives than did our ancestors. Physical survival beyond early and middle adulthood is no longer an immediate concern. Even considering recent bouts of terrorism, our enemies today are more internal than external, more personal than international. Mental and emotional stress, job concerns, and interpersonal relationships now consume much of our time as we seek solutions that will make our lives more tolerable, if not more comfortable.

How did we get to this state? Each of us has stories to tell, and together we have a culture to transmit. The rich and famous cannot do it for us. We must all take responsibility, individually and collectively. No one else can speak for me—or for you. Which brings us to the most significant, if not the most common, response that I encounter, the "I'm just a ..." retort.

Consider Your Own Greatness

The exact words vary and are unimportant, but the communication is clear and precise, if not purposeful. "I don't have anything important to say." "What could I possibly contribute?" "Who would want to hear about my life?" "I've never done anything important." "I'm just a ..." (You fill in the blank). These are all variations of the same theme. Despite the outward bravado of our narcissistic society, the most commonly seen human animal is the jellyfish, or perhaps chameleon. Like any animal protecting its territory or its young, we flap our wings and bare our teeth. But it's all a façade, as we seek only to protect our manufactured ego, which is always willing to sacrifice truth and genuineness for "looking good." Believing we're really insignificant, we compensate by trying to pretend we're big, tough, and self-assured when internally we're uncertain and insecure.

Nevertheless, it is precisely that truth which could inspire and motivate future generations as they struggle with their worlds. Relationship experts tell us that empathy—the ability to mentally and emotionally view and appreciate situations from other than our own perspective—is a fundamental key to productive interpersonal connections. What better way to initiate such empathy than with recorded honesties about our quandaries and dilemmas, thus encouraging future generations to expand their own perceptions! Despite our frequent beliefs to the contrary, younger generations can and do learn from older ones. But relevant information must be available to them—communicated with emotion, sincerity, passion, and truth (as each of us sees and experiences it). We all possess those attributes; they are not reserved for the rich, the famous, and the educated; they are universal. And who's to say which perceptions will best serve future generations?

Our world has been punctuated with biographies of great visionaries, philosophers, and artists who were scorned during their earthly lives, only to be understood and revered for their thoughts and deeds long after their deaths. Which raises the question, why didn't their contemporaries really care about what these out-of-step people were doing or saying? Could it be that their works were far too advanced or different to be taken seriously at the time they lived? Lacking immediate significance, the outcome for many was isolation, despair, and even suicide. Yet, like Van Gogh and other such victims in history, their impacts on future generations have often been enormous. Are there issues in life whereupon you find yourself in substantial disagreement with our present culture? Most likely there are! Do you have some off-the-wall suggestions that might improve certain conditions—locally, nationally, and worldly? Most likely you do! Are you concerned that your perspectives might be ridiculed or rejected? Most likely you are!

Such is occasionally the price for greatness; it may go unrecognized for decades or even centuries. As noted earlier, no matter how profound an individual's ideas, suggestions, or accomplishments, it appears to be a common perception that, if we know (or are) that person, s/he can't be all that important or knowledgeable—another way that we directly or indirectly diminish our own importance.

Lack of Time

Another reason people cite for not recording stories about their lives is that they don't have time. Of course, lack of time is an excuse so common as to lack credibility. Nevertheless, it may well be a plausible response for those whose lives are so focused on physical survival that they can concentrate on nothing else, or for those whose lives are so full of meaningful and rewarding activities that lack of time is truly a problem. For most of us, however, neither of these conditions applies for an entire lifetime, even though we can all rationalize ourselves as exceptions.

Lack of time usually means lower priority. We all have the same amount of time available to us. How we use that time depends on that human characteristic of choice. And therein rests the difficulty. We have far more choices available to us today than did our ancestors. Some of those additional choices are due to inventions and advances in technology, some to the development of organizational skills, and some to alterations in culture.

While the Industrial Revolution of the nineteenth and twentieth centuries has provided luxuries far beyond the comprehension and imagination of our great-grandparents, many of those luxuries have now become economic, mental, emotional, and social necessities. We have simultaneously developed a deprivation mentality and luxurious lifestyles. CDs, DVDs, digital cameras, cell phones, computers, cable and satellite TVs, video games, and GPS devices highlight the more recent communication inventions that take up our time. Add to these the creations of modern travel that dwarf the planet and increase the dangers, and we possess enough distractions to easily justify a lack of time for that which we perceive as personal indulgence or wasteful activity (i.e., writing life stories).

On the surface, better organizational skills might seem to give us more time for sharing life stories. But initial assumptions and reasoning can be deceiving, and reality often overrides predictions. During my school days in the mid-1900s, as we mulled over George Orwell's leap into the world of 1984, we fantasized an adult existence of monitoring machines, pushing buttons, and recreating. Naïve as that perception may have been, thirty years after Orwell's projection into the future, we find life far more complex than we ever imagined, as we struggle with personal concerns about organization, consolidation, evaluation, and decision making.

Multitasking is now considered an essential skill for both home and workplace as personal and occupational functions become more profuse and entwined. Many businesses and industries are operating with fewer employees, often requiring not only more work for those remaining but also more versatility. Lucrative home businesses provide a major source of income for many, and a burgeoning day-care industry exists for the benefit of those who work elsewhere. Corporate greed, fraud, and mismanagement have turned once-loyal workforces into angry mobs as laborers struggle with credit card debt and erosion of benefits. Meanwhile, politicians argue about ideologies, entitlements, and the role of government in never-ending standoffs, too often using whatever rhetoric they can muster to ensure their self-serving reelection bids by tearing down opponents rather than building up themselves.

Unlike the conditions in many third world countries, however, most Americans fear uncertainty more than immediate poverty, often resulting in what psychology has called "choice anxiety." To allay those concerns requires a reorganization of priorities, and recording stories of life is far down the list. "Once I get organized," the saying goes, "then I'll be able to focus on other things." As though that will ever happen, because we are continually bombarded with new options and new opportunities—and new arguments for the inclusion of each choice into our already hectic lives! These new choices are always intriguing and inviting, as commercialism and profit dominate our environment. Where once survival meant basic sustenance and shelter, today it means possessions and acquisitions. Poverty now means the absence of luxury. Handouts, bailouts, grants, and loans are considered entitlements. Individual accountability has taken a backseat to blame and greed amid demands for social engineering to assure equality of life's rewards.

Cultural changes have both resulted from and caused such transformations. Our historical dream of becoming a melting pot for the world's dissidents has indeed emerged, though probably not in the manner our ancestors anticipated. Our European heritage is about to be trumped by the influx of a massive Hispanic movement and a steady Asian influence. With the adoption and integration of these and other such cultures, we have begun to accept an "anything goes" philosophy, as we strive not to offend our new inhabitants.

Concepts of "right" and "wrong" are more blurred than ever, resulting in additional options never even imagined by our grandparents. Prolife, prochoice, gay rights, civil unions, and other such terms were unknown or unexamined just a few decades ago and have led to a concept of political correctness that often impedes daily conversations. With each new choice comes more confusion, more rationalization, more options—and less time to relax and enjoy the stillness of life, less time to philosophize, less time to tap into the spiritual side of life. And certainly less time to think about what each of us can offer to future descendants and generations.

This complexity of modern life keeps most of us on automatic pilot. We tend to react far more than we act. We tend to behave first and think later. We tend to protect what we have and grieve about what we don't have. Greed, envy, and rebellion have replaced charity, acceptance, and compliance. Not that all of these changes have been bad. Far from it. But some have, and the sorting process has been difficult for many; some have succumbed to dangerous new behaviors, while others have held steadfast and refused to budge from the ways of their ancestors. Neither stance is particularly productive in the multicultural society we citizens have tacitly approved.

It has been cited often that the Chinese symbol for crisis means "danger plus opportunity"—an apt description for the conditions I have described. As in most such situations, the danger is more obvious than the opportunity. But opportunity there is! Out of confusion and choice comes clarity for those who seek it. As with the thousands of neurons and synapses in our brains, where one variation can result in vast differences in behavior and thought, so we can come to thousands of conclusions about life from so many choices and options. Our real priorities are represented by what we do, not by what we think we ought to do or would like to do. Desires are only rhetoric until acted upon. In the end, lack of time for recording life stories is still only an excuse—understandable but pointless.

Trying Isn't Enough

Procrastination is another obstacle many of us face and is related to the perceived lack of time. Don't do today what can be put off until tomorrow. "I really want to do it, but later—when I'm retired, when the kids are grown, when I can find the time, when ..." Translated, this usually means, "I'm not interested, but I want to appear that I am, so I'll just make a promise for the future." In another context, a similar rationalization is found in the phrase "I'll try," which was earlier described as a commitment to "failing with honor"—an attempt to convince the listener that our intentions are honorable, and the effort will be made. It's usually another way of politely saying no. Socially it guarantees that no one will be offended, but such retorts are meant to cut off conversation, and they generally do.

For some, writing stories—even personal ones that might live beyond death—is just too much trouble. Few admit to that directly, for it can appear lazy, selfish, and uncaring. Nevertheless, their nonverbal and tonal behaviors often convey just that attitude. "What's in it for me?" is their communication. Worldly materialism seems to be their main focus. If there is no immediate reward for their efforts, it is considered a waste of their time. They do not view life with any broad-based perspective, mental or spiritual, but are instead consumed with perceived earthly necessities or pleasures. They may fit any of the behavioral categories described in chapter 3 and could be of immense help to future generations, for they have experienced the essence of much of twentieth and twenty-first century life. But their hearts are more aligned with consuming the present than with sharing the future, and their field of vision is narrow and self-absorbed.

Who Cares?

So it may be that the truthful answer to "Who cares about my perceptions of life?" is that no one cares—for now. At the beginning of the Broadway show *Carousel*, Billy Bigelow looks up into the stars and mutters a phrase whose general meaning is all too familiar to most of us: "I'm just a tiny speck of nothing in the universe." Who hasn't felt that way? Life has a way of humbling us, of knocking us around, of italicizing our self-doubts. By the time we've reached mental and emotional maturity (whenever and whatever that is), we're too beaten down or cynical to access the wisdom that comes from struggling, sacrificing, and surviving. And who cares anyway?

Who cares that you've had a life? That you've worked at a boring job? That you've raised a family all by yourself? That you actually had a childhood? That you squandered opportunities? That you never married? That your children disappointed you? That you spent time in the military? That you ...? Who cares?

I'm sure that when my great-grandmother, Dorliska Dean Vincent, wrote her diary as a young twenty-two-year-old mother in 1865, she had no idea of the impact it would have on her descendants nearly 150 years later. Wouldn't many of us like to know the inner feelings of life experienced by our direct ancestors centuries ago? The genealogy craze today focuses on names, dates, and places because, for the most part, that's all we have available to us. How exciting would it be to be able to read or hear about interpreted experiences as well! Yes, writing stories about life as we are living it may not bring immediate rewards, but who can judge with certainty the impact on an unknown future? Perhaps a more significant question than who cares about our legacy is, "Do we care enough to leave one?"

We might ask, did those few life story writers of the past really care about future generations? Were their motives for greatness altruistic? Or were they merely following some inner drive, some fatalistic predisposition, some spiritual destiny? We can only speculate, based on our own internal impulses. That is, do we really care enough about others, present and future, to give them the benefit of our own appraisals of life? How we respond to that question, in addition to our own self-perceptions of importance, will ultimately determine our decisions about legacy, about leaving records of our lives for future generations.

Our response will also have an impact on what our children and grandchildren come to believe about their importance to us. As the Hallmark commercials say, do we care enough to give our very best to them—even before we ask the question, do they care enough to receive it? Moreover, since we can control only ourselves, it is the first of those two questions to which we need an answer.

Where to Begin?

Occasionally I encounter people who appear willing to record their stories but lament that they have no idea where to begin. Usually this happens because they're looking at the process as all or nothing. Either the task is utterly overwhelming or a trivial pursuit.

In the first instance, rather than conveying short stories about life in some recorded form, they think "autobiography" and just give up the challenge. Truth is, in one way or another, most of us share vocal stories about our lives every day—at the coffee shop, in the fitness center, by the water cooler, on the telephone, or in line at the grocery store. Seldom do we need prompting at these times. At certain times and in certain places, our stories just seem to flow, as in the campfire example mentioned earlier. Even watching movies or television can bring to mind events and stories perhaps long forgotten.

Who has not had emotional responses to certain types of programs? Why do horror pictures bring out fear in some of us and laughter in others? Why do we feel sadness or compassion in one instance but not in others? Why do animals, babies, westerns, war movies, romances, athletic events, and other program types conjure up certain kinds of feelings? Can the cause be other than our unique background of experiences?

One possible solution to the problem of where to begin is to seek an environment that stimulates these emotions, with the premeditated purpose of creating a story. Awareness must be the initial goal—to remove the automatic pilot of life and focus on commitment to an end result. We must think about that which we wish to bring about! At every minute of life, a potential story is brewing. Finding that story and creating our own ways of telling it can be satisfying, meaningful, and fun.

Initial paralysis may also come from thoughts that we have nothing significant to say—a variation of the "just a ..." mentality described earlier. If we believe we have nothing much to offer, of course we will struggle with where to begin. But take off the blindfolds! There's the first story—the struggle with where to begin. Think about that struggle. What is the foundation of it? What are its symptoms? Why is it happening? What does this tell me about my life history? How did I arrive at this point in life, with these thoughts about life?

Out of this initial story, which blends the past with the present, will come many more. Trust me! Writing about these present struggles will uncover memories about past events, which will lead to more stories. Each of us has an unending supply of such stories, and no one else has your or my perspective because no one else has lived life in exactly the same way as you or I. Indeed, it is our uniqueness of interpretation in a world of personally experienced events that makes our stories valuable. No one else can have quite the same perspective.

How Do You Wish to Be Remembered?

For some, writing stories about their lives to be passed on to future generations is a no-brainer, though few do it on a regular basis. The more usual way is to wait until old age or retirement and then write memoirs. Unfortunately, much is lost or transformed in the process of remembering, and long-past events become clouded, distorted, or completely forgotten. Time and emotional distance may allow for a more objective and mature perspective on life but also undervalues the ongoing thoughts and feelings that life provides. Both scenarios are essential to a more complete understanding of life, and this book is dedicated to making that happen—for us and for our descendants. Fact is, only a tiny percentage of people ever record *any* stories about their lives, so they leave behind neither perspective nor spontaneity.

Too many older citizens consider themselves too tired, too insignificant, too uneducated, too depressed, too frightened, too guilty, or just too boring to begin conveying details about their lives. Yet, if we were to record these stories on a regular basis—daily, weekly, monthly, or even yearly—throughout our lives, we would be more energized to explain our thoughts and behaviors as they occur, a process usually far more accurate than hindsight. In so doing, we might lose perspective but gain credibility. We might lose objectivity but convey genuineness. And we can always update, reexamine, and rerecord our entries at a later date, if we wish. To cite a well-known quotation, "Nothing is ever written in stone"—at least until the writer dies!

To record stories as they are occurring obviously requires great purpose and discipline, but there are many rewards for those who do. There can be great personal satisfaction in leaving a legacy of life experiences for future generations. Of course, we cannot know how or even if our records of life will have any great impact on descendants—or even if such records will survive. Such is the mystery of existence. Still, the mere possibility of influencing the future, of some form of immortality, can bring goose bumps to the most demure of us.

As children, our imaginations took us everywhere. There were no boundaries to our adventures and heroism. We could be anything, do anything, and have anything—and we still can. Age need not diminish this magnificent childlike enthusiasm. Indeed, involvement in adult society should be an addition to, not a deviation from, the magic of childhood. What the mind can conceive, actions can achieve! What might the future look like if each of us had that attitude?

We need only imagine, centuries from now, families crowded around a table, observing some advanced communication system, ingesting and discussing ancestral manuscripts, recordings, and pictures, perhaps marveling at our immense survival skills during this primitive era known as the twenty-first century. Consider your own sense of awe and excitement if you suddenly came across a diary of life as recorded by an ancestor centuries or millennia ago. Findings in 2007 of a perfectly formed baby woolly mammoth in Siberia produced world fascination and interest. And ancient skeletons of primitive people have enthralled us as we continue to investigate the beginnings of existence. How much more exciting would be written stories from a known family ancestor!

Alternatively, consider that same group of your descendants discussing their heritage amid the sadness of wishing they knew something about their genealogy, as they rummage through sparse remnants of family history. Your name is mentioned, but they know nothing of your essence, so they can feel no emotional connection, only frustration at wishing you had left some explanation of life through which they might better understand you and, ultimately, themselves. Unfortunately, this has been the usual scenario, and will continue to be until we take action to change it.

Thoughts/Activities to Consider

1. What internal obstacles to writing stories about your life have you encountered? External ones? Write a short personal story on this topic and conclude with what you have learned about yourself.
2. When urged to "consider your own greatness," what feelings emerge?
3. What activities could you eliminate so you'd have time for story writing?
4. When you encounter strong emotions in your daily activities, do an internal investigation as to their causes or origins.
5. How do you wish to be remembered by future generations? What can you contribute now that might influence such an outcome?

CHAPTER 6

What to Tell Your Descendants

From Ideas to Stories

Discussion so far has concentrated on the why of communicating stories about our lives, the pros and cons of both verbal and written modes of delivery, and some of the self-imposed obstacles to getting started. Understanding a rationale is an essential first step to either motivation or inspiration, both of which can lead to action. As was suggested earlier, motivation begins with an idea formulated in the mind and carried out by the body, while inspiration is more mystical to most of us, beginning with a spiritual force that seems to work with, and yet to transcend, both mind and body in its application. Many choose to link inspiration to a religious concept, such as the Holy Spirit, while others may attribute such overwhelming energy and focus to more worldly phenomena.

My purpose is neither to argue nor convince anyone to change beliefs, but rather to encourage participation in a process dependent only on a desire to help future generations to better understand their roots and thus themselves in attempts to extend reason, hope, and progress in the universe. En route we may experience many or all of the personal rewards and tribulations discussed in earlier chapters.

Time-consuming as this might appear at first glance, it is a massive win-win course of action for all.

Convinced as some may already be of the importance and potential significance of recording our stories, we have to begin to take action somewhere. Out of an intangible commitment must come tangible outcomes. There must be results that can be read, heard, watched, or somehow experienced. So how do we get from an idea to an end product?

As mentioned earlier in the Introduction, writing instructors tell us that a good story should include answers to the following questions: Who? Where? When? Why? What? How? How much? The first three elements need little discussion, as they are quite obvious. To reiterate, when referring to our life stories, the who is you or me or whoever is doing the recording, the where is wherever that who has lived or experienced life, and the when is the time or era in which the who has physically existed in the where of this world. How specific we wish to become in any given story will depend on our objectives, but as long as we're writing about our own personal lives and experiences, these questions of who, where, and when answer themselves.

Throughout these chapters I have tried to explain the importance to future generations, and secondarily to ourselves, of leaving behind a record of our physical existence on earth—a legacy, a personal library reflecting beyond our human similarities the uniqueness of each one of us, famous or anonymous, rich or poor, old or young, criminal or philanthropist. No one should be left out. Every person's death diminishes each of us, unless every life is remembered for the wisdom and value it contained or generated. This is the essence of why.

All that remains is what to record and how to transmit it. With all that life throws at us on a daily basis, how do we decide what to write or talk about, and how do we communicate our life experiences and conclusions in such a way that they will be useful to, and understood by, future generations? As we write, we will also convey the essence of our personalities and values, a secondary goal likely to be treasured and appreciated by our descendants. It is impossible to totally isolate these items, as they blend and overlap on many levels. Nevertheless, some distinctions must be made in order to avoid confusion and enhance understanding.

Basic Guidelines

When beginning any new venture, we usually need some guidelines, a map or path to follow, a model to which we can refer, an outline of ideas that gives us some direction. Without some frame of reference with which to begin, a vacuum exists, and chaos and frustration rush in to fill it. Quitting usually results.

So our first task is to develop some focus, some guidelines for sharing. In considering such guidelines, we need to ask some fundamental questions. Number one on the list is: *What would you like to know or have known about your own ancestors?* What information would be most meaningful to you about their existence? Your responses to this question can provide you with a place to begin, for those responses provide clues to experiences about which your descendants might also wish to hear.

Each entry in my great-grandmother's 1865 diary began with a weather report. How boring! Does that help me to know her? Not really, unless I consider how the weather may have influenced other aspects of her life—her moods, her activities, her worries, her daily plans, and so on. Today I turn on the Weather Channel each morning to see how the weather might affect my plans for the day. Seldom does it change those plans. The information merely begins a thought process about how to utilize the forecast or how to overcome it. At worst a rainy, snowy, or windy forecast presents an inconvenient challenge, but rarely is it life-altering. Those who have survived major hurricanes, tornadoes, blizzards, earthquakes, forest fires, floods, mudslides, avalanches, and other natural phenomena may initially disagree, but objective reflection will usually recognize these as exceptions which few of us experience even once and which almost no one experiences again in a lifetime.

Today we have instant access to global information and predictions that allow us to prepare for and circumvent weather conditions that often proved disastrous in 1865. If planes are grounded, I drive. If the outdoor heat or cold is oppressive, I turn on the air conditioner or heating unit, usually with a flick of a switch. If the electricity goes out, I plug in the generator. Bad weather today is an inconvenience for most, not a life-threatening prohibition. There are exceptions, of course, and if weather has accorded you horrific results at one time or another, make the most of it. You have survived, and you now have a story to tell!

But on a day-to-day basis, would I usually begin any of my stories with a weather report? Not likely. Had great-grandmother Dorliska realized that her diary would be available to future generations and could have an effect on them, would she still have begun each day with a weather report? Probably—unless she had the vision that weather would have far less of an impact on her descendants than on her own generation. But it's unlikely that she would have imagined the magnitude of weather technology continuing to burst on the scene of humankind.

As a student of history I have some idea of worldly conditions in 1865. I also know that my great-grandfather—Dorliska's husband,

Wilbur—spent the majority of his working life sailing cargo ships on the Great Lakes. His safety was dependent on unpredictable weather conditions, and his wife's emotional and economic states were dependent on his safety. Armed with this understanding, her weather reports acquire a much greater significance. And even more so, her responses to the weather give me additional insight into her being, as she struggled daily to maintain her household and her sanity while experiencing often below-zero winter weather herself and imagining her husband battling storms on the Great Lakes for three-fourths of each year.

She birthed six children, only one of whom—my grandfather, Will Vincent—lived long enough to give her any grandchildren. The comments he made to my mother when she was a teenager in the 1920s only reinforce the difficulties in predicting and preparing for the future. Infatuated with the sophistication of the household radio, he would often say, "Imagine if we could actually *see* those people who are talking hundreds of miles away." Then he would laugh heartily and add, "But that's impossible!" Unfortunately, he died of an occupational disease in 1930, before his eyes could reveal what his mind could not conceive at the time—several color TV sets in millions of homes over the entire planet and satellite reception in every part of the globe.

We can only speculate about the enormous changes that technological advances will create in the lives of the yet unborn. But that such changes will come is assured. I recall the amusing story about a worker in the US patent office, following the initial onslaught of the nineteenth century Industrial Revolution, who once remarked that his office might as well be eliminated because everything that could be invented had already been thought of. So much for predictions.

How then can we be certain that our stories will be meaningful to future generations? The simple answer is that we can't. The best we can do is to provide the stories—our stories. We cannot control the future, but we can certainly try to influence it. We can describe the stepping-stones that will eventually lead to whatever life circumstances our descendants may be facing. Our task is to create and report the stories. Their task will be to decide how to use them. But they cannot make such decisions without the information. So we must do our job first, before they can do theirs.

Besides considering our own desires for information we would like to have received from our ancestors as a basis for what we record from our own lives, a second guiding question might be this: *What has influenced us to become the persons we are?* Usually that query into our own development will bring up a myriad of responses, and each one is a story with great potential. These stories do not have to be factually accurate, for who knows for certain exactly how and why we have developed as we have? But our responses will reveal to descendants our experiences, our perspectives, our thought processes, and our motives. In addition, such investigations will undoubtedly aid us in making sense of our past lives, making connections between seemingly unrelated events, and determining how we wish to use our future time on earth, however long or short that may prove to be.

A third guideline might be to ask ourselves: *How am I both different from, and similar to, others from my generation?* As each of us has developed over the years, such differences and similarities must have become obvious. For example, I can cite many similarities to my older brother. We have many of the same small-town values; we both graduated near the top of our high school classes; we were both active in athletics; we both became college teachers; we even acquired PhDs within a year of one another; we both married strong but sensitive women who were educators; we both adopted a child; we are both very family oriented, and so on.

But there are also significant differences in our development and in our conclusions about life. He thrived in leadership situations; I didn't. He seemed comfortable in social situations from his early childhood; I wasn't. He was outwardly devoted to a relationship with God; I hardly thought about it, only going through the motions. His personality was very outgoing; mine was very reserved. As we have aged, his political outlook leans liberal; while mine leans conservative. There are more similarities and differences, to be sure; these are merely samples. But if these exist between brothers, raised by the same parents, in the same location, with access to the same people, might we conclude that our similarities and differences with those outside of our nuclear family should be even more evident?

The problem is, of course, that in growing up many of us learn to hide our thoughts, feelings, and ongoing conclusions, even from ourselves sometimes. We learn to conform to what others think we should believe and we become robots, behaving by remote control and default systems tucked away in the pockets of significant others. We become alien beings, forever struggling with that inner core of individualism that defines us all. Can we turn things around? Can we escape the shackles that imprison us? I believe we can. At any age!

Children will obviously have fewer chains of social bondage from which to break, even under the worst of living arrangements. Depending on their ages, they have fewer years of social and political propaganda to endure. They generally have fewer inhibitions and greater openness to change. That's why we must begin to encourage them to share life stories while they are young; to foster a habit of genuineness and self-examination before conformity to the dictates of others becomes calcified.

Beyond these basic guidelines (What might descendants want to hear about? What has influenced each of us to become the kind of person we have become? How are we both similar to and different from others in our generation?) are general categories and themes into which we can channel our perceptions. These might include: accomplishments/successes, perspectives, turning points, politics, values, aspirations, ideas, philosophies, opinions, habits, education, and experiences. Also: pets, family, friends, jobs or employment, regrets/mistakes, home/living arrangements, travel experiences, hobbies/interests, talents (used, unused, misused), idiosyncrasies/quirks, personality traits, technology, crime/terror, and "local color."

Self-Centered Is Not Selfish

A further consideration is whether to focus on self or others. It has been said that we humans are all self-centered. Often this is phrased as a criticism, but how could it be otherwise? No matter what our goals in life, no matter how altruistic and honorable, we seek to feel better, act better, and be better according to our own standards; and we all create agendas to meet those standards. Whether these standards and agendas are acquired or inborn in origin matters not to that bottom line. Our agendas may be helpful or not to the populace at large, and what seems to help in the present may prove disastrous in the future. Likewise, we can sacrifice in the present for anticipated personal rewards in the future, but there are few guarantees. Whether in private or public life, we act according to our goals, knowledge, insights, conscience, and experiences.

In 2008 President George W. Bush left office with apparently the lowest approval rating in history. His presidency was defined by world conflict, enemy attack on our soil, internal strife, and a term-ending economic crisis. Were his policies and responses self-centered? Of course they were. Should we be concerned about that? Not in the least! He behaved in ways that would enhance his own satisfaction with doing what he thought needed to be done. Martin Luther King Jr. did the same thing. So did Mahatma Gandhi. And so have Barack Obama and all others who will follow. Will history show their behaviors and beliefs to be helpful or not? We can only speculate. Which ones have done the right things? God only knows. The only thing we can know for sure is that each one behaved as he thought best, which is inherently self-centered and self-enhancing, at least in intent.

Each of us ordinary citizens is no different. Our thoughts and behaviors may be less far-reaching, for the moment at least, but they are no less important. Certainly not for our lives and for those we influence, now and in the future. Let us not confuse, however, self-centeredness and self-enhancement with the common definition of selfishness. The latter connotes that our behaviors and attitudes are deliberately hurtful, intentionally designed to rise above others, to put others down, even to destroy them or their possessions if they get in our way.

Selfishness is regarded as a competitive sort of greed and may be a root cause of comparison. Self-centeredness is a basic foundation of all life; selfishness is not! Selfishness is ego-created and socially engineered. We are born self-centered but not selfish.

The recognition of self-centeredness promotes reason and cooperation, the antithesis of selfishness! It understands that self preservation and desires for enhancement are common to us all at birth but that we are all different in our pursuit of specific goals and ways of attaining them, so why not help one another out? It assumes abundance and expansion, an infinite universe, a belief that there is enough for all, so why fight over morsels?

In contrast, selfishness thrives on ideas of scarcity, limitation, and finiteness. Comparison and aggressive competition are its cornerstones, often with brutal consequences, as shoppers maul one another for the last latest electronic game at Christmastime, athletes do "whatever it takes" to disable their opponents, bright students resort to cheating on exams in order to ensure top grades, and parents seek to humiliate their children's classmates by sending false or indicting information to colleges just to gain an advantage in admissions.

All of these scenarios have been recently reported in the press. "I'm more deserving than you, and there's not enough (money, glory, opportunity) for all" is the message. These ego-driven, covetous components of selfishness are often associated with the religious concept of "original sin" (to be discussed at length in part 3).

But is selfishness "original?" If we are born in the image of God, with the spirit of God within us and with an undeveloped brain, as many believe, then are we not born with original divinity? (For atheists, it might be original neutrality.) Perhaps that's why the presence of a newborn is so precious to us. We instinctively recognize in all the purity, love, and innocence of an infant that which we really are!

Then we teach that godly infant the ways of the world—how to win rather than how to help, how to overlook or defeat that inner spirit that keeps trying to influence us in the form of conscience. We bask in the glory of church, in news reports of philanthropic and humanitarian gestures, and in those occasional TV and movie stories that tearfully touch our emotions when relationships are mended or enhanced.

Moments later we're back to screaming and scheming as our ego once again overtakes the divine spirit that we momentarily released.

What does all of this have to do with writing stories about life? All personal stories have, at their base, beliefs about who and what we are, as members of the human race and as individuals within that category. What stories we write and how we write them will be influenced by our concepts of self and others. If we see ourselves as originally divine and seek to peel off our many layers of socialized ego, our stories will somehow reflect that belief. If we look in the mirror and see original sin, then our stories will be congruent with that premise, either attesting to that sinful nature or struggling to overcome it with artificially construed good deeds.

We need not struggle if our divinity is innate—just let it flow! But if we believe ourselves to be inherently sinful, then in order to live in inner peace, we must strive to be something we believe we're not, fighting our nature instead of our socially developed ego.

So then, should we focus on our inner selves in our stories or on our relationships or on life circumstances? It really doesn't matter. By definition, most personalized stories will focus on the writer as the center of attention, but if the writer's primary intent is to teach upcoming generations, then the specifics related to the writer's life might be peripheral sidebars, with the focus on external conditions and situations, and on other people. Again, the writer's objectives should be the determining factor.

Testing a Basic Orientation

You can test a significant personal orientation with a simple experiment. When something very bad (or very good) happens to you, do you tend to say, "Why me?" or do you say "Why not me?"

The former response suggests that you consider yourself to be somehow "above" (or below) others, in an elite (or dummy) class, immune (or predestined) to the situation or circumstance in which you now find yourself. It is basically a selfish response in which you see yourself as competing and comparing. Since we tend to view ourselves as we view others and vice-versa, we assume that others feel the same way—and are therefore competitors.

When reacting to an unpleasant circumstance, the usual implication of a "Why me?" orientation is that "I've suffered enough" or "I'm too important to be suffering at all" or "This should be happening to someone else, not me." When the circumstance is pleasant, the "Why me?" response implies a putdown of self, but with the same issue of comparison and competition at the core—"I don't deserve this" or "I'm not as important as others" or "This good fortune shouldn't be happening to me."

The "Why not me?" response accepts that you are equal to others in universal importance, that there is no inherent reason why a given condition has fallen upon you, that you are neither more nor less deserving than anyone else. In fact, is it not a premise of Christianity that God's grace is not based on anything we "deserve" by our behavior?

Of course, we have an instinctual desire for self-preservation, whether physical, emotional, or mental, but the word "self" can be viewed narrowly or broadly. When we run from or avoid a situation that we deem risky to our personal preservation, we are viewing self narrowly. But when we rush to save a child at the risk of our own safety, or when a soldier flops down on a grenade in order to save comrades from injury even at the likelihood of certain death, we are viewing self broadly, as part of a larger, more important body. In all such situations, self-centeredness is at the core.

By these examples, the reader may have already surmised that self-centeredness is not necessarily the safest personal response to the momentary situation, nor is selfishness necessarily the least useful response to life circumstances. The critical difference is basic philosophy and intent, neither of which most of us are inclined to examine within ourselves, making it very easy to blame, disregard, rationalize, and ignore. When these differences are not clearly understood, confusion often results, as when we mentally convince and fool ourselves that our behaviors and attitudes are honorable and helpful while portraying the exact opposite to others. For these reasons I have included a chapter (9) on the philosophical beliefs that may guide our behaviors and our stories.

Ethics is Common Sense

In terms of what to write, there are also practical and ethical questions to be considered. What effect might my stories have on present relationships, and who might gain access to them? What might living persons object to, and do I care? Are my conclusions stated as the opinions or perspectives that they are, and not as objective facts? Do my stories unfairly portray individuals or families, either in what is said or in how they are recorded? Are my motives to help future generations or to gain vengeance on past or present ones? Have I sufficiently examined my own role leading to the outcome of significant experiences?

Of course, answers to some of these questions will come only after determining the destination for your stories. Do you intend to make them public, eventually housed in a museum perhaps? Are they strictly for the internal use of your family (realizing that your control over this aspect is lost at your death)? Have you revised and edited your stories so they communicate to others the essence of your thoughts, realizing that some misunderstanding is probably inevitable? Have you considered getting "prepublication" feedback (perhaps even permission in some cases) from significant others, such as people you've mentioned in your stories or their families? Can you find or create a small group of strangers to give you objective, unemotional feedback on the possible impact on those whom you've mentioned, explicitly or implicitly, in your stories?

Thoughts/Activities to Consider

1. Close your eyes and think only about some positive events in your past or present life. Pick one and write a short story about it.

2. If, in the process of doing no. 1 above, your thoughts wander to some unpleasant stories, consider writing a short story about that, but only when your mind is ready!

3. Consider one thing you would have liked to know about one of your ancestors and write a short story about that same aspect of yourself.

4. Write a short story about one thing that you think influenced your development as the person you've become.

5. Choose one trait or characteristic of yours that you believe is similar to others of your generation and one trait that you believe is different, and write a short story about it.

6. Write a short story about your inclination to say, "Why me?" or "Why not me?" about either a pleasant or unpleasant event in your life.

CHAPTER 7

How to Tell Your Stories

Once the content of a given story has been determined, some thought must be given as to how to tell it. This is an essential and crucial component and overlaps the companion issue of content. In part 2, I will illustrate with several of my own stories a few of the options available, which I will briefly describe in this section.

Once Upon a Time

Most stories can be told chronologically or topically. We can create a beginning and follow the story through time until we reach some ending point, as many TV programs do. This provides an initial setting and leads to a dilemma, situation, or crisis, eventually resulting in some sort of final outcome or interim stopping point along the way of life. A story about married life might begin with an initial meeting, followed by courtship, marriage ceremony, early years of marriage, birth and raising of children, retirement years, and so on. Depending on the writer's focus, such a story might include employment, community activities, and other peripheral issues, or it might concentrate only on the marriage relationship, eliminating any reference to children, jobs, friends, and the like. Depending on one's age and the nature of the topic, chronological stories tend to require more time and length, especially for those who wish to include lots of details and intervening events.

Alternatively, the goal could be to describe one aspect of the marriage relationship, such as the resolution of conflict on the honeymoon. In this topical format, chronological time may be diminished or eliminated altogether. Examples of conflict situations could even be divided into those that were happily resolved and those that were less so. Or, the topical and chronological aspects could be combined, as when conflicts are described in the order in which they occurred in the marriage. The possibilities are endless, depending only on the experiences and creative desires of the author. Whatever the goal, clarity is the key to usefulness when writing for the benefit of others.

Laughter through Tears

It has occasionally been said about a difficult situation, "Years from now, when we look back, we'll laugh about this." Yes, there are times when perspective can glean humor from what was originally a very serious event. We cannot know for certain the ways in which many things will turn out, but we do know that worrying about the future sometimes seems inevitable, even though ultimate life experiences may not have yielded the horrible consequences that were initially foreseen. So we often have the option of recording a story in the way in which it was originally experienced or in the more humorous vein that may have developed with the passage of time. Both formats have value.

Some of my own stories were written with tears dropping on the pages as I revisited some very emotional scenes. Others I could barely put on paper because my hands were shaking uncontrollably with laughter. Pleasure and pain are part of existence, though each of us handles those feelings in unique ways. I happen to be a rather emotional person, though it took a special type of adult education to release me from earlier social indoctrinations. Boys don't cry. Boys show toughness. Boys are leaders. Boys take charge. Boys are dominant. Boys are adventurous. Boys take risks. Boys like violence. Boys are unemotional. These and others like them are unconscious thoughts that I absorbed in childhood, not from any deliberate attempts by others to inflict confusion or chaos, but rather from my own cultural observations. These "mandates" were often not good fits for my nature and led to some painful, even traumatic, social experiences, many of which were experienced internally and not obvious to others.

But there was also a very pleasant side to my development. Family relationships were awesome! My parents were consistently loving and totally accepting. Paternal grandparents lived nearby and always welcomed my frequent visits. My athletic abilities were acknowledged and supported by peers and helped to compensate for my social inadequacies and academic success, the latter not always a plus in this tiny rural school where advances into higher education were rare. I was respected by classmates but seldom involved with teenage cliques, occasionally known for behaviors and pranks of which I silently disapproved.

Assuming that all of us have experienced both tears and laughter, and pain and pleasure, in our development (and likely still do), what stories do we want to write about? A surface view of the issue might conclude the obvious: avoid revisiting tears and pain because such memories can only trigger discomfort in the present. Who would want that! A less obvious view might be that such revisitations could be helpful by providing therapeutic catharsis of previously buried issues. Reframing those issues, with the aid of emotional distance, could lead to a less painful perspective, perhaps even internal resolution and emotional healing. As with the death of a loved one, burial removes the issue but not the memories.

Sometimes we may think that humor is trivial and wasteful. We tell jokes when we're relaxed and not serious. So how can such stories of pleasure and laughter be helpful to descendants? We have only to consider the value of humor in our own lives. Medically speaking, there is evidence that laughter can be curative—physically, mentally, and emotionally. In ways I don't thoroughly comprehend, worry, stress, and negativity seem to have deleterious effects on the human body that can be countered with relaxation, laughter, and positive humor.

By including both tears and humor, not only can descendants come to know us as emotionally balanced in our experience of life, but they can also gain insight into our culture and coping skills. In the process, we can take a step toward self-healing, self-acceptance, guilt reduction and the enjoyment of memories. Seeing humor alongside concomitant opportunities for self- and other-forgiveness, in what were otherwise painful and tearful experiences, can be eye-opening and therapeutic. Readers are encouraged to write the same story from both a humorous and serious perspective to gain the full impact of an emotional experience.

Who can tell if a given descendant, at a particular time in life, will benefit more from a story written in a humorous light or a serious vein? Each of us has a remarkable ability to reframe virtually any subject or experience. As beauty is so often in the eye of the beholder, so is perspective. Like a prism or a house of mirrors, as we change the angle we also change the view. The outcome depends primarily on which way we choose to observe the subject. What seemed serious yesterday may seem humorous today, as we realize that our greatest fears were quite illogical and highly unlikely.

Alternatively, what seemed humorous or harmless yesterday may seem serious today, as when we played teenage pranks that, in hindsight, might have led to dangerous consequences. Sometimes we can gain clarity on a given event by recording it both ways. This process can provide greater understanding of the situation and shows unequivocally the power of the mind to impact feelings. Providing two or more versions of the same story might be incredibly helpful to future readers who might learn to view life from a more balanced perspective when they see that they can have considerable control over their beliefs, interpretations, and emotions. An example from my own life of writing the same story from two perspectives is given in part 2.

Changing Negatives to Positives

Closely related to the humorous/serious dichotomy is the positive/ negative one. Too often the painful/harmful experiences of life can create traumas that last a lifetime and keep mental health therapists in business, while the plethora of positive/helpful experiences go virtually unnoticed. Instead of focusing attention on gratitude for the beings that we are, the blessings that we have, and the favors that we do for one another, we all too often emphasize bitterness, sadness, blame, and anger for what we aren't, what we don't have, and what we don't do for each other. Much of that process is accomplished by default, as when we habitually believe we're entitled to what we lack, or that our goodness is somehow unworthy or trivial. Somehow it seems to feel better to attack and blame those whose lives appear to be happier and more successful or to degrade ourselves for failing to achieve that which we have defined as legitimately ours.

Still, where we wish to focus our minds is a choice. An old song suggests, "Into each life some rain must fall." Doesn't this also suggest that most of life is rain free, perhaps even sunny? But even if we experience much of life as essentially cloudy or rainy, we can choose to focus our attention on the sunny times—the times we were helpful to our neighbors, our society, and our humanity. There is not a living person, or one who has ever lived, or one who will ever live, whose existence has not been of some significant value. By withholding judgment, blame, and comparisons, we can find that value in everyone. For those of us still living and yet to live, we can demonstrate and model such value by sharing our stories, experiences, knowledge, and advice. Armed with our stories and experiences, our descendants will never have to walk alone, even if they carry no beliefs about a Supreme Creator. Our stories can make a difference in their lives.

Are there times when we should portray negative aspects of our lives without pointing to some potentially positive directions? I can think of none. Even the most negative experiences contain the implicit advice of "Don't do it" or "Don't put yourself in this position" or "Figure out a way to cope with this, if you should face such a situation, and here are some suggestions."

There may be occasions when we would wish to challenge future readers to find their own solutions by emphasizing only the negative. However, should that be our intention, we might be advised to state that intent as part of our story or to use stories that implicitly contain an obvious solution or two. As stated earlier, only the most discouraged, vengeful, angry, and bitter individuals would deliberately wish to encourage those same attributes in descendants.

Thoughts, Feelings, and Behaviors

When we contemplate life stories, our focus can be on thoughts, feelings, or behaviors, or some combination. In our most memorable situations, feelings and behaviors usually take precedence. Only the most mature, sophisticated, or nonhuman of us think carefully about each life experience as it's unfolding. Much of the time we feel and then act, or act and then feel, leaving mindful consideration for later scrutiny. It is tempting to evaluate this process as a mistake—and often it is, especially when our attitude is suspect and the situation is painfully emotional.

But when the situation is a positive one, and our attitude is loving and nondefensive, acting spontaneously on our feelings can be freeing and enhancing to our relationships. Too much thinking before we act can not only paralyze us from acting positively but can also lead to a diminished ability to access our more tender emotions—with nonhuman, robotic consequences. Check out my story "The Irony of a Kiss," in part 2 for an example.

Writing life stories as they are evolving can be much like writing a daily diary or journal. Concentration is usually on the immediate past but often with current feelings about that past and, occasionally, with wishes or fears about the future. The older we are, the more past we are able to access, though with limited reliability; the younger we are, the more future we are tempted to access, though with obviously limited vision. Perhaps that's why middle-agers, in the prime of life, can be potentially the most helpful to future generations. That's where the essence of life is lived for most of us. That's when we are raising families, engrossed in our work, physically and recreationally mature, still with hopes and dreams but with a more realistic outlook on life.

Does it really matter whether we emphasize behaviors, feelings, or thoughts? Not in the slightest! Certain of our stories naturally lend themselves to one or more of these. I can't imagine writing a story about the loss of my dog (see part 2) with only mental objectivity. While that story necessarily includes some of my thought processes in order for it to make sense to readers, there is a heavy concentration primarily on my feelings and secondarily on my actions. I wrote the story primarily as a personal outlet but with the belief that other pet lovers would identify with my experience, so I was aware that I needed to communicate with some clarity. If I had only been writing for my own catharsis, much of the story would likely have been chaotic and nonsensically emotional, as I would have had little incentive to describe the situation clearly.

As long as our purpose for writing personal stories is for others to read and appreciate, some description of our feelings, behaviors, and thoughts will probably be desirable. However, it is not essential that the story be so detailed in these descriptions that the reader faces no ambiguity. It is only necessary to convey enough understanding that a connection and interpretation can in some way be made to the reader's life. We are not responsible for what that interpretation might be, only for encouraging it to take place. (I had no previous thoughts about how the story of my dog's death would relate to, or impact, individual readers.)

Fortunately, we humans are similar enough in our basic makeup that making such connections is rarely problematic. Witness responses to dramatic or humorous movies and TV shows. The emotions we feel and the thoughts we have during viewing are evidence of the connections or potential connections we're making to our own lives. And perhaps no better example exists than some poetry and artworks, created with such ambiguity that their only pragmatic value (beyond the beauty of their expression) is what the eye and mind of the beholder concoct.

Of course, some of our memories or stories may contain little that is as emotional as my dog story. Suppose you want to discuss political views, personal philosophies, ideas, accomplishments, travel experiences, or the like. Your focus would then be more mental and academic, though how you came to believe and behave as you do might well contain both affect and action.

Similarly, if my dad had told the story of his recovery from a near-fatal teenage car accident in the 1920s, he might have emphasized behaviors that pertained to the cause of the accident and to his day-to-day efforts at physical rehabilitation during his six-month stay in the hospital and thereafter. Or he might have discussed the many sacrifices of his family as they invested in his recovery. Or he might have contrasted driving habits in the 1920s with those sixty years later. Or he might have stressed what he learned about life through his ordeal. Or he might even have included some spiritual or religious component. The possibilities are endless, but readers might expect some reference to several aspects of his recovery, though a main emphasis might be evident. How we choose to tell any of our stories is totally a function of our memories and preferences. That's the way it is and that's the way it should remain!

Learning about Life

We experience life, but we also observe life. Either way we learn about life. Much of what we learn is unintentional; that is, we absorb information by internalizing data of which we're unaware. That seems to be how most cultures develop. As we see certain attitudes, interpretations, beliefs, emotions, and behaviors consistently repeated by family and friends, we are inclined to copy them without much cognitive scrutiny. Our eyes and ears seem to do the work while our brain rests. We do not evaluate or judge, but we are indoctrinated, nevertheless. We assume that what we observe and experience is right and that opposing forces are wrong. So we evaluate and judge dissimilar cultures and their conclusions instead, usually to the detriment of empathic understanding. The imperialism of past centuries and the terrorism of the present one seem to be products of such observational and involuntary learning.

The process of writing personal stories serves to reawaken the brain. It makes us think about what we're doing and how we're feeling, what we've done and how we've felt, and what we might do and how we might feel under changed conditions and circumstances. In a sense, it can teach us empathy and tolerance as a side effect, and even more hopefully, respect, as a main effect.

Sometimes we may wish to emphasize our experiences of life, and sometimes our observations. Experiences tend to be more action-oriented and observations more passive. But the differences may be more apparent than real because many observations lead to internal experiences. Our stomachs may churn and our minds may explode while our outward appearances remain calm, as when watching movies or television. Cultural expectations, gleaned from years of socialization, can be a smokescreen for internal experiences.

How we begin a story makes little difference. An observational story can start out quite detached, but if it's important enough to write about, some explicit or implicit experiences will likely intrude at some point. It is nearly impossible to communicate a personal story as an objective news reporter would. In fact, veteran reporters may rewrite their news stories many times in an effort to remove their own emotions and biases. However, as with columns, editorials, commentaries, and opinion articles, *our* stories need not be concerned with patent objectivity.

When writing for family or descendants, our purpose is to convey our essence, our personhood, our experiences, our observations, our interpretations, and our conclusions. We want readers to know how we have lived, what we have valued, how we have interpreted life, and what experiences have most influenced our development.

Action, Reaction, and Inaction

The process of life is a series of actions and reactions, and sometimes it's difficult to tell the difference. We act and others around us react to those actions. Part of their reaction is usually additional actions, related to the issue at hand but unique to their perception of the situation. We then react to their perception and add some fresh material of our own, and so on. Such give-and-take is vital to meaningful dialogue and is an essential part of learning.

The tragedy is that too many of us too often and for too long become mindless reactors who behave with inaction. When we withhold our own perceptions and meanings, that withdrawal motivates others to fill the resulting vacuum (and therefore to lead and control). By our silence, we may hope to avoid potential conflict; we may evaluate our own contributions harshly ("I'm just a ..."), or we may have little interest in the interaction or issue. Everyone does this occasionally, but if such behavior has become a common occurrence, I encourage you to reevaluate the possible significance of your own experiences and observations for future generations.

In chapter 3 I discussed five categories of human behavior and tried to show the potential contributions of each one. However, a total absence of *commenting* on what we observe, evaluate, and endure helps no one. It may seem the easy way out by avoiding some work or conflict in the present but produces little of value for the future. Ask yourself the following types of questions:

How helpful is it to describe yourself as having little long-term value for your years of life, however many they may prove to be? How insulting to your creation is diminishing or renouncing your impact on important life events? How self-enhancing is it to think of your influence on future generations as being a microcosm of what it might be if you left recorded stories of your existence to descendants? How valuable will your silence be to the yet unborn?

You don't have to be a pioneer, an initiator, or a leader; each of us has all the raw material necessary for acting on our own experiences, perceptions, observations, and conclusions—whatever they may be. To the extent that we have kept these concealed in the past (often for purposes of socialization), we may have made a mockery of our lives. We have lived falsely. We have lied to others and ourselves. But we can still correct our negligence and conclude life—whenever that may occur—with honesty, authenticity, and integrity. We can tell our descendants anything we wish. We can truly act on the truth of life as we have interpreted it. We can aid and influence the future by restoring vitality to our lives through communication of our stories.

Social Credibility

Earlier I addressed cautions about making some of our stories public. The US Constitution assures us the right of freedom of speech with few legal limitations. But it cannot protect us from social or political consequences, as "Joe the Plumber" found out during the 2008 presidential election campaign. A simple question to a candidate led to a thorough and apparently unwarranted investigation of his life circumstances in an obvious attempt to discredit him and to dissuade onlookers from posing other uncomfortable questions in the future. Any of us could experience a similar fate when our stories conflict with others' thoughts, experiences, and ideas.

On a broader scale, witness the threatened citizen boycotts of the state of Arizona over border issues, even before our courts passed judgment. Our legal system may weigh such issues carefully, but our social and political systems are not so patient. Political correctness has been both a blessing and a curse. Our margins are smaller, our consequences harsher. We must carefully examine what we say and what we write, and we must determine when, how, and to whom each of our stories is released.

One of the best ways to avoid difficulties associated with others' varying perceptions of a situation is to make certain that we emphasize in our writings that we are communicating our own unique perceptions and interpretations and that others' assessments may differ substantially. To garner the most potential credibility, it is important that we support our thoughts, feelings, and behaviors with as much "evidence" as we can muster (how we came to believe, feel, and act as we do). In the process we may modify, reject, or strengthen some of our earlier perceptions.

At the very least, we will gain a greater understanding of the situation or ourselves. At best we may become more aware and respectful of legitimate differences in beliefs and conditions. In the end, our open-mindedness can only make us more believable to future readers.

As I'm writing this in the spring of 2014, a potentially devastating global economic crisis has been upon us for the past few years. Blaming is rampant. Billions, even trillions, of dollars are being proposed and have been offered and spent in bailouts—for banks and other financial institutions, for automobile companies, for state treasuries, for health-care subsidies, for homeowners—and this may be only the beginning. This entitlement mentality appears to be contagious and far-reaching. Excessive government spending, perceived flaws in the Affordable Care Act, and the threat of defaulting on our national debt led to a political impasse and partial government shutdown in fall 2013. Virtually no one has accepted responsibility for choices that put us in this situation or has acknowledged the consequences of their own political behaviors. Our leaders are behaving as if blameless and helpless—like children.

In my earlier career, as a graduate school professor charged with developing counselors and mental health therapists, the following scenario was common and may be apropos to the current political situation. When a student was challenged regarding the background of an acknowledged self-defeating belief or behavior, the following interchange would sometimes take place:

Student: "That's the way I was brought up" (or "That's what I was taught as a child.")

> (The implication being, "So how can I be responsible for what I believe or how I behave?" (i.e., "I can't help myself.") And the likely expectation was that our interaction would end there, for how could I respectfully challenge their upbringing?)

Me: "Are you still a child?"
Student: "No, but ..." (I never let them finish this sentence.)
Me: "Are you still a child?"
Student: "No, but ..." (With slightly more indignation)

Me: "Are you still a child?" (This could go on for several exchanges, but my interruption and response was always the same.)

Student: "No, I'm an adult!" (usually expressed with loud indignation.)

Me: "Finally, we're getting somewhere. Now act like the adult you say you are and take responsibility for what you believe and do, and stop blaming others." (Sounds like good advice for our elected and appointed government officials, doesn't it?)

Our message to future generations must emphasize both our responsibility and our credibility. In relating our stories, we must additionally communicate something like the following: "According to my life experiences, and to my interpretations of those experiences, this is what I believe (or conclude, or suggest, or perceive, or judge). Reality, like truth, is often in the eye of the beholder. I make no claim to total, or perhaps even partial, accuracy in my stories. I am a fallible human being—but also an important and significant one, equal in value to any other man or woman who has ever lived. And I deserve to tell my stories in the ways in which I perceive them."

Suspend the Rules

Another related consideration when conveying our stories is our subjectivity. How much can we deviate from the absolute truth? Must our stories be accurate reports, or can we add some drama and even fiction? Do we stick with reality, or can we include wishes and even imagination? How do we separate objective facts from subjective opinions? Should we focus on entertaining readers or on conveying messages? When is a summary appropriate and when might we need to provide specific details?

There are no mandated rules. It really depends on the content of an individual story and your purpose in writing it. Are you just trying to have some fun with your reader? Go for it! Are you attempting to convey a serious message to a future generation? Have at it! Is your goal to struggle with your own doubts and conflicts in the presence of your descendants, to allow them to experience aspects of your life while living theirs? Be my guest! Are you trying to deliver facts about life at the time of your existence? By all means! Do you wish to show aspects of the personality that you have developed and the conditions and circumstances that influenced them? Do it! The only barriers and limitations to your stories and how you deliver them to readers are those that you create and maintain.

Respect Your Readers

Let me offer a few additional guidelines. First, consider how each story relates to you personally. In many types of stories, it will be obvious, but in others you may have to include some reference to that relationship. After all, it is your life that has conjured up these stories, and it is your descendants who may be reading them, and they will want to know just where you fit in, and perhaps some background information about how and why you chose your stories.

Next, while you have virtually unlimited freedom in what you choose to write about and how you decide to convey each story, your intent may not be clear unless you make it so. There is an ethical aspect to this. Authors have an unwritten contract with their readers, based on truth and honesty. That is, if fiction is being written, this most basic information must be stated initially, as should nonfiction. Sometimes books, movies, and TV programs combine fiction and nonfiction, in which case a partial disclaimer of "based on a true story" can be displayed. This tells the reader or viewer that the foundation of the story is accurate, but that many details have been added, subtracted, or modified for the purpose of clarity, entertainment, propaganda, or some such goal usually unrelated to the initial story. As long as the audience is made aware of the amount of truth and honesty in the story, no problem exists. These same ethical standards should be utilized in our own personal stories.

If we can't remember all the details of a story (as is most often the case), let readers know that. We can provide such disclaimers in a variety of ways, perhaps specifically in the introduction of a story or in the process of writing it. In the latter case, we can occasionally and simply include words or phrases such as, "I believe ..." or "I think ..." or "My opinion/conclusion is ..." or "What I remember is ..." or "I was told by my parents that ..." All such conveyances suggest the possibility of error and actually add to our humanness and credibility. These types of sentence beginnings will likely be far more plentiful than those starting with "I know ..." or "I'm absolutely certain that ..." or "It's a definite fact that ..."

Be aware that readers often interpret perceptions as absolute facts in the absence of disclaimers as suggested above. For example, "The teacher told me I was not college material" might be taken as a fact, and the reader would probably be annoyed or angry with the teacher (and perhaps teachers in general) and sympathetic to the writer. Compare this with, "I interpreted the teacher's comments as meaning I couldn't succeed in college." Most of us can't remember, especially if many years have elapsed, exact conversations, but we can remember how we felt. It may be that the teacher said something like, "You'll probably have a tough time in college" or "Unless you get more serious about your studies, you'll never make it through college."

Bottom line: when we take responsibility for clearly conveying not only the truth but our part in interpreting what we see, hear, and feel, our integrity and credibility soar, and our writing becomes more influential.

Finally, write with positive intentions. No matter what your present circumstance or condition, no matter if you're reading this in a lifelong jail cell or in a high-rise corporate office, no matter if you're intensely lonely or happily gregarious, your stories can be written with either the goal of helpfulness or vengeance. No matter how any of us actually behave in this world, we have all had evil, hateful thoughts and feelings, and we have all had helpful, loving ones. Painful stories, citing evil situations and unpleasant behaviors, can always be truthfully told, but with the intention of advocating behaviors, thoughts, and feelings that would lead the reader toward happier and more productive and useful consequences.

Every life, no matter of what age or stage, can advocate positive actions leading to more joyful outcomes. When we write stories about our lives, we are role models to our readers. With our last breath, we can decide to make those models positive. It's our choice!

Thoughts/Activities to Consider

1. Write a short personal story from two or three different angles. Experiment; be as creative as you wish.
2. Examine a personal event that has angered you in the past and write about it in a positive way.
3. Choose a personal story and write three paragraphs—one with only your thoughts about the event or situation, one with only your feelings about it, and one with only your behaviors exhibited.
4. How has the culture or subculture in which you were raised brainwashed you?

CHAPTER 8

Learning Our ABCs, etc.

How Valuable Are You?

Nearly fifty years ago, radio commentator/philosopher/motivator Earl Nightingale narrated an inspirational segment about the impact of thoughts on behavior. His basic message was, "You become what you think about." A simple yet profound statement that must include not just thoughts but also attitudes, beliefs and concepts—the end results of our minds at work, the ABCs of our intellectual powers. And where do these attitudes, beliefs, and concepts come from?

While there is obvious overlapping of these categories, it seems that we gain our *attitudes* primarily from our interpretations of life experiences. To the extent that these experiences are viewed as pleasant and fruitful as we develop, our general attitudes are usually quite positive. Whether they remain that way depends on the impact of future experiences. If we continue to find our world pleasing and friendly, that attitude solidifies. If not, it crumbles. This generalization, of course, does not negate the possibility— even likelihood, perhaps—that in certain areas of life we may find our outlooks alternately eroded and repaired by conditions and circumstances.

Our initial *beliefs* about life's components tend to emanate from what we're told and what we observe, though these beliefs interact with our attitudes in such a way that each influences the other. Our familial, social, political, theological, and educational institutions are the major providers of our belief systems, indoctrinating us with various forms of cultural values and rhetoric, some useful and some not so. Most recently the media, formerly expected to be objective and unbiased, has burst onto the scene and become a major force in influencing, determining, and modifying those beliefs.

Concepts are generalized ideas about features of life and convey our understanding and mental comprehension of those traits. While definitely influenced by attitudes and beliefs, they are often vague but powerful intellectual abstractions of the mind that can unconsciously affect behaviors.

In short, the meanings of ongoing events as each of us interprets them arise from unique explanations of life happenings as determined by those attitudes, beliefs, and concepts acquired through what we've experienced, what we've been told, and what we've comprehended or learned.

Years ago, my wife informed me that she and many others learn by associating new ideas with familiar expressions. Therefore, this chapter's title represents my attempt to help readers remember what's been stated. Attitudes, beliefs, and concepts represent the ABCs, to which is added the means by which each is basically absorbed— by being experienced, by being told, and by being comprehended (etc.). I'm reminded of the Broadway show *The King and I*, in which several times the king issues opinions or proclamations and ends with "etcetera, etcetera, etcetera"—a way of saying that much more could be said, but that it's time to move on. Given all the possibilities inherent in the above-mentioned components of life, however, how can we expect our stories to be anything but unique? And that's why we need everyone on earth to contribute! Everyone!

If we truly care about our descendants, our community, and our species, and likewise believe our existence to be valuable, important, and significant, we will contribute. How can we do otherwise? Whether guided and goaded by ego, spirit, or conscience, some such outcome is almost mandatory. Therefore, the most powerful image we can create is a positive view of self, because how we view our "selves" encourages, discourages, reinforces, and reflects those feelings of value and significance, which will then affect our desires to leave stories of our memorable lives to descendants. As a significant side effect, if we truly value our own lives, we will more likely value the lives of all others, and encourage them to contribute as well.

Yes, when we feel esteemed, worthy, appreciated, and useful, we are more likely to see others in the same way. Only a deranged or extremely narcissistic person would see oneself in this way and others differently, and only a severely depressed person would see others as more highly prized than oneself. Neither of these extreme conditions would likely lead to life stories—one because of a false sense of superiority and arrogance that might be exposed or damaged, and the other due to internal feelings of uselessness, worthlessness, and inferiority leading to lack of confidence, social withdrawal, or repressed anger. In either instance, caring enough about others to leave a legacy would be quite unlikely.

How Golden Is the Golden Rule?

Jesus commands those of us who would follow his lead to love God fully and unconditionally and furthermore to love our neighbors and even our enemies in the same manner as we love ourselves. The clear implication of such teaching is that we should love ourselves wholeheartedly so that we can love all others in the same manner.

Similarly, Christians and non-Christians alike often cite as an antidote to inappropriate social behavior some reference to the Golden Rule: "Do unto others as you would have them do unto you." This assumes, of course, that we would like others to show authentic love, caring, and kindness toward us. But what if we believe that we deserve punishment? What if we're guilt-ridden? What if we secretly believe we're unimportant or even evil, or that we're "just a _____?" What would that do to the rest of Jesus's directives? What if we don't love ourselves?

Some have said that our problem is not that we don't follow the Golden Rule and other such decrees but that we do! We sabotage ourselves with varying forms of self-defeating beliefs and behaviors in attempts to satisfy our ego; we then hate ourselves for our weakness and stupidity; and we secretly convince ourselves that we are therefore undeserving of anything but punishment. So we seek redemption by further behaving in ways that ensure getting what we believe we deserve—some form of punishment. Following the Golden Rule, we must now do to them what we have convinced them to do to us. Instead of loving our neighbors, our enemies, and even God, we think badly of them because that's how we think of ourselves. Of course, little of this process is done consciously, but does that matter?

The ego's job is to protect us from such harmful thoughts and internal damage, so it must find a way to divert the danger. Blaming those whom we've identified as enemies (sometimes including our "neighbors" and even God) we project our inadequacies elsewhere, while denying any personal ownership. We can then safely destroy the real culprits and continue life self-righteously.

So how do we extricate ourselves from such madness? Only by confronting our manufactured ego and replacing it with attitudes, beliefs, and concepts that lead to truly valuing all lives. Believing that we humbly deserve only the best in life (minus the presence of arrogance and narcissism), we can behave toward others in like fashion. Such positive attitudes will more likely lead to productive behaviors that will in turn generate concepts more useful to future generations, and our personal stories will reflect that!

Behavior is the key. Attitudes, beliefs, and concepts are intangibles; we cannot see them. We can only infer their presence or absence by the observation of behavior; yet, it is exactly that presence or absence that determines behavior in a reinforcing and circular pattern. Putting a positive spin on any portion of that circle affects the entire circle. Thus, if we make small positive changes anywhere in the circle, we can produce better outcomes.

The Golden Rule and showing love to others emphasizes behavior, what we should do to others, but it also assumes that we are self-centered, that we should behave toward others (and ourselves) in ways that benefit our own lives (i.e., "as you would have them *do unto you*"; "love thy neighbor *as thyself*"). In more modern words, it proposes a win-win interaction (the basis of which is self-centered but hardly sinful as some theologies might suggest). Intangibles may provide the background for our behaviors but cannot be the focus.

For example, hatred is an attitude, not a behavior. It may or may not be manifested. So when we say, "We hate ourselves, and therefore we hate others," purists might counter that this distorts the real meaning of the Golden Rule because that attitude of hatred reveals how we assess ourselves and others internally rather than what we want done to ourselves and others externally. No doubt this is an important distinction. Still, when we hate ourselves and believe that we are unworthy and undeserving, seldom can we hide that self-sabotaging conclusion from others. Though we may be unaware of our own behavior, it usually remains consistent and congruent with our beliefs and attitudes and invites others to verify that image when relating to us.

Of course, some of us, consciously or not, berate ourselves in an effort to gain compassion and praise from others, thus engaging in trickery and manipulation—like fishing for a compliment—and that is dishonest. Statements such as, "This may be a stupid question," or "I can't do anything right" often fit that category. Such behavior is either self-condemning or manipulative, and serves to influence or control the listener's responses. Whether that is our conscious desire becomes a moot point. Mentally we may not want such results, but behaviorally and emotionally that's exactly what we ask for and, in the process, that's exactly what we deliver!

Though our egos are often reluctant to admit it, feelings of uselessness, worthlessness, and inferiority are rampant in our society. We have developed institutions, policies, and methodologies that have both caused and reinforced these feelings, and the outcomes are obvious—crime, drugs, broken relationships, abuse, and, of course, low self-esteem, all of which discourage those who consider themselves among "the ordinary" from blessing the rest of us with their perceptions of life as each has experienced it.

The Golden Rule presents a disturbing incongruence between the anticipated pleasantness of how we would like to be treated and our mindless perception of how we deserve to be treated. This is especially true of Christians and Jews because there is so much emphasis put on guilt and ultimate retribution as the consequences of "sin"—an explosive, controlling word that can have devastating results for our self-image. Of course, religious institutions have then manufactured antidotes that keep their pews filled—rituals (baptism, communion, confession, praying, chanting, etc.) designed by the various churches to expunge misdeeds and strengthen their institutional control. Though such potential guilt could easily be reduced by substitution of the much less toxic secular word "mistake," that might remove the need for repentance and severely constrain the power of the church! And the pursuit of power is too often the hidden motivating force behind institutional desires for influence. (See part 3 for a more complete discussion of the interaction of power, control, and influence within institutions and how that concept affects our life histories and stories.)

Because it is so difficult for most of us to view ourselves as inconsistent, incongruent, and fragmented in any basic sense, it's imperative that we feel worthy and deserving. Otherwise, we sabotage any good treatment from others in order to match and reestablish congruency with our own poor self-image. In addition, as I have repeatedly stressed, liking ourselves is an essential step toward liking others, and we cannot fool ourselves or fake a positive self-image for long!

What Is the Purpose of Life's "Dash"?

Because institutional dogmas and policies both reflect and create many negative aspects of our society and culture, generating a positive self-image may require a significant amount of reframing and reinterpretation of events in our lives, and even a reexamination of our philosophies and religious beliefs used in the initial interpretations. This reexamination can be part of writing our life stories, as we retrace the steps of our past. As with many memories, this process can be both painful and exhilarating, but the essential component is openness to different interpretations of those stories. The concept of reframing is considered later in this chapter, but for now keep in mind that events that initially appear unpleasant, distressing, and regretful can always be redefined in more positive terms.

Some of this reframing may motivate or inspire us to grapple with the most basic questions of life. Who am I? Where did I come from? Where am I headed? How did I get here? What should I be doing with my life? What happens to me when I die? These are questions we all ask at some point in our lives. Deep thinkers, spiritual leaders, and worldly philosophers ponder them on a daily basis, while others may consider such thoughts only on their deathbeds. Most of us lie somewhere in between those extremes. The human brain is so full of wonderment and imagination that try as we might to block out such thoughts as some of us do, we cannot ignore them forever.

In seeking ancestral answers to such questions, genealogists must often be satisfied with nothing more than names, gravesites, past residential locations, birth/death dates, and a few scattered facts. What most excites us, however, are written stories of life experiences. We crave to know how our ancestors handled "the dash," their time between birth and death, the same as our descendants will wish to know about us. Often underlying this inquisitiveness is the desire for some revelation about the purpose of life itself, the answer to which has eluded us for millennia. Yet we still think about the question, and so will our descendants. When actively engaging such thoughts, though, we tend to either quickly dismiss them and give up out of frustration or pursue some elaborate scheme we attribute to an unknown universal force, which most acknowledge as God or by some other sacred name.

Consciously or not, the purpose of life is our foundation for living, the pursuit that gets us up each morning, keeps us going, and provides our stories. We may not be able to explain our purpose or even to define it, but our behavior shows our belief about it. For some, the purpose is to accumulate wealth and possessions. For others, it's to serve their Creator, advance our civilization, provide safety and security for their families, learn and grow as human beings, maintain a certain way of life, or just survive each day. Most would probably like to attain all of these goals, though the awareness that their strategies often conflict with one another and with those of other people provides daily doses of worry and stress—and the fodder for lots of stories that we could record for posterity and perhaps also for our own edification or our current family's pleasure. (Some basic philosophical issues will be discussed more extensively in chapter 9 and part 3.)

Given the condition that there are so many different purposes possible for so many people, and that one size does not fit all, we may be missing the obvious. Perhaps the only real purpose of life— at least for present generations—is simply to try to figure it out! All of us do that, anyway—some intentionally, some unintentionally. In the process, we all play a part in advancing civilization. Some provide discoveries, breakthroughs, and pathways, while others put up potent obstacles, benign barriers, and difficult challenges that the formers must learn to go over, around, or through, thus providing opportunities to use the potential endowed by our Creator. Many more seem to stand around and watch, ignore, or evaluate.

Everyone has a role (see chapter 3), and what may at first glance seem least productive may turn out in the long run to be most productive. Only one thing is for certain. If everything went smoothly for all of us, we would likely stagnate; there would be few incentives to use our humanly endowed gifts to progress and advance. Perhaps that's exactly what the Creator had in mind! We humans seem to love challenges, be they mental, emotional, spiritual, or physical! Unfortunately, they too often lead to political, social, or religious impasses, or even worse, armed conflict.

Instead of helping one another, we fight one another. Instead of cooperating, we seem to prefer competing, and we justify that behavior with rationalizations that competition stimulates the advancement of our civilization. Considering our daily goals of wealth and acquisitions that may be true, but has it led to universal peace, safety and well-being? Do we all enjoy life, liberty, and the pursuit of happiness? Some might say that our only hope for those deeper goals is the first or second coming of some spiritual savior, as though the original Creator of life forgot to include the right ingredients when we were made.

But to turn things around, we may need only to tweak our knowledge and creative abilities. Mentally we already know how to get along; we do it with our friends; it's not that complicated. We just need to do it more often through changes in our ABCs! For the moment, though, our concepts of unconditional love and the Golden Rule seem to have lost their glitter.

Reaching Our Potential

Considering the sometimes-catastrophic consequences of our behavior, and the widely accepted estimate that we use less than 10 percent of our potential, what might we accomplish if we used the other 90 percent? Maybe that's the overriding purpose of life—to access 100 percent of our potential, at which time there will be no need or desire for fighting, assuming that part of what we haven't yet learned is how to avoid, defuse, and transform conflict. If that's our mission, our descendants have centuries of challenges ahead of them, considering how long it has taken to get through the first 10 percent. Consciously or not, we are all responsible for this meager beginning—everyone who has ever been born, without exception! The only questions we need answer for a more productive future are: what roles do we each wish to play, how long will it take us to get to 100 percent, and can we finish the job before we extinguish our species?

The goal is indeed formidable, but it appears we have everything we need to accomplish the task: (1) a body designed with enormous flexibility and an uncanny ability to heal itself and withstand abuse; (2) unparalleled mental powers to comprehend and create whatever we need, and to aid, control, and encourage the body to maximize its usefulness, and (3) an emotional/spiritual component that allows us to connect intangibly with our inner selves, one another, and a possible Creator.

The unseen mental, emotional, and spiritual components are, for the most part, responsible for our physical behavior. Without the mental ability to choose, reason, and decide, our bodies would be controlled by instinct or involuntary behavior, as is the plant and animal kingdom; and without our emotional and spiritual components we would be robotic and inhuman. The overall ability to determine our will and then to act with compassion and generosity or antipathy and greed is what defines our species and enables us to learn in noninstinctive ways. Of course, modern psychology has shown that we can be conditioned to behave in much the same ways as plants and animals, but also that mental awareness and desire can thwart such outcomes. We are as free as we collectively wish to be.

So where does that leave us? If our purpose really is to use 100 percent of our potential (and why not?), how do we get there? How do we access all of it? When we think carefully about it, hasn't all human progress been made through the process of trial-and-error? When confronted with a challenging situation, we sort through our feelings, brainstorm our thoughts, and try out behaviors—and often make lots of errors until we find a solution that is workable and acceptable.

The same process is evoked whether the issue is individual, national, or worldly. All inventions and ideas, great and small, are a result of trial-and-error evaluations, as are all decisions. Carpenters, doctors, electricians, lawyers, plumbers, politicians, corporate executives, teachers, families, and all others use this process, despite the all-knowing arrogance of innate superior knowledge claimed by some. Once we find a workable solution to one issue, we go on to the next one, always ready to revisit and reevaluate previous ones, if and when conditions warrant.

Of course, we build on the previous knowledge of ancestors, but they acquired their knowledge in the same manner. Both ancient and modern civilizations have advanced through this pragmatic process of trial-and-error, which is the antithesis of certainty, that arrogant attitude that impedes progress because it invites discord and discourages exploration.

As a consequence of trial-and-error learning, over the course of time we earthlings seem to have progressed remarkably in communication technology, industry, medicine, and travel, though lagging miserably in others, such as interpersonal communication, conflict resolution, and relationship-building and maintaining. Such disparity is likely the result of our ego's obsession with gadgets, comfort, comparison, and meaningless longevity—and our neglect of intangibles such as emotions, spirit, philosophy, and purpose.

Still, our history indicates that for centuries we can wallow in the wrong direction (defined as a direction ultimately unacceptable to a relevant population), but eventually the course is changed to a more productive one. Wish as we might that advancement would be smoother and faster, trial-and-error learning will likely continue in our human laboratory, much of it under the designation of "science." So far we've been able to avoid a species-ending mistake, though it may appear we're getting closer to that unfortunate outcome.

Polarization

Will we recognize and correct some potentially disastrous error in time to save some aspect of humanity? Probably, but with many sacrifices of life and lifestyle along the way, if power and might continue to dominate the scene. Does that really matter? Who knows but some Universal Intelligence?

Many of us revere all of life and seek to preserve it by whatever means and at whatever stage. Others calculate the beginnings and endings of life differently and with much less passion; while for some, life is most valuable when sacrificed to please some spiritual, moral, or theological purpose or deity. But these are all just human theories, manufactured currently or generations ago by beliefs that certain people or parties have the right answer to the origin, meaning, and purpose of life.

Veiled in this guise of certainty, opposing leaders emerge and use rhetoric and propaganda to consolidate their power at the expense of masses of confused and unsuspecting people, who then obligingly become followers of a particular outlook. The same history has been repeated again and again throughout the world. Such polarized certainties prevent integration and compromise, or at best delay solutions and, therefore, human progress.

Studies of current political and ideological systems bear witness to such polarization and have raised increasing concern about threats to world peace. Our leaders' behaviors—locally, nationally, and worldly—suggest that many would rather risk mutual destruction than modify their beliefs or give up power, an obvious sign of mental and emotional madness! Nazi leader Herman Goering's powerful statements at the time of the Nuremberg trials following World War II confirmed the ease with which entire populations can be quickly brainwashed. Acknowledging that common people in every country wish to avoid war, Goering stated that they are nevertheless easily manipulated by telling them that they are being attacked and that any peacemakers among them are dangerous traitors. He added that it makes no difference what kind of government is in place; it works the same in dictatorships or democracies. With only a very slight change in semantics, doesn't this sound similar to the preelection campaign rhetoric of our political candidates?

Obviously, in our trial-and-error learning we are only in the beginning stages of what's possible, but polarized pendulum swinging has stifled much potential progress; and the scenario described above shows how easily we can be manipulated. History as taught is primarily a story of wars and desires for power over others or a defense against others. History as programmed learning then becomes how to defeat others in order to gain power or how to defend against defeat. Out of this teaching/learning process emerges an atmosphere of fear, suspicion, and aggression, resulting in an attitude of "I must get them (or avoid them) before they get me" (a passive/aggressive stance). The politicians and media thrive on this fear-based scenario because it fuels their business and lines their pocketbooks.

We go from extreme to extreme in much of our political, social, and religious lives. When one approach doesn't work, we adopt an opposite strategy. When aggression doesn't work, we try appeasement.

When prayers aren't answered according to our wishes, we give up religion or seek alternatives. When far-left liberalism appears to be failing, we insert far-right conservatism. This discourages and negates our desire and ability to cooperate and compromise, thus further restricting our advancement.

Questioning Religious and Cultural Assumptions

Religion is a "hot button" these days. Worldwide, we humans make assumptions about a Supreme Being, based on ancient manuscripts likely written by fallible human beings whose motives, experiences, and resources are suspect or unknown, at best. Then we interpret those writings in whatever way suits our ego's purpose and conclude that the hand of some deity is behind it all. To add to this mockery is the fact that we tend to believe as we do based on accidents of birth—the part of the world into which we were born, the family into which we've been placed, the culture into which we've been raised, and the time span into which we've been given life. How profound does that make the saying, "There but for the grace of God go I?" And yet we fail to recognize or accept that all religions make the same types of arguments to justify their own beliefs!

We are aware that most theologies and philosophies are based on "faith," a word that Webster's New World Dictionary describes in its primary definition as an "unquestioning belief that does not require proof or evidence."

By this vague but all-encompassing definition, every major world religion can claim its own significance by promoting its faith, though that faith may render harm to others or be based on wholly bogus or fabricated assumptions. The history of both the ancient and modern worlds reveals widespread destruction resulting from such faith as this. For all their good intentions, radical Christians, Jews, Muslims, and all other religious zealots share responsibility for such destruction, when so convinced of their "rightness" that they use psychological or physical power and scare tactics to keep their members in line and to recruit new adherents. Often their agendas are hidden, but their goals are similar—to secure or convert but rarely to explore beliefs or seek new truths!

Acceptance and exploration of other ABCs (attitudes, beliefs, and concepts) are openly or tacitly discouraged, and the questioning of current theological assumptions by parishioners in order to determine their own beliefs is looked upon with suspicion or disloyalty. The implication seems to be that each dedicated parishioner adds to the certainty and proves to all others (and to the clergy) that they are indeed on the right track—perhaps an apt description of a theological "numbers game."

We use religion-based concepts of sin, evil, and hell as weapons to control behavior and limit trial-and-error processes, as though moral and ethical behavior is inevitably tied to a religious precept. Heaven, or some such blissful destination, is looked upon as a rewarding resting place but available to only a select group following earthly death.

But what if that is the only destination there is, that heaven is for everyone, no matter what his or her earthly circumstances and behaviors have been? Or perhaps this life is only a way station and there's more to come? And what if God is not a punishing or vindictive force just waiting to judge us, as many believe? What would these changes in beliefs do to the power of the church and our subsequent outlook on life's purpose?

The universe is vast. We are bundles of energy, according to science, and we are told that energy cannot be destroyed, only transformed. What if our spirit or soul or energy merely moves on to another galaxy? What if we have more to contribute to another part of this universe or even to another universe?

How much effort in our earthly existence is being used to stifle such speculation? Those entrenched in closed-minded thinking (brainwashed?) will scoff at such questions, for closed-mindedness is safe and secure. Or is it? If indeed the truth will set us free, why are we so afraid of seeking it, of questioning our own and our like-minded colleagues' thoughts, beliefs, and conclusions about life and the afterlife?

Scientists, historians, inventors, and even genealogists are making new discoveries on a daily basis, so why not those who are mentors to our religious, philosophical, and spiritual beliefs? What if all that our Creator desires from us (if anything) is see how much we can accomplish with our endowed abilities? What if this Universal Intelligence has no human ego, as we seem to want to give It? What if being worshipped and fought over is not even on Its radar?

What if all that's really important to our Creator is our existence and the accompanying freedom to choose our own responses to whatever life brings? Isn't that what most of us desire for *our* children? Maybe that's what love is really all about, creating children and encouraging them to be all that they can be, without indulging them in all kinds of entitlements, indoctrinations, and possessions.

If we are indeed made in the Creator's image (and not vice-versa), or if there is at least some connection with that Force which created us, might not that same goal be applied to us? We have a whole universe to explore and use. The possibilities are unlimited. Yet we spend our time, energy, and resources competing, comparing, and crushing rather than cooperating, caring, and creating. Whether we are homeless drifters, government bureaucrats, elected politicians, community organizers, business owners, prison inmates, entertainers, educators, or clergy, we all are perpetrators, and we all are victims! We have our beliefs (though we rarely are aware of their origins), and we staunchly defend them. We stubbornly advocate unproven answers, rather than risk losing personal or organizational power by posing thoughtful questions that might lead to disturbing, opposing, or contradictory conclusions. We seem terrified of being wrong, so we clutch certainty!

How much time, energy, and anger have we spent on sociopolitical issues such as pro-life, pro-choice, gay marriage, premarital sex, religious truths, and equal rights? We engage one another on philosophical, religious, and moral grounds where there can be no winners and no losers—just hardcore beliefs that lead only to animosity and frustration. Such issues tear us apart as our egos staunchly defend past and present territories and refuse to explore new horizons and creative solutions!

I am generally pro-life when it comes to abortion and pro-choice about contraception, but because of pragmatics not some moral conviction. To me abortion robs us of life already conceived that could contribute to our progress. Still, I am not appalled by anyone's death (though I am deeply and humanly saddened by the loss), as there will be many more contributors to come, and eventually we'll "get it right"—whatever that may come to mean! I believe in a Creator who loves Its creations and will take care of every departed spirit, soul, or energy by recycling it to another being, transferring it to another task or universe, or providing a final resting place. No creation really dies, so why worry about it! (And if I'm wrong, and there is no afterlife of any kind, what's the sense of worrying about *that*?)

How might it all work? Is there an end somewhere—like heaven? Is there reincarnation? Are there mansions in the sky? Is there some sort of spiritual transformation? I don't know, and I don't care! It's enough for me to believe that something good will somehow happen. I don't wish to waste time trying to figure out the Creator's unknowable purpose for us, other than to use the gifts of creation to ourselves create! Staunchly adhering to any uncompromising religious, political, or social belief detracts from our basic task of making productive use of our own existence. Therefore, I'm not opposed to the concept of pro-choice, either, and certainly not when the issue is contraception. After all, the power of choice is one of our gifts, procreation notwithstanding.

It may be that what pleases the Intelligence (if "being pleased" is even a concern of It) is that we earnestly try to fulfill the purpose of figuring out what we're here for, or that we attempt to use the abilities with which we've been blessed. Even so, I can't envision a Creator who would be vindictive to those who don't try, because each of us automatically contributes in some way (see earlier references to the movie *It's a Wonderful Life* and the chapter 3 description of people types). *It's impossible not to contribute, but it's quite possible not to understand or reveal our contributions.* For those who may have lost track of the purpose of this book, recording our stories for the use of future generations is one way of detailing our efforts, contributions, and essence, no matter what those stories divulge!

Is There One True Religion?

I recall an event in my childhood in which a young female acquaintance was told by a clergy person that only members of that faith could access heaven. All others would go to hell. She went home devastated because her grandmother was of another faith. What a terrible image to portray to a young child—or to an adult, for that matter!

Aside from belief, can anyone be absolutely certain that any one religion in the world is better than another? Isn't religion merely an attempt to answer some elusive philosophical questions: Who am I? Where did I come from? What am I supposed to be doing here? Where am I going after this life?

In answering such basic questions, why are there so many sects and denominations even among Christians? Why do we pay so much attention to such small details and variables that we have to build separate churches to answer the same fundamental questions? Even if we profess to believe that our church is no better than (but merely different from) others, the concept of "separate but equal" may be as prejudicial in religious affairs as it's considered to be in the educational world. Is there not an inherent underlying supposition of rightness in our selections? If not, then why in our rhetoric and choices do we bother emphasizing the differences? Perhaps the rise in nondenominational community churches is an attempt to counter such traditions.

One might argue that capitalism demands competition, even among churches, and that business, industry, and religion operate more productively for the consumer when someone produces a better mousetrap or more accurate belief system. But emphasis is on the words "better." and "more accurate." Can we actually prove that one belief system is better than another, and does not "more accurate" imply judgment or worthiness? Can we imagine someone making a pitch by saying that his or her product or service is worse than, or even merely equal to, the competition? Whether it's pizza, politics, property, prune juice, or piety, we all look for the best (or right) product or service available to us.

Sometimes we personalize our choices without any intent of evaluating options, but all too often we behave judgmentally in the process. When only one of a kind is within our grasp, we lose options and either go without or accept what's available. In a crisis or when there is no choice, we are resilient and lose our zealousness! So why not in everyday life? By providing ourselves more choices, and vocally or silently evaluating the choices of others, have we invited unnecessary discord?

Can we not just appreciate that we all have meaningful options and variations and be done with it? Or perhaps only focus on similarities and ignore differences? What difference does it make that you and I have alternative beliefs about our origin, or that we pray to some other deity, or that we pray at all? Aside from the dictates of ancient manuscripts (some or all of which may be fraudulent) and our individual or collective interpretations of their contents, how can we yet be certain of any such beliefs?

If we broaden the concept to other religions and philosophies, our beliefs and behaviors become even more fixated. We argue and fight over prophets and symbols; past and present signs from some sacred being; and gurus, each of whom has been arbitrarily picked as the main or only true messenger from a Creator. And all of this is mere speculation and interpretation because none of it can be proven! Yet we assume we're right, and sometimes sacrifice our lives and the lives of others in order to keep those assumptions alive.

When what we value most is at stake, as when outsiders threaten our very existence (i.e., Pearl Harbor, 9/11, neighborhood crime, etc.), our differences magically vanish, and we become united. Using that logic, perhaps what we earthlings really need is an attack by aliens from another planet! *Star Wars* may not be that far-fetched, anyway, considering our recently acquired knowledge of space travel, missiles, rockets, and other terrifying weapons. But will we use them to fight one another or to peacefully unify against some exterior enemy—be it aliens or ignorance? Either way, science fiction may not be fiction much longer!

Ironically, there may be many more similarities among, than differences between, most of our warring religions. Is it really likely that a benevolent and loving Intelligence cares about which messengers provide spiritual philosophies to earthlings? And is it likely to matter whether those messengers are called Abraham, Buddha, Jesus, Mohammed, or some other name? Maybe none of them are messengers; maybe they're all frauds. Or maybe they're all virtuous and righteous, and it's our interpretations that make them seem different. Or maybe ... Or maybe ... Or maybe ... Or might it be that trying to figure out how best to use our endowments is enough, that the process and not the end result is the goal?

How many of us have ever considered that you or I might be a guru that a Creator is working through? Certainly many of the biblical characters were just ordinary people, facing the same types of struggles that you and I face on a daily basis—and making the same kinds of mistakes. How might some Universal Intelligence be using you and your life? Is that blasphemy or is that a possibility? You decide. If it's blasphemy, then I admit to guilt because much of what I'm writing in this book has come through inspiration that I can only identify by labeling myself a conduit. If that's blasphemy, then I'm in good company, for haven't all religious gurus, prophets, saints, saviors, and visionaries been blasphemous in some way? When I revisit some of this manuscript that I wrote years ago, it seems strangely mysterious, as though I typed the words but the thoughts were planted.

Consider your own situation. Are you willing to "bet your soul" that your life has had no meaning to Whomever or Whatever put you here on earth? Are you willing to let your existence vanish into oblivion as though you had no purpose? Do you suppose that such thoughts might be an affront to your Creator? Even if your life has been as devastating as the biblical Job's, will you leave some stories that will prove to your descendants, and acknowledge to your Creator, that you were indeed a valuable link in their heritage and in the pursuit of human progress?

Openness to Reframing

One of our mental gifts is the ability to "reframe" any belief or concept that we have acquired. Whatever our past beliefs and opinions about ourselves and the world we live in, we can revisit and reinterpret any that we later question, or that have not served us well. Reframing, of course, requires considerable forethought but doesn't necessarily require any change in personal beliefs; it does require a change in attitude, however. For example, this world would change overnight if we all reframed some of our certainties into inconclusiveness (with a footnote "further examination needed") and our often-silent arrogance into respect, starting at the personal level. Not only would we positively affect both our neighbors and ourselves, but the eventual effects on international policy and behavior might be enormous. Would this be risky? Possibly, but isn't a meaningful life about taking risks? The alternative is to stay on the path we've taken for centuries—to rope off our territory and stand our ground. How peaceful has that turned out to be?

"Reframing" is a term often used in the helping professions, and means viewing a situation or condition in a different way from the usual, from a different frame of reference, taking an alternate view with perhaps different basic assumptions, thinking outside one's own personal box, and thereby respectfully considering an alternate conclusion about the subject being discussed.

We do this automatically at times, especially while dealing with a painful or traumatic event. Rather than dwell on the sorrow of a tragic death, we may communicate our sympathy but also indicate that the suffering is over now and that he or she is in a better place. Please note that I am not suggesting a callous remark; our sincerity will be revealed through our tone of voice, facial expressions, and physical mannerisms. But we have mentally reframed the event, thus providing greater comfort by focusing on a more pleasant or positive aspect. We have changed nothing but our interpretation of the event.

One of the common sayings in our family when someone faces a difficult situation is, "That builds character," thereby emphasizing a potentially productive outcome arising from an unpleasant experience. The experience hasn't changed, only the perception and conclusion. As indicated in the preceding paragraph, it is imperative to the positive reception of such a remark that it be accompanied nonverbally by conveyance of empathy and compassion. Wallowing in negativity and unpleasantness may be realistic to a degree but is rarely helpful. Since it is dependent only on mental reinterpretation, absolutely nothing is exempt from reframing.

Unfortunately, reframing can go in both directions. Pessimists and optimists provide the best examples. Those who are accustomed to viewing the world with fear and skepticism will often reframe the best situations into dis-ease and negativity; those who've been programmed with confidence and trust, though, will reframe the worst situations into promise and optimism. While the former may be useful in certain situations, optimistic reframing is a healthier approach since it changes our outlook from negative to positive and leads to a more satisfying life.

Reframing would rarely be necessary if our social and public institutions were more positive in their attitudes, behaviors, and communications. Unfortunately, much of their nature is competitive and comparative, and the strategy for gaining equality or domination is commonly based on bringing down those who succeed rather than lifting up those who don't, and insisting that the former is an essential prerequisite to the latter. We often go to great lengths to try to lower another's self-esteem when we could better use the time and energy to raise our own.

Nothing is more indicative of this tactic than the actions of leaders in political parties. Negativity, distortions, name-calling, deliberate misinterpretations, and fabrications are their main strategies, and while the electorate voices a general dislike for these maneuvers, it continues to put into political offices those who do it best. We have accepted negative campaigning and good-sounding rhetoric because it's what we're accustomed to, and it seems our only choice. Even politicians who appear initially different too often succumb to the nefarious advice of their power-driven strategists. Where did this obsession with winning and pursuing power originate, if not with the institutions of our youth where we learned by both experience and observation how life should be lived in our culture.

We should be wary of all politicians and leaders who are unwilling to reframe their rhetoric and soften their attitudes toward others who believe differently. Instead, we put them on pedestals and reelect them as though it's a virtue to be tough and uncompromising. Willingness to "reach across the aisle" is now a virtual death sentence for many seeking political office. Even though voters with moderate outlooks generally determine national elections (thankfully), they are often maligned as being wishy-washy fence sitters, and frequently must choose from among extremist candidates.

It's a sad but fortunate commentary that extremists usually balance each other out in a democratic election. A politician who actually shows an inclination to seek pragmatic solutions rather than promote an ideology risks a label of treason by mainstream party constituents or at best is considered an unfit candidate. Recall that former US Senator Joe Lieberman, a moderate Democrat from Connecticut, was denied backing by his own party for reelection because he didn't quite fit the party platform; fortunately, the voters rebelled and elected him, anyway, as an independent! Willingness to seek solutions to challenging problems by being reasonable is no longer an asset, and stubborn adherence to political doctrine is no longer a liability. Compromises and concessions are no longer tenable with an attitude that makes the attainment of power the primary goal.

But has our core of humanity really bought into this way of thinking? Have we given up our natural inclination toward honesty, love, compassion, truth, and other forms of goodness? I hope not. We can and must free ourselves from acquired (brainwashed) ways of thinking. Tolerance begets tolerance, but tolerance is only half way home. We must accept as a viable alternative that which we cannot prove otherwise. If not, how can we expect acceptance for our own beliefs?

Accepting does not mean absorbing; rather, it means respecting! We all have thoughts, ideas, and experiences—and resulting stories— that have defined our lives and that could be left to descendants. All we need as incentives to express them is the confidence that our thoughts and conclusions about the lives we've led are equal in value to those of educators, attorneys, physicians, historians, entertainers, industrialists, inventors, politicians, and the like.

So far we have concentrated on the importance and value of transmitting our individual life stories to future generations, some of the logistics involved, and the institutional and cultural obstacles to doing so. But there is a broader picture to be understood, one that takes into account our place in the entire universe and the philosophies that guide it, and that is the subject of chapters 9 and 10.

Thoughts/Activities to Consider

1. Examine the origin of one of your most basic beliefs and write a story about it. Try to choose one that cannot be absolutely proven and consider why you continue to hold on to it.

2. Write a short story about the purpose of your life as you see it, and of how well you have satisfied that purpose.

3. Write a short story about your religious beliefs or faith (or lack thereof) and examine its origin. Have there been changes in viewpoint from how you were raised? If so, how do you account for them? If not, why not?

4. Write a short story about your open- or closed-mindedness.

5. "We seem terrified of being wrong, so we clutch certainty." Write a short personal story about this quote.

6. Choose a past or present personal experience that has caused you anguish and try to reframe it in more positive terms.

CHAPTER 9

What Principles Guide Your Stories?

Our Own Personal Wisdom

No one writes a story from scratch. We all have backgrounds of experience and learning that influence our present perceptions and state of mind. Out of those backgrounds we have carved a way of life that makes most sense to us. It isn't perfectly consistent and may even be totally contradictory at times. Our feelings, thoughts, and behaviors too often travel on different highways, try as we may to place them on one interstate and seal off the exits; we like to portray this appearance of consistency in order to convince significant others of our stability and reliability. In addition, steadiness satisfies our ego by enhancing its ability to protect us from criticism, although the ego also has many other weapons at its disposal for that purpose (rationalization, denial, avoidance, counterattack, submission) and usually defends itself quite adequately. It thrives on fooling others but is less concerned about internal conflicts.

Few of us can quickly articulate the principles that guide our lives because we spend little time considering them. But guide us they do! They're usually part of the unconscious 95 percent of our mind that some experts say dictates most every move. Little of what we experience and learn throughout life remains at the conscious level, and what's in "the back of our minds" may influence us most.

Students cram for exams and then go on vacation for a couple of months. How much do they consciously retain following that time off? Not many of the details. Still, conscious review restores learning to an extent that varies with each student but provides evidence that much of our initial education is preserved somewhere in the mind. Like the ability to ride a bicycle, the fundamental principles are unconsciously retained long after the initial skill is developed.

Incidental learning from our cultural activities is no different. We pick up new ideas and reinforce others just through the process of social living. There are many variables to our retention patterns and many different environments away from the classroom that influence lives; we only know that some learning sticks. We can test for the academic portion, but the rest merely gets absorbed and sits there until reactivated by life experiences.

The end result of this chaotic dance is the formation of guiding concepts that steer our behaviors in certain directions (see chapter 3). To the extent that these directions have some consistent and congruent organization and depth, some might be called philosophies. Technically, the word "philosophy" means love of wisdom, but its most common usage refers to a particular system of principles for the conduct of life. Congruent or not and conscious or not, we all have a system or a set of principles that guide our behaviors.

Is it important that we understand our own personal system? How can that be useful to our descendants, our contemporaries, and perhaps even to us? It is tempting to downplay the need for a well-thought-out direction in life, since most of us have never consciously had one and may consider it a needless endeavor.

As children we followed parental and cultural dictates, then later modified or rejected many of those as future education and life experiences intervened. But seldom have we been totally satisfied with the outcome. Life is just too complicated, and there are too many times when our current desires conflict with our ideals, and our behaviors contradict our deepest values, resulting in underlying guilt and social worries that we then unwittingly pass on to our children. These internal conflicts and contradictions can even become socially agitating and result in wounded or destroyed relationships. The only ones who profit from such unfortunate disruptions are therapists and attorneys!

Present generations may have paid a heavy price for our lack of conscious direction, but future ones need not follow our examples. We can search out and examine—perhaps in hindsight for some of us older generations—the principles that guide us and offer our hard-earned wisdom to the future of our species, giving the yet unborn the head start on a solid foundation that may have eluded us. They too will have a philosophy grounded in principles to guide their lives, but of what will those principles consist? We can influence their choices by bringing into consciousness for their examination those principles that might otherwise remain unconscious but powerful determinants of their behavior.

The preponderance of this chapter will present my own attempts at defining a personal philosophy, in an effort to model an admittedly fallible process rather than promote any specific content. I have examined my own thoughts, feelings, behaviors, and experiences as I have interpreted them throughout life; then I've measured them against some "pure" philosophies described by academic scholars. Though much of philosophy is timeless, interpretations vary considerably, and newer versions continue to surface as modern scholars probe the possibilities. Please bear in mind, however, that I have no desire to evaluate or compare, only to interpret and personalize according to my own understanding and experiences.

Pragmatism

Like many Americans, I have always had a strong pragmatic focus, but there are logical and ethical limits involved in practicality, in "doing what works." Like many human philosophies, what works in the short run may vary considerably from what works in the long run, and we can't always predict long-term consequences of our actions. Even in the short-term we are prone to mistaken or self-defeating behaviors. Still, it makes little sense to be excessively cautious and forego many productive activities because of the fear of something going awry. This is one of the many foibles that we must confront with a pragmatic philosophy. Perhaps this is why forgiveness of self and others is such an important attitude for pragmatists to have and convey.

I appreciate and embrace many aspects of pragmatism. It is action-driven, science-focused, and process-oriented. "Doing" based on logic and solid research is considered more valuable than "talking," yet *how* we accomplish our goals must take precedence in a democratic society. For the pragmatist, certainty and absolutism is rejected in favor of context and relativism. No problem can be solved permanently because situations and conditions are always changing. Truth must be constantly pursued but with the understanding that it is always an ideal never to be reached.

Pursuing a goal that can never be attained may be troublesome for some in our problem-solving society, but if we perceive our lives and progress as links to the future rather than ends in themselves, our entire focus changes. Since all solutions are temporary, relative, and contextual, the pragmatist is very concerned about what we leave for others to inherit. Therein lies a most significant responsibility— preparing new life for different circumstances and conditions. This is not to deny the cyclical nature of the universe (see chapter 10), but only to recognize that thousands of years and many hundreds of generations may pass before similar circumstances and conditions actually return. Therefore, our closest descendants will need to capitalize and build on what immediately past generations have learned and experienced. They cannot merely copy our examples, but our stories may still be crucial to their mission, if only we will provide them!

As Kaplan notes in *The New World of Philosophy*, knowledge (even history) is not just a record of the past; "it is a reconstruction of the present directed toward fulfillment in the emerging future" (1961, 27). Knowledge is a precursor of logical thinking, and pragmatists are very absorbed with using logical thinking to solve problems of daily living. Surely, our logic is sometimes flawed, especially when strong emotions are generated at the same time, but the pragmatist's emphasis on education, science, and technology helps to counteract or neutralize faulty logic.

Pragmatism is always open to new possibilities but is thoroughly committed to democratic values. As such, there is a strong belief in both the capabilities and responsibilities of every individual. With our capabilities there is little we cannot accomplish in this world, but too often we sell ourselves short and leave our responsibilities to elected and appointed representatives who promise to carry them out for us but have little knowledge of (and even less investment in) our lives. They supply mostly rhetoric and are themselves too often irresponsible in those promises to us, making each life ultimately a do-it-yourself project!

Religious fundamentalists will likely take issue with many pragmatic views. Pragmatists may consider the Bible and other such documents as temporary fixes, forever subject to scientific scrutiny and revision. Ultimate truth is forever pursued, never to be settled with certainty. But pragmatists need not be atheists. Gregg Braden, for example, has shown that much scientific analysis confirms the likelihood of some sort of superior intelligence having created humans and the universe. (See chapter 10.)

As explained earlier, many past generations in all parts of the world have fashioned their own theories about how creation took place and the various messengers sent to earth by a Creator. While these accounts have generated many good works and much charitable behavior among believers, they have also contributed to many highly destructive conflicts between those with opposing theories. We argue, fight, maim, and kill over beliefs and ideas that cannot yet be substantiated and may never be proven, thereby diminishing the value of human life and replacing it with the worship of power, speculation, and wishful thinking.

Existentialism

Man as a *species* has been carelessly tossed aside, while the minds of *living* men have argued politics and ideals about what "things" are most important. We have great concerns about the preservation of nature and natural resources, about the characteristics of a universal Creator and the means to obtain Its favor, and about the policies of government that should guide our collective thoughts and behaviors. In addressing these issues, however, we have neglected to emphasize the centrality of human life itself and of the individual's living circumstances and conditions. We assume that money and rhetorical attention will somehow accomplish the goal of satisfying basic human needs—physical, psychological, and spiritual. But the more we spend and the more we talk, the further behind we get. This has led to the rise of existentialist beliefs throughout the world, and I have found some of those beliefs quite in accord with my own.

The idea of existentialism is that each person exists and then becomes something; that is, existence precedes essence. We are born, and then we develop our individual lives. Little is innate or inborn. As an aside, this philosophy also assumes that everything else that defines our daily world begins in our mind first; that is, its essence precedes its existence. If we can't even imagine the possibility of something existing, how can we define it? We must first create its essence in our mind. Then it exists, and we can name it. But humans are different because we are at the top of the global intelligence chain. According to existentialists, we exist first and then our essence is created. Why is all of this significant?

According to this view, as members of the human race we are responsible for who we become, and who we become is determined by the choices we make throughout life. We invent our own meanings and values simply because we are free to do so, and that freedom can never be exhausted. We cannot put the responsibility for our choices on anyone else. Though our choices may be limited and substantially controlled by environmental conditions, some choices always exist, as Holocaust survivor and author Viktor Frankl so aptly pointed out in his book *Man's Search for Meaning.*

However, our choices may have consequences for others that must be considered, so there is an ethical and social aspect as well. Above all, integrity and authenticity are emphasized in the existential philosophy. Whoever we choose to become, it is vital that it remains our choice and not that of others who may try to selfishly influence us. We may choose to ask for their advice, but whether or not we accept and act upon that advice merely represents another choice. Moreover, what gives meaning to life is not what we experience but rather how we interpret and respond to those experiences.

This emphasis on personal responsibility can result in feelings of isolation, loneliness, and depression, and has often been looked upon as a cause for despair among existentialists. But need this be the case? No doubt, such freedom can be scary, and ultimate responsibility for one's choices and essence effectively eliminates the use of blame, one of the ego's premier weapons of protection. But freedom from influence also opens up more possibilities for self-improvement, without the will and interference of others.

To the extent that we are responsible for our conditions and situations, we are then capable of independently changing them; whereas, when others are responsible for our lot in life, we must await their good will and accommodations if our conditions are to be improved. In other words, if another person, group, or organization *caused* our (pleasant or unpleasant) emotions, interpretations, or behaviors surrounding an experience, then by implication that entity must somehow remove that cause if we are to get a different result. In that case we would choose to be helpless, that "state of being" described by Martin Seligman in his research work on the art of helplessness at the University of Pennsylvania.

The common phrase, "You make me feel (whatever)," is an example of how we blame others for our emotions and implies that we cannot feel differently until those others who are responsible decide to change back—which they are unlikely to do, further reinforcing our presumed state of helplessness, of being unable to control our own emotions and circumstances.

Since a basic tenet of the existential philosophy is that each person is responsible for his/her own choices, how can the life histories of past generations (us) be of much help to our descendants? Again, the answer dwells on the issue of choice. First, there must be some things from which to choose—our stories help fit that bill! In this case, *our* essence precedes *their* existence; we portray the essence of our lives by putting our stories down on paper. Only then can our descendants decide how to use them to enhance their own lives.

Through their own examinations and analyses, they can choose what to discard and what to retain, just as they do with our material goods when our physical bodies cease to exist. Descendants are always influenced to some degree by intergenerational relationships, but their decisions about how to use our experiences and interpretations are commonly made without much examination. Mindless conformities or thoughtless rebellions are common results of these relationships, but such unconscious behaviors belie integrity, authenticity, and thoughtful choice. Our stories can insert conscious behavior into this process and, by providing an alternative to cultural brainwashing, therefore increase the likelihood of more beneficial choices.

Hinduism

After centuries of disregard and scorn by Westerners, Asian philosophies have more recently been given their due respect, and I find many of my own beliefs leaning in that direction. Much of the traditional Indian view of life is based on the acceptance of religious diversity—not just tolerance but true acceptance. It might be phrased in this sentence: "We all worship the same God, and that God accepts whatever form we use."

What would happen in this world if we all believed in that concept? Perhaps we could wipe away all the speculation about our origin and purpose and get down to the issue of helping one another solve earthly problems. By acknowledging the possible legitimacy of all ways of conceptualizing and worshipping a Creator rather than merely tolerating an assumed illegitimacy of all but our own way, we would open doors of communication that have rarely existed and pave the way for solutions not otherwise considered. Is there anything more divisive than telling people they are wrong in their beliefs, thus setting up an immediate barrier to further discussion?

There is no such thing as original sin, proponents say, and the only hell we need to be saved from is what we ourselves create on earth. Much like the Christian philosophy, there is a strong belief in cause and effect; we reap what we sow. But there is hope, because this life on earth is not the end. There is an ambiguous, often undefined transformation into another type of existence, not necessarily reincarnation. In Western terms, this might be stated as "we are energy, and energy cannot be destroyed, only transformed"—into *what* would be mere speculation!

There is a belief in finality in much of American culture that is alien to Indian beliefs and causes us extra grief (i.e., life ends in death, never to return; our final destination is heaven or hell; the grave is our final resting place). In contrast, even with the traditional Indian caste system, the kind of life one lives in her/his present circumstances has an effect on the next round of life, whatever that may be. The possibility of a better upcoming life provides ethical and spiritual direction in this life and hope for the future.

There is a strong emphasis in Indian philosophy on knowledge and understanding. "Life is experienced as a problem only because we do not understand it, and just this is the only thing to be understood" (Kaplan, 222). The goal of life is truth, and increasing our knowledge is the way to get there. Everything is intermediate and in process until that absolute truth is attained, far away as it may be.

Theism and atheism are equally in error. Each is taking a different road in the pursuit of truth, but neither has found it yet. Pragmatic logic would suggest that they work together by gathering more knowledge, instead of belittling each other's efforts and beliefs. Unfortunately, reality does not always mirror logic.

Finally, Indian thought is action-oriented. Actions speak louder than words, and works speak louder than faith. As with pragmatism, relativism is emphasized and rhetorical conflict minimized. Unity is underscored. But it is the lack of certainty, the lack of arrogance, the lack of righteousness, and the attitude of acceptance of all forms of religion and knowledge in the pursuit of truth that is especially appealing to me.

Buddhism

In recent decades the Buddhist philosophy has grown considerably in Western thought and has had substantial influence on my beliefs. According to Kaplan, Buddhism arose out of Hinduism much like Christianity arose out of Judaism. Like the Indian philosophy, Buddhism emphasizes the prominence of knowledge and understanding as solutions to life issues. The main Buddha considered himself a teacher and model for living, not a religious savior. Similar to Jesus, his followers added the worshipping aspect.

As a philosophy, Buddhism is atheistic, considering man to be master of his own fate. There is no god, no immortal soul, no creation, and no last judgment. Individuals must find their own truth to life. Nothing should be accepted on faith alone; all aspects of life should be examined by each of us, and we each must judge for ourselves their worthiness. Our ancestors who have preceded us in life can be guides on our journey, but each of us must be his/her own ultimate decision maker.

Regardless of how we arrived on earth, our presence is proof of our own existence but not the proof of a special Creator. Therefore, service to our fellow humans is more important than the worship of an unproven deity. This is accomplished through action, not rhetoric. We must pursue insight and convert it to responsible earthly behavior, not to eternal salvation. Our obsession with the afterlife and our addictive attachment to "things" here on earth has blinded us to our responsibility to others.

Instead of compassion for people, we demonstrate passion for gadgets. This shows up both in our occupational lives and in our worshipping patterns. Technology is king of the former, and symbols, rites, ceremonies, and attitudes of righteousness are elements of the latter. By such passionate attachments we also inflict pain on ourselves. We agonize and despair when those attachments are taken from us and needlessly worry ourselves that we might someday lose them even when we have them! What sense does that make? This self-inflicted psychological and emotional pain needlessly directs energies inward for protection and discourages us from acting to help others.

Besides emerging from the Hindu tradition, there is much in the Buddhist philosophy that is also common to pragmatism and existentialism. Life is as we make it; we reap what we sow, and it is our responsibility to choose our own pathways, recognizing that we are at the same time both alone and not alone. Religion, if even a factor, is peripheral at best. Concepts such as heaven, hell, original sin, penance, and atonement are rhetorical distractions to our responsibility to help one another. They may provide some control over our ego's selfish behavior but often at the cost of increased guilt and decreased self-esteem.

Buddhism cites four basic truths. First, life is imperfect, incomplete, and often painful, trivial, and meaningless. Few of us would disagree with that assessment. But life is also dynamic and always in process, allowing us ample opportunities to make changes. Life has no special meaning or purpose, leaving it up to each of us to determine that for ourselves. Eventually we die and others are born. That's what life is, and if we don't become too attached to it, the loss of life (our own or others) need not be devastating.

Second, most of life is based on the principle of cause and effect. Evil is man-made and thus erasable by different behavior. We must identify, understand, and remove the causes of our problems, and our powerful minds give us the capacity to do so.

Third, the source of this man-made evil is the aforementioned emotional and psychological attachment to "things," including money, consumer goods, institutions, concepts, ideologies, political parties, other people, and even our own bodies—breeding frustration, anxiety, anger, guilt, competition, despair, and the illusion of certainty. The ultimate attachment to such things can even be suicide, as when we attach ourselves to death in place of life. We must detach ourselves from both the good and the bad in order to live a life of responsible citizenship. Otherwise, we surrender to the illusion that what lies outside of self is essential to our happiness, and such thinking then causes selfish and evil behaviors.

Fourth, the prescription for living responsibly is the renunciation of our selves (egos?) with all our external and internal attachments. Eliminate selfishness and replace it with selflessness. Replace our passion for the illusions of life with compassion for all living things.

Compassion implies detached sorrow accompanied by a desire to help, not the callous and uncaring feelings generated by selfish passion. Such detachment frees us from self-inflicted pain and encourages responsible behavior toward others. Moreover, we are better able to seek and absorb knowledge and enlightenment in a life filled with compassion. This, of course, would mean replacing many subjective feelings with more objective understanding. "The Buddhist idea of the wise man, the sage, is of one who is never overwhelmed by his feelings, yet never acts unfeelingly" (Kaplan, 262).

To many modern Westerners, the idea of detachment might indeed seem callous, but it does fit somewhat between two extremes that currently polarize American politics—the heartless behavior attributed to some (ultimate detachment?) and the bleeding heart mentality imputed to others (excessive attachment?). In so doing, many seem to equate emotional distress with love and concern, and emotional calmness with neglect and disregard. Buddhists see this quite differently.

Zen

The Zen philosophy is an offshoot of Buddhist thinking. While agreeing that humans are far too attached to exterior and illusional aspects of life, Zen adds that we talk too much. Life should just be accepted, not pursued or understood. Talk gets us into difficulty. It abstracts and distorts reality and leads to misunderstanding, mistakes, and miscommunication. We create additional problems by engaging in long, drawn-out discussions trying to prevent imaginary problems for which there can be no solutions. Talk merely interferes with life and complicates it by trying to explain things. When politicians exclaim, "Let me make this perfectly clear," we can usually anticipate a drawn-out, foggy message!

We purport to use talk for its content, but the real message is in the delivery process, say Zen enthusiasts. Our words are distractions and smokescreens. The only real meaning stems from that we talk, why we talk, how we talk, when we talk, to whom we talk, where we talk, and how much we talk. Like Marshall McLuhan has said, "The medium is the message." The fact that the speaker utters a number of words here and now in the manner chosen is the real communication, hidden as it is by the illusion of verbal meaning.

While many of us intuitively understand this, I am constantly amazed at the rhetorical ability of successful politicians to fool an educated public. Zen considers such talk a distraction from wisdom. "The wise man does not pursue wisdom, but lives his life, and therein precisely does his wisdom lie" (Kaplan, 311).

Zen is a style of life focused on the acceptance of reality. What we see is what we get. There is no hocus-pocus. We do not need to understand and interpret life, just accept it as it is. Trying to solve it is what creates problems. Then we try to fix the problems we've created by figuring out more solutions, and in doing so we create even more problems.

Nowhere is that scenario more evident than in our various legislatures, where thousands of pages are often used to explain one article of law. Interpretations become so onerous and detailed ambiguous explanations so preposterous that politicians resort to passing laws before knowing what's really contained in them, causing more problems, which courts have to sort through and then make their own wordy judgments, few of which are unanimous and many of which involve controversial interpretations, often just more talk creating more problems. Witness this last sentence for an ironic example!

Life is simple in Zen philosophy. Work and love both have great value and are emphasized. Yet we spend enormous amounts of time trying to find solutions to nonexistent issues. "Chill out, relax, and enjoy life as it really is," might be the advice that many proponents would give—if they gave advice at all. For adherents also believe that each of us must learn about life through our own experiences, that no one can teach another person how to live. Life is not empty but may seem that way when we look for fulfillment outside of ourselves. As for how we conduct our daily lives, Zen offers this suggestion, "Live as though we died yesterday." With no worries, obligations, duties, or other encumbrances, how would that affect our lives?

Chinese Culture

Another philosophy that has intrigued and influenced me is taken from ancient Chinese culture. Though there are differences between the Confucius and Tao versions of this culture, my only interest is conveying that which I have absorbed in my experience with life.

A fundamental orientation of Chinese philosophy seems to be an appreciation for many different viewpoints on a given issue. This differs considerably from a more Western polarizing mind-set that states outwardly or at least implies that "if I'm right, and I know I am, then you must be wrong." Virtue, morality, and social ethics are held in high esteem, and duty to family and community command far more attention than does regard for any religious doctrine or worldly affair. The value of religion is not denied, only put in its place of secondary importance to service to one's fellow humans.

Man is innately good, according to these beliefs, and if he would only rely on his positive core, many difficult problems could be overcome. However, his virtue can be compromised by conditions and circumstances, and when that happens, his behaviors can be evil. Education and socialization are often the cause, shackling the unsuspecting with promises of material pleasures and spurious propaganda that overwhelm our innate perfection.

To avoid such outcomes, we must limit our desires, simplify our lives, and gratefully make do with what we have. By abandoning ambition and material success, we can concentrate on being what we innately are and diminish the worldly pressures to become what we're not!

Much of Chinese thought is pragmatic and contextual, with little emphasis on rigid rules, though virtue and morality are always at the core. While virtue (goodness) is inborn, ideas vary on where the acquisition of morality (how that goodness should be displayed) comes from—the dominant culture, education, religion, or self-examination. Taoism is suspicious of both government and cultural institutions and cautions against education being the source of moral instruction, which would seem to eliminate schools, churches, and many organizations, all of which (as in America) generate some suspicion as to motives.

The worst mistake institutions make is to tamper with people's hearts, that virtuous part of our being that serves our family, friends, and neighbors. "The efforts of the educator and moralist are at best futile, and at worst destructive of every human good" (Kaplan, 294). By creating reams of laws, governments define criminals; by preaching religious doctrines, churches create sinners; and by setting arbitrary standards of achievement, schools identify failures. Are these the best ways to promote our goodness?

The Taoist's answer to many of life's dilemmas is nonaction, doing by not doing, letting things happen on their own without outside interference. In this way our core virtues can be released and cultural obstacles overcome. A personal example may demonstrate.

In my graduate school teaching experience, charged with developing competent counselors able to help others with emotional and behavioral issues, part of my work involved helping my adult students acknowledge and examine their own internal and relational dilemmas in life through ongoing semester-long small group interactions. My usual method in facilitating these groups was nonaction. By being initially present but very still, and avoiding the lecture process that collegians have learned to expect from teachers— through this lack of direction, tension was soon created.

Describing the process of learning that resulted from attempts to lower that tension is well beyond the purpose of this example and would take pages to explain. Nevertheless, the nonaction of letting things happen on their own without much outside interference was nearly always successful, as my observations and student feedback consistently verified. Though the process was always time-consuming, usually emotional, and often painful, eventually cultural masks and protective disguises were discarded and replaced with the core virtues that the Tao says will be released.

One semester I decided to team-teach the class with a colleague whom I greatly respected and admired but who had a very different philosophy, one more in harmony with student expectations. This esteemed teacher was considered a role model by many students and lived up to that reputation by verbally providing viewpoints and ideas through stories and activities that were usually very relevant to student experiences.

However, our teaching philosophies were so different that we were unable to work together effectively after that initial experiment. While I wanted to do my job by not doing what students expected but probably would have liked and by my nonaction stimulating them to somehow collectively figure out their own solutions to the lack of structure, my colleague's verbosity and directive nature never gave me that opportunity. Nevertheless, we continued to refer students to each other's classes for a curricular experience that each of us could provide alone.

In Conclusion

I have not done justice to any of these philosophies. I have intentionally pulled out parts of each one that have most influenced me and with which I could most identify. I have likely misinterpreted some and distorted the purity of others, and I have definitely omitted many—due to lack of knowledge, opposition to basic tenets, considerable overlap with those I've chosen, or assumed familiarity (i.e., Christianity). But none of that really matters! If completeness and total accuracy were of prime importance to my message, I would have written a very different book.

Instead, what I have tried to convey is a process through which we all decide, albeit unconsciously, the principles that guide our lives. A few scholars over the centuries may have organized these principles into what they believe to be logical, coherent systems, but who cares? Their academic conclusions are of little interest to the general public because we are creative, dynamic, ever-changing individuals, not robots chained to others' interpretations of life.

Nevertheless, our descendants will be counting on our help to determine the direction of their lives. If we can make conscious for them those guidelines that have previously been unconscious to us but that have significantly influenced our behaviors, we can provide them with choices they might not otherwise recognize.

In this chapter, I have mixed and matched some elements of the better-known philosophical theories to convey my own unique outlook on life. It's important to note that this outlook has been determined over time by my developmental background and initially preceded any knowledge of academic principles or theories. Nor is it suggested that any reader should know or understand those or any other theories. A few were provided merely to show the variety of categories from which to choose and the numerous options available. Some such awareness of guiding principles could be of value to you and your descendants by eliminating some future trial-and-error mistakes and replacing them with responses having more beneficial outcomes.

As you develop your own awareness, try not to judge, criticize, or evaluate what you discover in your own life situation. Question your own past and present choices only as other options make sense to you, and by all means do not compare your principles favorably or unfavorably to mine as I have described them herein. As gestalt therapist Frederick Perls has emphasized in his famous philosophical prayer, our task in this world is to meet our own developing expectations, not anyone else's. If we happen to agree, so be it. If not, then accept the differences, respect the differences, and build on whatever similarities there may be—and there will always be some.

Now let me summarize my thoughts, as I hope you may someday do yours. As the Perls Prayer suggests, individuals may have very significant differences but also very important similarities, and that likelihood describes one of my core principles—that we are all unified in an intangible web that I call "spirit" but separated by a long series of tangible events and situations created by our need for socialization that I call "life." We develop egos to cope with that socialization, and when those egos get out of control and begin competing with one another in quests for personal self-enhancement, "all hell can break loose." An intentional return to that which unites us might be the antidote and could both trigger and reflect changes in attitudes, beliefs, and concepts. But first let me begin with a belief about our origin.

It's difficult for me not to believe in some sort of universal creative Intelligence. Both nature and the human form are too perfectly made to be accidental, and it's difficult to comprehend a beginning without a beginner. I understand that this is a speculative concept, but it's one that I find compelling, even after realizing the futility of trying to determine how that universal intelligence itself could have been created.

Somehow humans came to be. Was it evolution over millions of years or a one-time design of a Creator? Did we arise from nothing (Is that even possible?), or were we created intact? Was there a Superior Being standing behind a curtain maneuvering levers like the storybook Wizard of Oz—experimenting to see what a configured body, a brain, and free will could accomplish? If so, perhaps our own curiosity about life and our fascination with experimentation is a reflection of our Maker! What is the spiritual and psychological nature of this creature that we identify as human? These and many more similar questions are so stunning that most of us just shrug our shoulders. Yet we destroy relationships, argue incessantly, avoid new ideas, and even kill one another for holding opposing beliefs and assumptions.

Is there really a Creator (or perhaps a galactic committee) who truly loves us, or do we represent some sort of scientific experiment by which It amuses Itself at our expense? When we clear away the self-defeating, selfish, and egotistical elements in our behavior and retreat to our core being, I see such love and caring for one another that the idea of an indifferent Creator seems highly unlikely.

If we consider our Creator to be a super-parent, as many seem to, isn't the greatest parental love shown by preparing our children and descendants for independent lives, free of external restrictions, free to make their own decisions even while acknowledging that some may be painful? Regardless of environmental situations and conditions, true love supports adult freedom of choice. To the extent that our man-made institutions encourage such freedom, we seem to be born with the desire and ability to determine how that freedom will be achieved.

As the highest level of intelligence on this planet, humans are blessed to have dominion over all other forms of life. Our descendants share in those blessings, and their existence includes genes common to their ancestors (us). If we look closely enough, we can view the evidence—sometimes in looks, often in talent, characteristics, and mannerisms.

Might it be the same for us, as offspring of a loving Creator? Might we have the same love traits, creative ability, and spiritual characteristics as the Creator itself? Might each of us have godlike spirits that spontaneously envelope us at certain times and that we can call upon at all times, but only when we choose to quell our egos? All of these questions I have answered in the affirmative. I abhor the idea of original sin and embrace the concept of original goodness, or even original divinity, since we are all the offspring of that Perfection which created us.

The above assumptions have been generalities. I have said little about specifics except that we are innately endowed with some very positive elements, including the wherewithal to work together to solve whatever problems of living we encounter. We have been given free will and the ability to think, create, reason, and use logic to accomplish mutual goals, though we access only a fraction of those innate gifts.

Because we are free to use our mental, emotional, physical, and spiritual gifts as we wish, we are often prone to using them foolishly and worshipping our own material creations, while neglecting responsibility to our human creations. But we also have the intelligence to make changes and alter our behavior. Unfortunately, what we have yet to learn is how to live peacefully, amicably, and in unity.

We manufacture problems that do not have to exist. For example, we create a god in our own likeness and then "demand" (often subtly in order to avoid open conflict) that others believe as we do. Such demands foster resentment and harm relationships, sabotaging our caring natures and promoting loneliness. We often need help from others, and such help is usually available, but we are frequently unable to access it due to our self-defeating behaviors. We have the ability to create loving and caring relationships but are obstructed by our competitive behaviors and materialistic desires. Nevertheless, our satisfaction with life is dependent not on the situations and conditions we face but on how we choose to interpret and respond to them.

Eventually our earthly bodies will die, but our spirits will return intact to the Creator for use in some other way. Death does not concern me because I look forward to the next adventure. I don't know what transformation will take place or how it will happen, but that's okay. I only know that it will be a positive assignment. In the meantime, my task is to use the abilities given to me at birth in the ways I think best.

As the Eastern philosophies suggest, we get far too attached to things, ideas, and beliefs, and pay far too much attention to words spoken, especially by those whose motives are suspect, whose positions pursue power, and whose egos are dominant. This would include nearly all politicians, far too many educators, and a considerable number of clergy. All of these positions rely on persuasive rhetoric, too often used to promise much, deliver little, and promote causes that are primarily self-serving.

Earlier I cited the Chinese advice that institutions should not tamper with the human heart. Besides being our most important life-sustaining organ, that heart may be the location of our core goodness, our inner spirit, and the vehicle through which our Creator speaks to and inspires us. When that heart stops beating, earthly life ceases, but the near-death experiences of some may lend credibility to the continuing existence of an intangible spirit.

In contrast, our egos are more rational and observable in their behavior but also more devious. They serve to protect us but might be unneeded in a world of honesty, truth, and mutuality. Selfishness is a tactic of the ego useful in combating fear and scarcity. It is usually considered socially harmful and morally wrong, and some philosophies prefer to replace it with "selflessness," an ambiguous term that implies elimination of the self, that which suggests individuality. But the self houses our core goodness and, in my opinion, should be enhanced, not removed. On the other hand, if selflessness only suggests removing the *ego* that each of us has manufactured as a protective response to social living, then such a long-term goal seems appropriate.

Like all of my fellow human beings, I am a significant person who's been blessed with a meaningful life; and I want to improve and better my world, not at the expense of others but rather in concert with them. That requires helping one another toward self-fulfillment and promoting human progress (whatever that may come to mean), using innate goodness, endowed abilities, and acquired skills. I can think of no better way to honor our creation.

Thoughts/Activities to Consider

1. Give some thought to the principles that guide your daily behavior. Write a short story about how one specific principle has affected your life.

2. As you read in this chapter about my interpretations of life and afterlife, at what points did you have a strong mental or emotional reaction? Trace those reactions to some experience(s) in your development and write a short story about one of them.

3. If you "lived today as though you died yesterday," how would your behavior be affected? What would you do differently, and how might others see you differently?

CHAPTER 10

The Broader Picture

Similar Conditions, Different Outcomes

Bogged down with daily chores and routines, we seldom pay much attention to the context within which our planet exists. On a clear night, we look upward and peer into an ocean of magnificent stars, those bodies of matter light years away. Ancient civilizations created all kinds of theories about the heavens, but the evolution of scientific inquiry has clarified a few for us. Through science we have visited the moon and sent unmanned spaceships to transmit information about the possibility of life on other planets. No doubt this is only the opening act of a play with no end in sight, one that will likely require the devotion of many generations to come. The only certainty so far is that Earth is a tiny part of a vast conglomeration of "stuff" that we know little about but that whets our appetite. The human mind is full of curiosity, whether we satisfy it ourselves or through the work of others. Ancient explorers risked their lives to know and understand what lies beyond the horizon, and modern explorers are no different.

But curiosity may be giving way to necessity! With increased longevity due to advances in medicine and nutrition and the subsequent explosion in population growth, along with exploitation of natural resources and possible climate change, we may be "outgrowing" earth. How much of this can we *control*? How much of this *will* we control? Adaptation takes both time and money, and we no longer have an inexhaustible supply of either. If we are to survive as a species, we need to understand our situation and conditions and inform our descendants so they can make appropriate decisions— while our politicians, institutions, and corporations argue and fight over morsels and petty issues.

Recently I've been intrigued by two books written by Gregg Braden. In *Fractal Time*, he combines the discoveries and theories of modern science with the ancient wisdom and knowledge of widely disparate ancestral cultures to create a fascinating model of the relationship between past, present, and future. His follow-up book, *Deep Truth*, continues on that track and emphasizes the dangers to humanity of teaching and maintaining outmoded versions of "scientific truths" which he suggests are still dominating our beliefs and behaviors.

For those readers who cringe at the thought of absorbing infinite amounts of confusing data buoyed by pages of wordy scientific explanations, meaningless charts, and complicated statistics, let me assure you that I understand your plight. I am not a scientist; it was my worst academic subject and held my least interest. I avoid such books at all costs. But these books are different, as is a third book, *Spontaneous Evolution*, by Bruce Lipton and Steve Bhaerman, upon which I will also comment since the authors' themes are quite similar.

Braden's research paints a picture of our universe as replete with patterns and cycles (fractals) that repeat at regular and identifiable intervals, creating similar *conditions* but not necessarily similar *outcomes*. According to this formulation, planetary existence is built on major world ages of about twenty-six thousand years divided into subsets of approximately five thousand years. While sometimes steeped in mathematical models and calculations, Braden's books are nonetheless quite readable and understandable. Of what relevance is this to personal story writing and the education of our descendants?

If the conditions occurring from generation to generation are determined to be cyclical, and if we can identify those conditions and the approximate times of their recurrence, could we not then potentially make more effective choices in order to capitalize on favorable conditions and neutralize unfavorable ones? Braden's calculations are based on information gathered from past human experiences and applied to future probabilities according to his research on patterns and cycles. How likely are patterns and cycles to determine the presence and timing of conditions throughout the universe?

It is tempting to assess our daily lives as distinct, separate, individualistic, and idiosyncratic—one-of-a-kind coping with a personal world never before known to anyone else. But might that be our egos talking? Look at some of the ways in which patterns and cycles govern our lives.

From birth forward we experience cycles and observe patterns in all of nature. We even recycle whatever we can of the inanimate objects that we produce. Moreover, we use phrases such as "what goes around comes around" and "the more things change, the more they stay the same."

We know about menstrual cycles; we recognize that each healthy fetus develops in the same manner or pattern; we take for granted that generations will follow one another and that physical bodies will develop similarly from birth to adulthood and deteriorate similarly as we age; most accept that death follows birth and rebirth follows death, if not in the form suggested by religious beliefs, then surely in the form of some sort of renewed universal energy.

Nature follows its own form of recycling according to the characteristics of each species. Insects, fish, birds, and land animals all have their own breeding, location, and eating cycles occurring by instinct. The plant kingdom has built-in cyclical processes. Trees and hordes of plants lose their leaves and flowers and enter a protective dormant state, only to reemerge later with new life, which begins a new cycle.

Weather follows its own mandates. We speak of weather patterns, and we prepare for upcoming hurricane and tornado seasons. Atmospheric conditions determine storms and droughts, and with the invention of new technology these conditions have become quite predictable. Even earthquakes and volcanic eruptions show patterns, though intervals between them can be decades or millennia long. Periodic floods and tsunamis can result from these planetary and meteorological conditions. Of course, we can't predict everything, but that's most likely because of our as yet limited knowledge rather than a disappearance of patterned or cyclical phenomena.

Perhaps nothing is more obviously cyclical than recurrent seasons. Summer follows spring and is in turn followed by autumn and winter in the northern hemisphere. Variations occur in the southern hemisphere, but whatever pattern is established is always the same. In the equatorial regions, rainy seasons and dry seasons are more observable, but the yearly cycles remain predictable. Topography within any region can provide variances but always in similar fashion until modified by some gigantic outside force or slowly generated by some gradual phenomenon, such as erosion, which then starts a new cycle. The earth's revolution around the sun defines our yearly calendar; its twenty-four-hour rotation gives us night and day; and its tilt toward or away from the sun's direct rays determines our seasons—every time and in the same way.

Our planet is hurtling through space at an amazing speed. That Earth is the center of the universe was proven false centuries ago. We are but a tiny missile in the grasp of the galaxy. Is it not likely, given the patterned behavior and circularity of our physical beings and our environment, that such processes also govern outer space?

The nature of a circle is that anything attached to it keeps repeating itself, following the line of the circle unless some outside phenomena, some extraordinary occurrence, propels it elsewhere, moving it away from the circle. Otherwise, the attachment continues in its original cyclical orbit, repeatedly revisiting each part of its path according to some intelligent or natural plan. Is it not logical to assume that any given location on that circle would maintain its conditions and have similar effects on any object that returns to that location?

But even if this is so, can the movement of the earth within different parts of the galaxy really have any visible effect on our daily lives? We know that the moon affects the ocean tides according to a predictable pattern. And many parents and teachers have provided anecdotal evidence of behavioral changes in children during a full moon occurrence. Additionally, SAD (seasonal affective disorder) is now an accepted psychological condition, created by a response to the seasons occurring because of the Earth's positioning vis-à-vis the sun—a predictable cyclical pattern already noted. Is it such an illogical jump to accept the possibility that broader and more powerful elements governing the outer wall of space also have an effect?

Note that I initially italicized the words "conditions" and "outcomes" at the beginning of this chapter. Conditions do not mandate outcomes. The critical intervening variable is choice, an attribute exclusive to humans. It may be that if we choose to ignore recurring conditions, we thereby put ourselves at the mercy of universal phenomena. But if we use the knowledge that humanity has uncovered in recent decades and centuries in order to make decisions, and take actions that could modify such conditions or our responses to those conditions, we might well ensure more positive outcomes—capitalizing on favorable conditions and neutralizing some of the effects of potentially unfavorable ones.

This is precisely where our stories could help. By accurately communicating conditions, outcomes, strategies, choices, decisions, and other variables that have influenced our lives, we can provide future generations with the vital information needed for coping most effectively with the conditions they may encounter. Without such anecdotal information, they will be unable to examine consequences of past behaviors and choose their most viable alternatives.

Because we don't have all the answers (or even questions) to the universe that we would like doesn't mean that our descendants won't have many more discovered in the future with which to increase their knowledge and make use of our stories. As that knowledge increases, how exciting would it be to future generations to combine their new findings with millions of stories from grass-roots ancestors!

Natural and Cultural Recycling

Every culture repeats its own cycles according to its political, philosophical, or evolutionary development. Government, religion, employment, and education often show cyclical characteristics. For example, as our bodies and minds age, we travel through the educational system. In elementary school we may begin in kindergarten, first grade, or even preschool. We move to the top level of fifth or sixth grade and then recycle back to the beginning of a more challenging set of skills in middle or junior high school. We are again at the top level in eighth or ninth grade but move to the lower rung of the high school curriculum in ninth or tenth grade. As seniors in high school, we have once again climbed to the top only to become freshmen in college or entry-level employees. From college seniors we become apprentices or entry-level professionals looking up at veterans of the workplace. Even as we gain years and status in our chosen careers, we face the prospect of being newly retired.

Each level of each phase of development shares remarkably similar characteristics. A freshman, a rookie, an apprentice, or a recruit at any phase in any walk of life faces newness, expectations, anticipation, uncertainty, and perhaps even loneliness and anxiety trying to appropriately fit into a new environment. Veterans in the workplace have their own set of maintenance challenges, as do preretirees anticipating a new start in a different kind of life experience. Maturity levels may produce different outcomes in a vertical sense, but conditions across categories remain intact. Differences in outcomes may be most attributable to differences in responses to similar conditions—and responses involve choice, that primary domain of humans.

According to Braden, citing many in the scientific world of space and astronomy, the winter solstice date of December 21, 2012, ended one world phase of approximately five thousand years and began another. At that time Earth began modifying its direction of movement away from the core of the Milky Way galaxy back toward the center. According to sparse but amazingly astute calculations, artifacts, and predictions made by ancestral cultures from different parts of the earth, this gradual change in our planetary environment may have a profound effect upon the conditions that present and future generations will experience. Just as these conditions have been experienced by generations before us, they will likely be again experienced sometime in the future. Even if that return takes thousands of years to complete, technology is giving us the ability to preserve our information and stories for the use of our descendants. What we need is a broader perspective of the universe to replace our narrow vision.

Being very distant from the positive core of our galaxy, the conditions have been quite unfavorable in the last few centuries for peace, unity, and tranquility. Nevertheless, humankind could have made different decisions than it did to avoid war, separation, and chaos. Perhaps it was ignorance of universal conditions that led to the action and inaction that allowed such violence. Let's hope so, because ignorance can be corrected! To the extent that we desire and believe, we can still make more positive decisions in the next few years to negate the unfavorable conditions that our planet may be experiencing. But we can only do this with intent, not indifference or apathy. To that end, Dr. Wayne Dyer's book, *The Power of Intention*, can be most helpful.

On the other hand, we may now be experiencing a movement back toward the galactic core and more favorable conditions for accessing our peaceful inner core of humanness. Though this movement will likely be gradual, it may also be noticeable to those who are open to such change. What a magnificent opportunity! As we cycle back to the core that has not been experienced by earthlings for hundreds, even thousands, of years, planetary conditions may actually be helping us.

Still, these effects may not be immediate or obvious in our lifetimes, so we must continue to focus on intent. Memories of recent wars and a plethora of habitual behaviors related to the violence of recent generations will continue to plague us with obstacles to the peace and goodness that lies ahead. We can still make decisions that destroy us unless we can learn to intentionally make those that enhance us.

The key to our rehabilitation is consciousness. With awareness, resolve, and intent, we can make more productive choices. This is where each of us can help. This is where each of us must help!

Collectively, we can provide stories to future generations that may help them avoid our mistakes and repeat our successes. Only grassroots individuals can do this effectively—not politicians, celebrities, academics, or otherwise famous people. They all ride on our shoulders and may be preoccupied with power, fame, or duty. They should provide their own stories, but they cannot comprehend or transmit ours.

Clearly, the stories that we provide will openly or subtly reflect our own knowledge and perceptions of the human species—as it originated, as it has developed, and as it continues. These stories will convey attitudes arising out of our experiences, beliefs emanating from what we've been told and absorbed, and concepts based on our comprehension of who we are. The reader can refer back to chapters 8 and 9 for a deeper discussion of these issues.

But suppose the conditions that I've described turn out to be inaccurate, and our stories just placebos, since little can be definitively proven, given our current knowledge? Does that matter? Is not religion also a placebo that has been enormously helpful to some, as we await absolute truth about our existence and purpose? Can we really afford to wait longer for final answers to our many questions? Can we afford to fiddle while Rome burns?

David A. Kendall, PhD

Evidence Is Not Proof

Braden details six "deep truths"—ones that we might consider when writing for our descendants. It is well beyond the scope of this book to provide minute details leading to Braden's conclusions, but I highly recommend that serious life story writers reflect on his work, which embraces the scientific method of inquiry.

Basically, his findings contrast previous accounts arising from faulty scientific assumptions with current explanations made possible by new scientific discoveries. As mentioned in an earlier chapter of this book, the speed at which these new discoveries are being made far surpasses the rate at which educators can process and disseminate them, leaving the public to live out lives that may have personal meanings but will be of little value to future generations, based as they may be on false assumptions. But does that matter? Aren't we all on a daily journey of investigation and analysis of life? Is not our understanding of existence a process of ongoing exploration and discovery?

Consequently, we must continually question our assumptions about life and leave a legacy based on uncertainty but also on the pursuit of truth. How we choose to pursue all truths about our existence, and the outcomes of those processes, will offer clues to our descendants about directions they should follow in their pursuits, a clear example of multigenerational trial-and-error methodology.

Braden emphasizes the differences between evidence and proof, noting that the latter is far more difficult to find. As in our legal system of justice, the two words are often confused. Proof is indisputable while evidence is more like the gathering of isolated facts that, taken together, may or may not end up as proof. When it comes to the origin of the universe, or the origin of humanity, very little is provable. But emerging evidence points in certain directions. Unfortunately, we rarely view this evidence from a clean perspective. Rather, we have predetermined beliefs (often ideological, theological, or political), which we tenaciously embrace and which cause us to view new evidence with suspicion, distortion, disbelief, and even hostility.

Psychologically, it's as if the value of our past lives is compromised when we allow new and possibly opposing beliefs into consciousness. Apparently, the thought that abandonment of old ideas and adoption of new ones might be evidence of mental and emotional *growth* is insufficient to overcome a perceived attack on the ego's prior convictions. We become programmed to that which is familiar and comfortable. As noted earlier, many experts claim that up to 95 percent of our behaviors occur subconsciously, arising from acquired beliefs that remain unquestioned forever—or at least until intentionally challenged and modified.

Braden's truths are based on factual evidence. Though little may be provable, much is gathered through scientific inquiry and logical conclusions. His views, therefore, represent a significant advance in the pursuit of answers to our existence and development. My interpretations of Braden's six truths and their effects are incorporated in the paragraphs that follow.

Exploring Braden's Deep Truths

We live precariously in this twenty-first century. We are living longer, healthier, and more luxuriously, but we are also using up our natural resources at an alarming rate. We have developed technology and weaponry that can both pleasure us and destroy us. We are great at inventing and creating "things," but have done little to understand our own beings and to develop peaceful and unifying social behaviors.

Globally, we have dismissed as archaic the possibility of many gods and substituted as fact the presence of one god (or no god) to whom we have given different names and characteristics, which we then argue about or fight over.

Moreover, we seem content to remain stuck in place and to continue basing our lives on outmoded ideas and outdated science. The key to resolving our planetary crises is cooperation, not competition. We have taken capitalism, socialism, and arrogance to a whole new level. Badgering one another, individually and globally, has not worked— and doing more of what hasn't worked well isn't likely to reverse the outcome. Moreover, we have assumed a know-it-all attitude toward issues that we cannot (yet?) control. Instead of working together to adapt to or modify these issues, we blame fellow humans and try to resolve them politically.

Climate change is but one example. Earthly evidence shows that severe climate changes have existed for thousands of years, long before industrial factories were built. Entire populations have been wiped out because they could not adapt to such changes. They had neither the knowledge nor the capabilities.

We have many fewer limitations today. But the outcome promises to be similar unless we learn to work together globally to control what we can and adapt to the rest. Implicit in that strategy is continuing to pursue understanding and knowledge that will enhance our efforts in the future.

Archeologists and other scientists are working daily to uncover more of our past and are finding evidence of very advanced civilizations that faced many of the same planetary conditions existing today. This lends credibility to the view of our world as cyclical, with conditions repeating themselves according to movement through time and space, much of which we do not yet thoroughly understand.

The fact that past civilizations did not survive these conditions may be evidence that they could not adapt or that they made poor choices. We must do better!

As I have done in the previous chapter, Braden also tackles the question of our origin and asks the same kinds of fundamental questions. Are we products of some universal accident created by inanimate objects that somehow fused to manufacture life as we know it, and the rest is Darwinian evolution? Or is there some creative Intelligence who carefully molded human beings, much like the Bible suggests?

"A growing body of scientific data from multiple disciplines, gathered using new technology, provides evidence beyond any reasonable doubt that humankind reflects a design put into place at once, rather than a life-form emerging randomly through an evolutionary process over a long period of time" (Braden 2011, 251).

So what does this mean, that we were designed? If so, then some "thing" (God?) must have designed us. But why? For what purpose? Or perhaps no purpose—why would an omniscient, omnipotent Intelligence even need a purpose?

How might future generations answer these questions? What will they see as they reflect upon life in the twentieth and twenty-first centuries and try to figure out their own destinies? Were we designed to malign one another, to hate one another, to kill one another, to compete with one another, to compare one another? If so, it would appear that our Creator is rather sadistic and perhaps the ultimate terrorist! Or do we have another believable option, a more appealing one perhaps?

Braden says that scientific studies are leading to a far more positive conclusion, that "violent competition and war directly contradict our deepest instincts of cooperation and nurturing" (252). Really? Who would have known by our behavior! But he says that all of nature and evidence left by many ancient civilizations confirm his findings, and that the desire for war is a learned behavior, not a human instinct.

Despite what we see and experience almost daily, most would probably agree with that assessment—as long as we feel no threats to our selves, our families, or our culture. Unfortunately, we live in a present world in which such threats are common, both locally and globally. The psychological shrinking of the planet and the desire to protect ourselves by eliminating or converting our opposition has put us all on constant alert.

Ironically, it may be the fear of planetary annihilation that will bring us to our senses. Fear can be a great motivator for finding solutions. Despite the extremely low rating of the US Congress in national polls, for example, most of these politicians crave reelection and fear defeat. The "whole truth" becomes irrelevant and sometimes totally absent, as candidates engage in "spin," partial truths, and downright lies. Yet the ones with the most persuasive rhetoric win! Then they can enjoy the fame, power, and benefits for another two to six years, while doing little to deserve them. It has been suggested, usually with tongue in cheek, that we eliminate their pay and perks until they give solid evidence of their ability to work together. Fear of such losses might open up their minds to either compromise or creative solutions.

Following World War II, the term "Cold War" described a nuclear arms race that paradoxically fostered decades of mild relaxation of global conflicts among the great military powers. While thousands were still killed in regional wars around the globe, massive destruction by nuclear weapons was curtailed, presumably due to the fears of total annihilation. The threat of extinction apparently created more fear than did our differences, so politicians and governments found at least temporary solutions.

Global terrorism is now the main focus. Individuals and small groups have found ways to disrupt and destroy planetary life. The civil disobedience led by Gandhi in India was annoying to authorities but rarely destructive or unpredictable. How long must we wait to unite and solve the differences that have led to the current international terrorism form of protest? Must we wait until small terrorist cells acquire nuclear weapons, as they undoubtedly will, and make hostages of the entire world? Our current choices will determine our fate. Will we choose terrorist cells promoting isolation, violence, and distrust, or tourist cells promoting peace, unity, cooperation, and mutual profit?

As Braden summarizes, "Our individual choices become our collective answer to our time in history" (255). Will we embrace love and cooperation or stay focused on fear and competition? If Braden is correct, and our human nature craves the more positive direction, then everyone's input is essential; governmental institutions designed by the most powerful nations, whatever the original intentions, are all flawed. Their policies of separation, protection, and intimidation no longer work in a global economy powered by instant and distrusting communication.

The current generation has an awesome responsibility, as will all future ones. But we must get the ball rolling so others can follow. Where do we begin? We can start from who we are, what we know, and what we have experienced—our individual stories—that vital link between where our species has been, where it is, and where it's headed. Since no other generation has done this on even a miniscule scale, we may represent the foundation for the future of mankind.

What kind of foundation will it be? What will we leave for our descendants to build on?

Explosive Evolution

Biologist Bruce Lipton and political philosopher Steve Bhaerman give us a message similar to Braden's, but with some significant additions. *Spontaneous Evolution* is a title meant to convey that, while much of the universe's growth has been due to slow and gradual evolution, some of the most significant changes were created by quick, massive upheavals. (Could the birth of Jesus and other religious leaders constitute examples of this?) Like spontaneous combustion, sudden explosions in life circumstances can emerge from seemingly stable conditions. The authors suggest that we may need such an occurrence if humanity is to weather current and future world crises.

They also believe that we humans are wired with the capacity to transcend our tendencies toward violent conflict by resorting to our more natural state of unity and cooperation. Like Braden, they see violence as a learned behavior absorbed by our subconscious minds in such a manner that it often becomes our primary means of defense and protection. But humans also have free will and can choose to reframe ideas and reconsider behaviors, both of which can affect emotions in a never-ending circle of entanglement and possible enlightenment.

The easiest but least effective way out of our dilemmas is to depend on some form of outside intervention, to wait for an earthly or heavenly savior to do for us what we have always been capable of doing for ourselves. As the authors indicate, "We are the answer to our own prayers" (xvi).

This book provides a very strong and positive message. It incorporates a powerful spiritual component with a firm belief in the capability of common persons, working together, to solve the problems of existence. In this sense it mirrors my own belief and that which I am trying to convey herein.

As Lipton and Bhaerman indicate, in an attempt to organize and enhance our lives we have developed political and social systems based more on violence than peace, competition than cooperation, and blaming than respecting. We opt for logical solutions that we believe will work. Following the trial-and-error model, when efforts work somewhat, we add more of the same in order to get better results. But when they don't work well, too often we don't abandon those efforts; we merely intensify them rather than alter outmoded beliefs. By doing more of what has already failed, we eventually strangle ourselves and collapse.

I used this "paradoxical intention" technique with great success in my former counseling work. By suggesting a dramatic increase or intensity of persistent behaviors that didn't work, formerly stubborn people began to recognize the absurdity of their misguided behavior and the beliefs that preceded and caused it, and were usually more willing to modify and replace both. This strategy can work well with intelligent, well-meaning individuals but is not recommended for governments that are so often neither intelligent nor well meaning. Yet that seems to be what's occurring—an increased reliance on what has never worked well!

The authors of *Spontaneous Evolution* stress that we must consciously recognize the prevalent but flawed beliefs that have later been refuted by scientific inquiry but are nevertheless incorporated into our subconscious behavior. The erroneous ideas that we learn early in life can be very difficult to erase, and we can thereafter tend to perceive the world according to predetermined conclusions.

To counteract these limiting perceptions, we must intentionally choose and practice alternate thoughts and behaviors. This is where we usually get stuck; it's so much easier to place blame elsewhere! To change ideas about life, about our human existence, about our innate capabilities, about our essence, requires considerable reframing and a whole lot of mental and emotional work that must then be translated into behavior.

The good news is that all of life, nature, and the universe are so intricately interwoven that determined changes in one area precipitate changes in the others. We have limited control over nature and the universe but potentially total control over our thoughts, feelings, and behaviors. And the best news is, according to these authors, that science is now providing solid evidence that those human components can actually influence *nonhuman* segments of our world.

Whether Jesus was God in human form may be debated forever but Jesus's statement that we could potentially move mountains with our beliefs may not be so far-fetched. That collectively we can create change through behaviors such as prayer, for example, has occasionally been demonstrated—which opens up a whole new aspect of spirituality and intangibility, an exciting but also frightening possibility!

Spirituality Is Inborn; Religion Is Contrived

We must begin to separate such "spirituality" from "religion." The former is an innate aspect of our origin and merely affirms our interconnectedness with each other, with nature, and possibly with a Superior Intelligence that created everything, even Itself! "Religion" is a manufactured method of acknowledging our subservience to a greater power, whose essence, intent, and purpose can never be known for certain. Depending on local conditions and circumstances, past civilizations and generations have created symbols, beliefs, and icons in attempts to "prove" their exclusive attachment to the originator of humanity, but these attempts have arguably caused more worldly discord than cohesion. We may live in an interdependent world, but we do so with suspicion and wariness.

"Not to be confused with co-dependence, interdependence means a community of capable, diverse, and co-equal individuals who recognize that self-interest and mutual interest are one and the same." (Lipton and Bhaerman 2009, 330) Thanks to modern technology, our individual existence, survival, and progress are intertwined with those of everyone else all over the world, both now and forever. What we are, what we become, and what we do today will affect future generations everywhere. Of that we can be certain; our stories are their foundations and must be based on truth, as each of us perceives and pursues it!

Perhaps, in time, all humans will discover and accept every ultimate truth about life that currently eludes us, but until that happens, we must be content with ideas upon which descendants can build. Since we cannot be sure that our evaluations of any given situation represent ultimate truths, we must encourage all others to contribute their conclusions—and then show total respect when they do.

Tolerance Is not Respect

Respect is a concept so misused and misunderstood that it has lost meaning. *Respect is not the same as tolerance.* When someone has a different view from ours on a given issue, and we respond, "You're entitled to your opinion," this phrase indicates tolerance, not respect, and is usually reinforced by an identifying tone of voice that additionally proclaims, "But you're wrong!"

A respectful response might be, "We seem to think quite differently about this issue. Let's talk about how we've come to such different conclusions." Or, if you wanted to learn more about a different viewpoint (vs. persuade the other person toward yours, which might be considered manipulative), you might respond, "I've never thought about it that way, but it sounds like you've thought about it a lot. I'd like to hear more." Such a response might also open the mind of your companion to further dialogue, which might result in closer access to the truth.

Showing respect for the thoughts, conclusions, motives, and interpretations of others is not difficult. It is a humble attitude that uplifts the self-esteem of your acquaintance and conveys your own sense of fallibility. Rather than beginning a game of one-upmanship and persuasion, it demonstrates an acceptance of equality, thus reinforcing both friendship and openness to other possibilities.

Respect, equality, empathy, and love are considered "issues of the heart" and can help us to transcend conflict and compromise (archaic and usually self-defeating solutions to world problems). Used properly, they help to promote unique solutions by first laying a foundation of trust through removal of mental and emotional obstacles developed by our egos. The nonthreatening atmosphere thus created, if genuine, encourages participants to reframe and redefine issues, therefore inspiring better results.

Years of experience facilitating sensitivity and encounter group discussions have led me to many of the conclusions I've proposed, but fear is a formidable opponent that terrorizes our egos. Few of us are willing to submit in public to the intense discomfort that facing our deeper selves entails. *Feel the Fear and Do It Anyway* is the title of a popular book by the late Susan Jeffers that was often required reading in graduate classes that I taught, but that philosophy is not one that most egos choose to embrace. Perhaps, as fear of the destruction of our families, our way of life, and our personal existence closes in, and these outcomes become more likely, we will be willing to risk new behaviors that may actually stem the tide.

What Options Do We Have?

Lipton and Bhaerman, in their chapter on "Healing the Body Politic" (chapter 15), refer to the work of Jim Rough, who suggests that the evolution of governance can be depicted by the geometric shapes of triangle, box, and circle. First is the top-down rule of monarchs and dictators that resembles a triangle; next is the "rules and regulations" style where a voting population compiles (usually through representatives) numerous agreements that can be put into a symbolic box (like a constitution) and referred to as needed; finally is a circle, where every individual is equidistant from the center and vital to retaining the shape of the circle. "In the circle, all are equal; there is no top or bottom, first or last, better or worse" (330).

The authors even suggest a better future form of government, a "box in a circle," which would incorporate the best parts of the last two shapes, ensuring some structure but within the context of equality, respect, diversity, and independent thinking, the most moral, ethical, and effective pathway to collective wisdom.

Unfortunately, for the moment we seem stuck in the first two forms. Moreover, the circle appears impractical given our planetary population explosion, though the invention of instant communication devices could lead to some interesting circle possibilities that might even utilize the "box."

The framers of our Constitution believed that the success of a democratic government depended on an educated and enlightened citizenry, but they also realized the difficulties involved in attaining that goal. Today we are playing out those difficulties. While we can gloat that we are a substantially literate nation, our public school dropout rate and lack of knowledge or interest about broad issues of life is disconcerting, making enlightenment highly questionable.

We have taken for granted our freedoms and our right to govern ourselves through the ballot box, even while watching those same liberties erode before our eyes. We pay lip service to citizen control of our government through voting rights but then stay home on Election Day noting, "It's only one vote. What difference can it make?" So we give up that control to unaccountable career politicians and bureaucrats who make up their own rules, reward their own special groups, and eventually ride off into the sunset with accolades and pensions gained from squashing their opponents as if victorious in an athletic contest.

Democracy thrives on the belief that the whole is wiser than any one of its parts, but it depends on each of those parts being different—unique, autonomous, and distinct, with each contributing to the goals of the group while not dominating the process. Is there a better way to do this than donating our life stories to descendants?

Recently I was privileged to hear Gail McWilliams on a TV talk show (Huckabee 1/19/14, on FNC). She was told years ago that if she did not abort her unborn child she would risk a lifetime of blindness. She refused the advice and indeed lost her sight. Her reasoning was inspirational, as she made her decision by looking at the broader picture, a vision of the contributions that child might make to future generations. When asked how she could maintain such a happy outlook on life in her state of blindness, her reply was, "How can others *not* be happy when they can *see*?" It is our attitude and the resulting responses to our life situations that hold the key to happiness and satisfaction, not the situations themselves. Our stories can confirm this!

Thoughts/Activities to Consider

1. Have you ever thought about life as patterned and circular? Or do you think of life as random and chaotic? Did this chapter alter your thinking about how you fit into this scenario? Can you write a short story about it?

2. Most of our beliefs are based on evidence, not proof. Do you sometimes confuse the two? Does that knowledge have any effect on the way in which you perceive others who have decidedly different beliefs from yours? Where does your evidence come from, and how can you be certain that it's reliable?

3. Write a short story about some part of this chapter with which you take issue.

PART 2

Sample Stories

Access to sample short stories from my life has not been difficult, for I have written many over the years, most of them since retirement. Deciding which ones to include in this book, though, has been challenging. In chapter 1 I gave a general accounting of some very early remembrances and my overall development in a small village in the 1940s and '50s. Astute readers will also detect some of my attitudes, beliefs, and concepts stated or implied in other part 1 chapters. My purpose in part 2 is twofold: first, to demonstrate the many types of life stories that can be created, depending on writers' objectives; second, to suggest the possible value of each story for future generations, or how that story might be interpreted by both writer and future descendants. I have deliberately chosen to use my own stories because I know them best. They remain a part of me, and I can communicate these stories with greater clarity and understanding and relate them more accurately to ideas and principles that I am trying to illustrate and express.

I have chosen a diversity of stories, some from early childhood and adolescence and some from my adult life. All have been written from memory and are therefore subject to the usual forgetfulness and haziness associated with long-term recall. Depending on the subject matter and my specific goal, the length of each story and amount of detail varies from less than one page to several pages. My overall objective is to show you, the reader and future writer, that there are many options, in both content and process, from which to choose.

When conducting workshops on this topic of life story writing, I suggest adherence to only four rules:

1. There are no *wrong* answers/stories/styles/modes of writing.
2. There are no *right* answers/stories/styles/modes of writing.
3. There are only *your* answers, your stories, your formats, and your approaches.
4. There are no *universal* rules, only the ones you impose on yourself.

One additional caveat: when writing for the benefit of others, give some attention to clarity. That being said, it is nevertheless important to recognize that interpretation is unique to the interpreter and that some misunderstandings of meanings are inevitable. Neither written nor oral communication can ever be perfect; that is, what is sent out and what is taken in is filtered by the goals, motives, mannerisms, and expressiveness of the sender, the background characteristics and state of mind of the receiver, and the quality of the relationship. Still, communication is the only roadway to interpersonal learning and understanding, and it behooves us to strive for improvement. Such is the case for the pursuit of clarity, whether writing a book for wide circulation, life stories for descendants, or diaries for catharsis. Want evidence? How often have you written something down, only to retrieve it later out of context and without a clue as to what you originally meant?

Before and after each of the following stories, I have provided only enough information to facilitate an understanding of the options examined in detail in earlier chapters. The specific content of each story is based on memories and conveys experiences, interpretations, feelings, and conclusions about parts of my life, which may or may not be of interest to a given reader; but my objective is to demonstrate a variety of content and approaches from which you may choose to express your life to future generations.

When I became serious about writing my own life stories seven years ago, I chose to enlighten any future readers with my motivations and initial insights. This is an optional exercise but one that helped me focus my thoughts and energies in a stream of consciousness. I wrote it with a sort of thoughtful nostalgia, as if I were talking to myself—which I was!

Getting Started

The time and date at this moment is 7:00 p.m. ET on Thursday, March 8, 2007. I am continuing to write stories about my existence. I know not whether these will ever be read, and maybe it doesn't matter in the long run. Who knows but God how much time I have remaining in this earthly state. In three months I will turn seventy years old. If I am fortunate, I will be writing about my memories for another twenty or thirty years. If I'm diligent in this endeavor, the final document should cover reams of paper and each subdocument will no doubt be edited and modified many times along the way. What would cause a very ordinary person to take on such a venture? Certainly, it's understandable why presidents, famous athletes, and others in the public eye are encouraged to write their memoirs, because so many people want to read them. But why me?

I don't expect anyone will want to read mine, except perhaps my descendants, if I have any. Right now I have two grown daughters, both in their thirties and both recently married. Who knows if either one will have children to carry on our genetic line! But I digress. The purpose of this little preface is to acquaint any reader with my motivation for starting this written journey of my life. Basically, I guess I'm doing this because I can and perhaps because I think I have something to say to future generations. What that something is, though, I haven't a clue at the moment. But I do feel it! Kind of like Charles Darnay in Dickens's *Tale of Two Cities*, when he fulfills the sentence of death for a friend he believes to be more worthy of life than he. As he awaits the strike of the guillotine, he says "Tis a far, far better thing that I do than I have ever done; tis a far, far better place that I go to than I have ever been." This series of writings will perhaps be my most important contribution to my days here on earth. This may be the "far, far better thing that I have done." Certainly I cannot point to anything that stands out up to this time.

One thing I'm sure of. As much as I've always liked to write, I can only write well from the heart. I've tried academic and research writing, and it bores me. During my academic career I started a few books, some alone and some in collaboration with colleagues. But it was always done with the idea that a promotion or merit pay might result, and money and status never motivated me much. After a little research and a few pages of writing, I quit all that I started. Yes, I did pen three or four articles in order to gain tenure back in the '70s, but that was it. It's amazing to me now, given these thoughts, that I wrote a dissertation to get my PhD, but I must admit that it was not very meaningful. Some of my colleagues used my study as a springboard for some of their own material, but I never did anything formal with it after I finished my degree. The dissertation was a means to an end. I wanted to teach college, and a PhD was the entry ticket. And the dissertation was the exit ticket for the PhD.

If I had my life to live over, would I have gone the same route? Not likely, though hindsight rarely proves anything. Fact is there would be many more choices now. Come to think of it, though, there were a lot more choices even then. But I didn't know about them. Or maybe nothing else but what I eventually ended up doing made any sense; nothing else "fit." I guess that's what growth is all about. If I were getting started today, I could see myself as a writer. Back then I loved to write, but writing for a living never seemed to be an option. It was like being a philosopher, or an artist, or a consultant—those weren't considered real jobs with steady salaries. Yes, I was a product of the Great Depression thinking of the '30s, when my dad and many others took any job available. Life was relegated to daily survival. And what jobs were available usually went to the better educated. That's probably why my parents put so much stock in my getting a college degree. Growing up, it never occurred to me that I had a choice; not that it bothered me. College was a status symbol for the whole family; it proved to all that my parents had done a good job in raising me, and it would lead to a life of happiness and wealth for me. Or so we thought!

Fortunately, I was a good student—bright, conscientious, athletic, and obedient—a real credit to the small village in which I was raised. I had little academic competition there, but it took college entry to realize how many much-brighter students there were in the world. But that's a story for later.

Right now, I'm excited about getting to some of the details, some of the themes, some of the challenges life has afforded me. And perhaps the real benefit will come to me as I examine further my life and memories and thus gain greater insight into my life's journey.

Still, I would like my life to be useful to future generations as well, if that's possible. Like everyone else, I have lived a unique life, and my story should be told. But how? To write a birth-to-death autobiography would be an overwhelming task and utterly boring—even to me—so I can't imagine others wanting to read it.

But life is not "a" story; it's really a series of stories with connecting dots, some of which have been obliterated over time in the process of daily survival. Perhaps if I reveal some of these stories as isolated events, the dots connecting them will reappear—insightfully. But I also want to communicate to others the essence of who I really am, beyond what some may have seen and heard and experienced, beyond what I have conveyed all these years—even to myself.

Can I do this, not through one long essay devoted to names, places, events, and times but through a series of anecdotes and stories, some of which may be serious, some humorous, some emotional, some thoughtful, some adventuresome, some mundane, some brilliant, some stupid? I hope so. The following stories will be dedicated to that result.

This early story was an effort to define some of my core self, so I wanted any future readers to begin to see me as I see myself—minus the trappings of social, career, and academic armor. I wanted to communicate a sense of confident humility, with much uncertainty but also thoughtful intrigue and hopefulness. Throughout my life, my head and heart have been in a constant battle between the outer world of human reality and the inner world of spiritual essence. Outwardly I was a social conformist; inwardly I was silently rebellious. Life experiences and the aging process have changed me but perhaps not all that much. I have an eagerness to tell the world who I really am, quite different in many ways from what others may have seen. Mostly I wrote this beginning story to show my similarities to the average person—the nonelitist—in small town and rural America, for those are the people who raised me, the ones I most admire, and to whom I feel the most connected.

cyc

When working on my genealogical roots, I was always curious about where my ancestors lived, not just general locations but very specific ones where I could actually see the specific house or land, walk where they walked, and envision their daily movements. In trying to be helpful to descendants, I have included this synopsis of all the homes in which I lived, from infancy to the present. In the process I tried to make a little story out of it. As you read this and succeeding stories, you will see references to specific events I may have already covered. This is not intentional but seems appropriate in the flow of my thoughts, as some events lend themselves to integral parts of several stories. Usually these repeat references are written from a different angle and emphasize the importance of the event in my overall existence.

On the Move!

My first move was out of the womb on June 16, 1937, at The House of the Good Samaritan hospital in Watertown, New York—the fastest move I ever made, according to Mom. She and I stayed there for over a week, as was the medical custom in those days. Where we actually lived at that time I'm not certain. The Great Depression was in full swing, and the family moved around a lot, settling in rental housing wherever Dad could find work. At the exact time of my birth, we may have lived right in the city of Watertown; if so, however, it was short-lived. Since Dad worked on Great Lakes freighters in 1938, it's likely that we lived with his parents at 633 Theresa Street in Clayton for months at a time. My first recollection is a move we made to LaFargeville (seven miles away) for about two years so that Dad could work in the milk plant. We were there when Pearl Harbor was bombed, though I have no memory of that incident. I know for sure that we moved into a rental home in Clayton (545 Theresa Street) in the summer of 1942 because that's where I began kindergarten at the age of five. By that time Dad had become an insurance salesman and was locked into that job until the end of the war.

Our next move came in 1947 when the owner returned to reclaim his house. We moved into an upstairs apartment (307 Riverside Drive) at the other end of the village; after about two years, the landlady (Delia Consaul) passed away, and we then moved into the downstairs residence where she had lived. By that time, Dad had taken a new job (as a truss-fitting specialist with the Wm. S. Rice Company in Adams, New York) that was to last until his retirement in the early '70s. In the fall of 1952 Dad surprised us with the news that we were moving to southern California, where he would lead a West Coast expansion for the company. Shortly after Christmas we traveled by car across the country to begin a permanent life in Los Angeles, living initially in a rental house at 720 South Broadway in Redondo Beach. Early in the fall of 1953, Dad received news that the company president in Adams had suddenly passed away, and the new owner was giving up the expansion idea and ordering him back to company headquarters. Just before Christmas 1953, the family returned to Clayton and moved into an upstairs apartment at 411 Merrick Street, where we lived until I graduated high school in June of '55.

My next move was into the dormitories at Cornell University, where I spent four years in North Baker Hall. Summers were spent at my grandparents' house on Theresa Street in Clayton so that I could work as a deckhand and later a pilot on the tour boats plying the St. Lawrence River. Following college graduation in 1959, I was offered a job teaching in the same school from which I had graduated four years earlier. Since I had massive college debts to repay and my relationship with grandparents was awesome, I remained with them for the entire teaching year of 1959–60. In the spring of 1960, however, I received notice from the military that I would be drafted at the end of the school year unless I decided to join the Army Reserves in the meantime, which would cut my active duty time to six months but then subject me to five and a half years of reserve duty, meaning weekly local training and two weeks every summer with the possibility of recall to full-time duty, if needed. So I joined the Reserves, served my six months active duty, and returned— now jobless—to civilian status in December 1960. It seemed like a good time to finish my master's degree in education, which I had begun during my teaching year at Clayton, so I enrolled full time at St. Lawrence University in Canton, New York, during the spring semester 1961—renting a room in a faculty member's home.

I applied for a teaching job near Rochester, New York, (where my parents had moved so Dad could operate the Rochester store for his company) for the following school year and was hired as a social studies teacher in the Wheatland-Chili School District in Scottsville, New York, living with my parents for that year on Ramblewood Drive in North Chili, New York. Meanwhile, I had begun dating my future wife (Cynie) during the summer, and we were married on February 24, 1962. She had been a vocal music teacher for three years on Long Island but joined me in Rochester in June, accepting a position at Greece Olympia High School.

We lived for a year at the Lee Garden Apartments in the suburban town of Gates but contracted to build a house in a new development near the town of Pittsford border in the town of Henrietta. Since the house completion was delayed by several months, we moved in with my parents for a few months, then into the model house in the development for several weeks more. Finally, in the spring of 1964, we moved into our first house at 10 Compton Crescent in Henrietta.

Exactly one year later I was accepted into a graduate program at Portland State College in Oregon for the 1965–66 school year, so we moved once again—this time into an upstairs apartment on SE Forty-First Street. We rented our house in Henrietta for the year and returned in the summer of 1966, remaining there until 1969, at which time I was granted a full scholarship to acquire my PhD at the University of Pittsburgh. So we moved again, to an apartment across from Mellon Park, for the year 1969–70, renting our house in Henrietta for the second time. Upon our return, I joined the faculty at the State University of New York at Brockport (a suburb of Rochester), and we decided to move once more to be closer to the campus.

In spring 1971 we sold our Henrietta home and purchased one on a two-acre lot at the corner of Widger and Stony Point Roads between the villages of Churchville and Spencerport, New York, just a few miles from Brockport. By 1978 we had a small family but a large workload and much property upkeep. After one of the worst winters in local history, we decided that we needed a townhouse where no property upkeep was necessary—and the only one that met our needs was across the city in the suburb of Penfield. So we moved again, but this time for twenty years, until my retirement.

Since many retirees were going south to avoid the harsh northern winters, we followed the trend. Cynie's brother had retired to Cary, North Carolina, a few years earlier and seemed very happy with the move. Since the heat of the Deep South did not appeal to us, we too decided to move to the Raleigh area and chose the small but expanding suburban village of Wake Forest, where we built a new home on Cottontail Court. We soon discovered that the summer heat was more than we had bargained for and sought to return to northern New York for the hottest months. We purchased our present home in 2001 in a summer resort area between Clayton and Alexandria

Bay and began renovations on the pre-1900 structure. Gradually we increased our time there from two months a year to eight months, so we decided in 2010 to sell the North Carolina home, complete winterization of our northern New York home, and move back to the Thousand Islands area full time.

All of these moves seemed reasonable and logical at the time, and who's to say differently? Some moves were job-oriented, some education-oriented, some weather-related, and some pleasure-related. Ultimately, my last move will take me where I started out, not in the womb of a human but rather back in the womb of the Universal Creator. Perhaps not a bad place to be, really!

This story was intended to give an overview of my travels in life, an overall perspective for my ancestors. Along the way they could learn a few things about my education, my career development, and the rationale for my many moves. I also tried to begin and end the story with a little levity, perhaps a tiny glimpse into my personality and character.

Life story writing can be not only informative but also gratifying and even exciting. Often I challenge myself to try a new approach, such as telling the same story from two different angles. In the following stories I have recounted my earliest memory, as I have reflected back and as I might have experienced it at the time. My mother verified the general details. How much of the rest is accurate or imagined is mere speculation, but does that really matter?

My Infant Story

I was born in June 1937, during the latter stages of the Great Depression. Economically it was a horrifying decade—few jobs and low pay. Like many others in the small village of Clayton, my dad worked whenever and wherever he could make a few dollars. In the spring of 1938, with the need to feed a wife and two small children, he found work on one of the cargo-carrying lake freighters, which meant leaving home in March and returning in late November or early December. Since Dad had been in a life-altering automobile accident nearly ten years earlier while a senior at LaFargeville High School, he had been left with a bad limp, which restricted the jobs he could handle on the freighter. So he spent most of his time in the bowels of the ship, shoveling coal into the boiler. My earliest recollection begins when he arrived home in late fall 1938.

I was almost eighteen months old, barely a toddler, experiencing the first freedoms of movement. I recall a particular evening when I was at my grandparents' house on Theresa Street. We were all in the living room, and the adults were talking and enjoying each other's company as usual. I was getting paid a lot of attention, running around crazily from adult to adult, tiring myself out—no doubt to their delight. Besides my grandparents, my Aunt Kathleen (Dolly) was there, as was my mother. I don't remember anyone else being around. My older brother, Bob, who was five and a half, must have been upstairs, or at a friend's house perhaps.

I found out later that the adults were awaiting the arrival of my father, due home that evening for his winter break. Of course, I didn't even know who or what a father was. He had left home nine months earlier, so the last half of my infant life had been spent without him around. I was barely crawling when he left home, and by the time he came back I was running around. He had long since left my conscious memory.

So when he walked in and greeted me, I was scared. There was something vaguely familiar about his voice and his limp but beyond that he was a stranger. When he bent down to pick me up, I was terrified and ran to my mother for protection. I recall crying hysterically as I tried to get away from this intruder. I can only imagine how devastating it must have been for him, watching me respond that way. But he had the good sense to leave me alone for a while and let me warm up to him at my own pace.

As I observed the hugging and kissing going on between him and the others, I must have begun to realize that he was okay. The trauma must have lasted only a few moments because, while that image of terror is still vivid, it was not long-lasting.

My Infant Experience

It's early December, just after Thanksgiving, and it's starting to get dark outside. I'm at Grandpa and Grandma's house on Theresa Street, having fun as usual. I like being there. Aunt Dolly and Mommy are also there. I'm one and a half. My older brother—he's five and a half— must be around somewhere, probably upstairs, or at a friend's house.

I'm playing a game with all the big people, running from one to the other, making the rounds and starting over again. They're just sitting around. What are they waiting for? Doesn't matter. I'm happy. I'm tired, too, but I don't want to quit, not with all the attention I'm getting.

What's that noise? Sounds like somebody's coming on the porch, kicking the steps. Grandpa does that to get the snow off his boots. But Grandpa's inside with me, so who can that be? Everybody important is already here.

I'm right. There is somebody! I can see the door opening from the porch into the dining room, and a man is coming inside. He's got a heavy coat on, and a big hat, but I can't see his face. How come he didn't knock?

Mommy jumps up out of her chair and runs to the door. She'll protect me. He won't hurt me. But wait … Why is she hugging and kissing him? Who is he? Grandpa, Grandma, and Aunt Dolly all have smiles on their faces. They're taking turns hugging him too. So he must be okay, but … I'm staying in the living room anyway. I can see him through the doorway into the dining room, and that's close enough!

Oh, oh, he sees me. He's coming toward me.

"David"—he's calling me by name. But how can he know my name? I don't know him. I've got to get away. I want to hide, but where? He keeps coming—and nobody's stopping him! I don't know what to do. Why isn't Mommy protecting me like she always does?

He bends down, puts his hands under my arms and lifts me up. I start to cry and squirm. I'm really scared!

"It's okay," the man says, but he must see how scared I am, and puts me down gently. I run to Mommy, crying harder than ever. She lifts me up, and I bury my head in her neck. Why can't he just go away and leave us alone? I was having so much fun.

Mommy strokes my head and walks into the kitchen, away from the stranger. That was a close call, but now I'm safe. I stop crying, and I'm very still in the safety of Mommy's arms.

She looks through the doorway and stretches her arm toward the man, waving her fingers. What is she doing? Oh, no! He's coming toward us. He walks funny; but I remember something about that … and that voice … I grip Mommy tighter, but her arms are loose around me, so she's not afraid. The man smiles at me, then stops a few feet away.

"David, this is your daddy. He's just been away for a while. You remember Daddy. He loves you."

I'm still not sure, but he doesn't seem mean. And everybody here seems to like him, especially Mommy. Now he's holding his arms out. Mommy whispers in my ear, "Go to Daddy. He wants to hold you. And I'll be right here."

Her eyes tell me that everything's okay. I slowly relax my grip, and my arms and body turn toward the man. Something about him says I should go to him.

Very gently he puts his strong hands under my arms and pulls me to his chest. Somehow it seems right, and I drop my head onto his shoulder.

And I feel safe once more.

Sometimes how one writes about self is as important as what one writes. Variety and flexibility have always been important to me, and perhaps these two approaches to the same story may give my descendants a glimpse of that value. Also implied is the significance of family in my life, beginning at the earliest age.

Preschool memories are necessarily scant for most adults, but isolated images often appear and may or may not be significant to our development. Still, they may help us connect some of the dots of later life and may serve as foundations for our descendants. I can recall only a smattering of events from my early childhood, but they all represent a part of the story of my life.

Preschool Memories

There are only tiny bits and pieces that I remember from preschool days. Why do certain events stand out in memory while others have long ago faded away? I wish I knew. Trauma perhaps, with *some* memories. But others seem rather mundane in hindsight; yet I remember them clearly. I know that we moved into a very large house in LaFargeville when I was three or four, and we left there to return to Clayton the summer before I started school; so it would have been 1942. Dad worked at the Milk Station there, as did his two brothers, Ralph and Walt, both of whom also lived in LaFargeville. Walt and Doris lived right across the street, and son Jimmy was born during that time. (Later, when Jimmy was a senior in high school in Clayton I was enjoying my first year of teaching there, and I recall that Jim was in the senior play, called *Shy Guy*, and I directed it for them.) I remember being over there one day while Aunt Doris was changing his diapers; and as little boys are prone to do, he "let her have it" right in the face as she was leaning over him. I recall being both shocked and humored, but the memory stops there.

Ralph and his family lived down the road a ways, closer to the Milk Station. He retired from there many years later, having risen to a very nice management position. Daughter Audrey was about seven or eight years older than me but I don't remember her at all during those days. We rented our house, just the downstairs, I believe. The home must have originally belonged to the town's founder, or a wealthy doctor, or somebody very important. It was old, and it was huge. It had a wood stove to cook on and to help keep us warm in the winter. I remember my tricycle being run over by a delivery man's truck—and getting a new one from the man, who felt very bad. Come to think of it, maybe I don't really remember it at all. But I heard my mother tell that story many times years later. It's sometimes hard to figure out what I remember from what I've been told.

I also recall that we had a chicken coop in the back yard, and I used to go out and collect eggs. But I was afraid of the chickens, who sometimes would flutter and cackle as I came near. So I didn't like that chore. I also remember an old car that had been left in the field behind the house. My brother, Bob, was playing around the car one day, and I believe that part of it fell on him. Obviously, he wasn't hurt badly but the incident stuck with me. I also recall spending at least one Christmas in that house. I had obviously been told not to divulge Christmas gift secrets, so I told Dad, "I'm not gonna tell you what I got for you, but it's something to comb your hair with."

Our next-door neighbors were Roy and Mida Newton. They were a wonderful couple, about the age of grandparents. I knew that they liked children, though they never had any of their own. Roy was a custodian at the local school, and Mida stayed at home most of the time. Roy was quiet and kindly, but Mida was a rascal—in a nice way. I'm sure I must have bugged her at times, but I was always welcome to visit and don't recall any feeling but fondness for her. One day she decided to play a trick on my mother, so she told me to go home and ask Mom for a "thingamajig for a bobbermarie." I dutifully plodded back home and tried to explain to Mom exactly what Mida wanted. After several tries, Mom finally went over to Mida's house to find out what she needed. Mida's laughter probably shook the whole village. Roy and Mida were marvelous to me but anything but cultured. They both could curse with the best. But when the same words came out of my mouth, they were not tolerated. I didn't know what they meant, of course, but I did learn that they weren't for me because I recall getting my mouth "washed out with soap" by my grandmother one day as she was visiting us.

Down the street at the main four corners of the village was the village barbershop. The barber's daughter, Rosalind Hughto, must have been my first girlfriend. I remember the name more than the person, but she was apparently my regular playmate. (Within the past year, Dad showed me a picture of Rosalind and me during that time; someone apparently sent it to him, and it brought a smile to my face.) Oh, yes, we had a dog at that time. We were always told it was a water spaniel, and we named her "Trigger," probably after Roy Rogers's horse. We got Trigger from a man in the village whose dog had had pups, and she was a faithful companion to me until I was about fifteen. By that time the dog was deaf and almost blind, and, fearing that she would get hit by a car, Mom one day had her put to sleep. We all agreed that it should be done, but no one would do it, so it was left to Mom. So what's new? Some things never change, I guess. I recall coming home from high school one day and not being greeted by Trigger at the door. When I asked where she was, there was a bit of silence, and I knew! By age fifteen, I had lots of other interests, so I don't recall mourning much, just accepting the inevitable. When she was young, in LaFargeville, she would chase cars. One winter day, as she was chasing a car up an icy hill, her leg slid under the wheel. We bandaged her up the best we could and took her home. I guess the leg was broken, but the local veterinarian made her as good as new.

During the summer of 1942 we moved back to Clayton, where I started Kindergarten in the fall. World War II was in full gear by then, but I really don't recall that it concerned me much. Dad had been exempt and was now working for an insurance company, a job he could not leave, by government edict, until the end of the war. Dad's exemption was due to the very bad car accident he survived during his senior year in high school, while riding as a passenger. His leg was severely damaged, and he always walked with a built-up heel on his left shoe, which caused a limp, after that. His accident was perhaps a blessing, though he almost died in it. But it did allow him to escape the horrors of World War II and to live longer than any of his family, before or since. (As of this writing, he is approaching his ninety-third birthday and can count many fine accomplishments among his years.)

The day we moved into the Amo house at 545 Theresa Street, just a block from my grandparents' house at 633 Theresa Street, a small boy from across the street, who turned out to be my closest friend for several years, came over to tell me he could "beat me up." He was David LaLonde, and was three years older than me, though no bigger. We were inseparable until he reached puberty and entered junior high school; then the three-year age difference began to show, as he entered his growth spurt and turned toward other interests and other friends.

It's very difficult to focus on just one part of life, because there is so much overlapping. As with many verbal discussions, going off on tangents is tempting and often inevitable. There is no reason to avoid such temptations, but they should be carefully monitored for clarity. Keep in mind that you are writing stories about your life that future generations will seek to understand. Tangential diversions can be very enlightening and add to that understanding, but they can also be confusing. Descendants will always have more questions than you could possibly answer or anticipate, so most of the time highlights that are meaningful to you may be your best choices.

For most of us, memories are a bit more vivid and plentiful as we reminisce our later childhood, but the same tangential concerns apply, and we must begin to be a bit more selective in our stories. The beginning of school was accompanied by some serious personal illnesses and by our entrance into World War II less than a year previously. Both of these events greatly affected our family and small village. To eliminate either of these issues from my story would be like trying to complete a jigsaw puzzle with several vital pieces missing from the whole picture.

Elementary School Years

I vaguely remember kindergarten. We were living in Clayton, in the Amo house at 545 Theresa Street. We moved there from LaFargeville in late spring or summer before I started school. My first teacher was Miss Reynolds. It was September 1942, and World War II had been raging for almost a year after Pearl Harbor. My teacher was very young, but she probably seemed old to me. She may have been right out of college, and this may have been her only year in Clayton. I'm not sure.

I remember playing and lying down for naps, and not much else. I do remember one student in particular who used to throw crying tantrums because she didn't want to be there. Everything else is very sketchy.

However, I heard my mother talk later in life about an incident that happened to me. Apparently, shortly after entering school in September, I began stuttering badly at home. That had never been a problem, so my parents were understandably concerned. One day, when Mom was discussing this with a friend, she was asked if I was left-handed. Mom answered affirmatively, and then asked why.

This friend had heard that, if someone tries to make a naturally left-handed person into a right-handed one, sometimes it causes the child to stutter. So Mom went to the teacher and asked. Sure enough, Miss Reynolds said that she had been gently transferring my writing utensils from my left hand to my right one—ostensibly because being right-handed is easier on the child throughout life. Mom told her to just allow me to be left-handed. In a few days, the stuttering stopped.

I later also had heard Mom tell people that she (Mom) asked the teacher if I was a handful, and the teacher told her that I was quiet, helpful, and cooperative—a perfect gentleman. Apparently, even at that young age, I had learned a lesson that was always gently stressed at home: "Don't embarrass the family; if you're going to be unpleasant or do 'bad' things, do them at home, not out in public."

My first-grade teacher was Louine Markham, a good friend of the family and a lifelong believer in me. Her husband, Doc, was a good friend of Dad's and a career officer in the Border Patrol. Doc and Louine never had any children and were quite a bit older than my parents. Doc died many years before his wife. In fact, I saw Louine only about five to seven years ago, as I was visiting my aunt (Mary Kathleen, or "Dolly," as we called her) at the nursing home section of E. J. Noble Hospital in Alex Bay. She was frail and fragile and nearly one hundred years old. She was lying on her deathbed, and was either asleep or unconscious when I saw her. Had she seen me, I'm sure she wouldn't have known me. In fact, I had to be told that it was Louine because I wouldn't have known her, due to her frailness. I remember her as very soft-spoken but serious about her work and demanding as a teacher, though always in a nice way.

During the late fall and much of the winter, I became very ill and missed about six weeks of school. The doctor, Dr. Pilpel, came to the house many times (That was when doctors made house calls.) over the course of my illness. Apparently, there was no indication what was wrong. It turned out that my older brother also became ill during the late winter, and his skin started to get rashes and peel. Then the doctor knew what I'd had—scarlet fever. However, since I didn't get any rashes, he said that I'd had a harder case of it because it was all staying internal. I believe it was during that same year that I had whooping cough. So I must have missed a lot of school. Fortunately, school came much easier for me than for many of my classmates, so I apparently caught up without much of a problem. I recall being very ill over Christmas and really not caring much about getting any presents. Santa came to visit on Christmas Eve. (I was told later that it had been the dad of older friends of mine, a man who sometimes went around to the children of the village dressed up as Santa Claus.) This all happened about a year after our entrance into World War II, and most of the young men in the village had gone off to war. Looking back with what little memory I have of those days, it was a somber time, with the village population depleted and everyone trying to aid the war effort in any way possible. Air raid warnings and blackouts were common, though no enemy aircraft ever came. Still, this early in the war, the effort was not going well, as the enemy forces were far more battle-ready and battle-tested than were ours. We had wanted to stay out of war, but Pearl Harbor forced us in.

I've always thought it fortunate that my dad did not have to serve in the military. He walked with a distinct limp and about a three-inch built-up heel on his left shoe. He never could have made long marches, so he was exempt. Still, with almost all of the young men his age serving their country, and many of them to be killed or wounded, those who did not serve were often chastised for not going off to war. I never heard Dad talk about any of that, but I'm sure it was difficult knowing all his friends were fighting, and he wasn't. He had been injured seriously in an auto accident on a narrow road between LaFargeville and Theresa. He was not driving but rather riding with a friend of his. They were seniors in high school in LaFargeville and were going to a dance, when they were forced off the road by a group of teenagers having some fun. That was before seat belts had been invented, and Dad was thrown through the roof and landed on the roadway with a crushed chest and a mangled leg. He was in the Watertown hospital for about six months and therefore did not physically graduate with his class, which numbered about five students. If that accident had happened today, doctors probably could have repaired his leg sufficiently to serve in the military. But perhaps the accident was a blessing, for he did not have to risk his life like so many others, and I have been able to have a relationship with him for many, many years. Today he still lives, at age ninety-two-plus, in the Mercy nursing home in Watertown, physically not well but still mentally doing okay, though even that is deteriorating now. Each year he lives has been a blessing, though I'm sure he's very ready to join Mom in the afterlife. I can hear tiredness in his voice, and life is becoming a real struggle. He probably won't live too much longer, and that's okay. He's led a full and meaningful life, and I've learned a lot from him. He's been a good father!

After that digression into World War II and my dad's life, let me return to my elementary years at the Clayton Central School, which had opened in 1941, so mine was one of the first classes to go all the way through, from K-12.

Obviously, the stories of my elementary school years continued. Like all of life, the years through the upper elementary, junior high, and high school years progressed and blended. Each year is a story in itself, as is in fact each day of our lives. My dad has now been deceased for many years, and I have written more about him in other stories.

Stories that reveal one's essence do not have to be long and wordy, as my next three stories indicate. Short as they are, each one adds a little background information about my emerging personality and outlook on life—from the fun-loving child, to the respected adolescent, to the reluctant leader with a sense of humor who eventually learned to laugh at himself.

Western Style

When I return to my hometown, even today, I'm sometimes accosted by an old friend who reminds me of a recurring incident in my preteen life. Time and again he would see me galloping up the street, with a skipping-type movement, slapping my backside with my right hand as though I were spanking a horse, while wielding a cap pistol in my left hand, and alternately shouting "giddyup" and "bang-bang."

Those were the days when cowboys were my heroes, and I never missed a movie starring Gene Autry, Roy Rogers, Hopalong Cassidy, Tom Mix, or, of course, the Lone Ranger. The good guys always won, and the bad guys always lost. On that we could depend. There was never any stress as to the outcome, and I learned that if I didn't look to do good in the world, some form of punishment would be the absolute outcome.

Of course, the Lone Ranger was also on radio, where I could use my imagination. Our radio was on top of the refrigerator, and I would stand on a chair, get my ear close to the radio, and listen intently, always knowing the outcome but mesmerized by the ingenious ways that the Lone Ranger and his sidekick, Tonto, would capture the bad guys—and my heart—at the same time.

Time would pass quickly with every episode, and I would smile with glee as I heard that final phrase, "Hi-Yo Silver, Away."

The Bracelet

I'm a sophomore at the high school in Clayton—academically near the top of my class, one of the better young athletes in the school, known by all in the village, surrounded by many friends. The football season is about over, and the world is my oyster.

My dad is coming home from his normal eight-week stint as a traveling salesman. He greets the family with the news that he's received a promotion, and we're moving to California right after Christmas. The news gets around fast, and the teachers and students tell me how much they'll miss me.

One night in early December, I'm attending a semipro basketball game in our high school gym, not an unusual occurrence, when I'm suddenly called out of the gym by one of the teachers, who said I was wanted in the cafeteria. *That* was unusual! I had no idea what was forthcoming.

When I entered I heard "surprise," a unison cheer given by my thirty-some classmates, who had prepared a going-away party. Dumbfounded and somewhat embarrassed, I sat down to a wonderful meal, after which I was presented a gift that I still own. It was an identification bracelet and was presented with a short speech by the class president. It was a memorable evening for me, a show of true friendship, a time that until recently I had forgotten about.

Our move to California was to be permanent, but through a series of events, we were destined to move back to the same school exactly a year later. But they didn't make me give the bracelet back, and sixty years later I still have it.

Bite Your Tongue!

"Children should be seen and not heard" was a common phrase among adults during my formative years in the 1930s and '40s. An obedient child, I learned that lesson well. I learned to be quiet and mannerly, and I became accustomed to the shadows of life. I did as I was told and rarely argued, even with my peers. I learned to be what others wanted me to be, what others expected me to be. I learned to bite my tongue.

As I grew older, I became an excellent student, and an excellent follower. As long as someone else made the decisions, I was very comfortable. But somewhere along the way, others' expectations of me changed. Since I did very well academically, more was expected of me behaviorally. Now leadership was expected—magically, I guess, because I never learned how.

So I had to learn another skill. Besides not being heard, I learned not to be seen. I avoided social situations, group situations, leadership situations—any situations in which I might be the center of attention, or even on the periphery of attention. I had learned to bite my tongue; now I added the skill of becoming invisible.

Life has a way of coming full circle. I eventually learned to become a leader in my chosen profession. I learned visibility, and I learned verbosity. I learned enough to earn a good living, to be both seen and heard.

But at age seventy-seven I still bite my tongue. I mean, now I *really* bite my tongue!

Aspects of my development, my peer relationships, and my internal struggles with the expectations of others can be gleaned from these very short vignettes. Not everything needs to be spelled out in our stories, because we reveal ourselves in many ways. Readers, of course, also add their own interpretations.

Sometimes writing stories in the first person, even for events experienced long ago, can be very informative, interesting, and powerful for the reader, and cathartic for the writer. In such instances, emotions felt may remain intact for years, while the exact details fade away. The following story depicts the unintended consequences resulting from a teacher's efforts to motivate me toward greater achievement. Due to the possible factual inaccuracies of long-ago memories, I have chosen to use fictitious names in describing this event. Even the specific grade level and teacher is subject to error, but the effect on me remains vivid and may have affected my life well into adulthood.

The Perfect Curse

"Frank, seventy-seven, good job. Jim, eighty-four, excellent. Jodi, sixty-eight; you need to study harder, don't you! Tammy, forty-six; you can do better than that." Our third-grade teacher continues to walk up and down the aisles reading off scores from our big spelling test as she hands the papers back.

"Ted, seventy-two; I need to have a talk with your mother. Laura, ninety-five; that's your best work yet; I'm so proud of you. Wait'll your parents see that." As Mrs. D. approaches each of us, in no particular order, she pauses, reads the score aloud, and makes a short comment.

It never occurs to me that maybe she shouldn't be doing that, but I still feel badly when some of my friends get poor grades, and everybody knows it. Some of the smarter kids giggle at them. I don't understand that. It seems cruel. I'm lucky that spelling is easy for me. I know I did well. Now I just have to wait until she gets to my paper. It'll take a few minutes because there're more than thirty of us in the class.

"David." She stops next to my desk and looks at the paper on top of the pile she holds in her hands. Now she looks down at me and slowly shakes her head. "David," she repeats, "98; what happened to you?"

Without waiting for an answer, which I can't give her anyway, she continues, "You missed two words. We went over those yesterday. Weren't you listening? I'm really surprised. I thought sure you'd get them all right. They weren't that difficult. You were very careless." She puts the paper on my desk. All I see are two big red check marks.

I'm beginning to panic. My heart is pounding heavily. The whole class goes totally silent, so I'm sure everyone hears it. I don't know if I'm breathing too fast or not at all, or both at the same time. My face is burning up, and I know it shows.

"Your face is getting red, David," teases Lois, a couple of rows over—and everyone laughs.

"Never mind," Mrs. D. responds as she glances around the room. I like Mrs. D., and I think she likes me. So why is she embarrassing me in front of the whole class! I don't think 98 is that bad.

I'm getting mad, but I don't know who I'm mad at—Mrs. D. for making a big deal out of it, or the rest of the class for laughing at me. All except Dick, the principal's son. He's my best friend, and he sits in front of me. He hasn't even turned around. He would never make fun of me, anyway.

Mrs. D. points to the first of the two words I missed. "Don't you remember the rule: 'i' before 'e' except after 'c', or ..." She stops and looks at me, waiting for me to finish it.

"When it sounds like 'a,'" I stutter.

"Speak up, so everyone can hear you."

"Yes, speak up," mimics Charlie from across the room. "I can't hear you."

"That's enough, Charles," scolds Mrs. D., without losing her focus on me.

"When it sounds like 'a,'" I blurt out.

"Did everyone hear that?" Mrs. D. glances around the room.

Heads nod.

She looks down at me again. "Do you think you can remember that next time?"

I nod. I'll never forget that, ever again.

She points to the second word. "You spelled a word we haven't even studied yet. You won't get that word until sixth grade. Do you even know what that word means?"

I shake my head. But I should be nodding. It's a word I've heard my mother and older brother use many times at home. But if I nod, she'll ask me to tell the class. And if it's wrong, I'll get balled out some more. And I just want her to stop.

"I thought not," she continues. "That mistake was just carelessness. If you'd have been concentrating on your work, instead of daydreaming, you wouldn't have missed it, would you?"

"I guess not." I look down at the paper. I can feel tears in my eyes. But I can't look up. Others might see them. And I'm a boy— and about the biggest kid in the class. I've got to keep the tears from dropping.

Mrs. D. goes on to the next paper, but the rest of the class period is a blur. When she goes to the other side of the room, Dick turns around and looks at me. "Forget it. She's a jerk," he whispers.

I nod, but I really want to cry. Mom has always said I should learn something useful out of every bad situation. But what can I learn from this? I can't figure it out right now. But I know one thing—it's okay for others to fail, but I have to be perfect. That's the only way I won't get laughed at. And if I can't be perfect at something, then I just won't try it. But what have I learned from this? I don't know.

I just want to cry.

At the time of this event I certainly knew how I felt, but only later in life did I realize its long-term effect on me. While I initially wrote this in the first person, it was from an adult perspective, so I did know what I learned from this. But at the end I chose to leave it to the reader's interpretation and conclusion rather than spell out the effect.

I am a philosopher at heart, in the common use of the word. I enjoy thinking deeply, beyond the obvious. I like to connect the dots of life, to figure out how events and processes are linked. I love intrigue and have little belief in coincidences. The following essay is an example of my view of life as circular and recurring, and further illustrates the intangible effects that each of us can have on those we touch.

Recycling Life

We all live under the illusion of life and death, as though life begins at birth and ends with death. But a case could also be made for life beginning at death and ending with birth. Probably neither is the whole truth. Science may even suggest that human form is merely concentrated energy, and energy cannot be destroyed, only transformed. It may be that beginnings and endings are like a revolving door, that once it gets moving, who can tell where it starts and where it finishes.

As I reflect upon my life to this point, it all seems connected. One event leads into another, and is itself the result of a prior event. What I previously considered a coincidence or an accident now seems perfectly related to other occurrences.

My chosen profession is but one example. Though I never saw violence in my home, I always despised fighting and would do whatever was necessary to avoid conflict. Fortunately, I was big enough, friendly enough, and wise enough to dodge teasing from schoolmate bullies.

My first recollection of occupational preference came in elementary school. I wanted to become a diplomat, someone who would help people resolve their differences and enable others to live in peace. I fantasized eventually becoming president of a United World.

That image downsized as world reality become more evident, but it didn't disappear. I graduated college with a major in international relations and prepared for graduate training at the American Institute for Foreign Trade in Phoenix, Arizona.

However, college debts and limited access to .noney forced postponement, and I took a position as a social studies teacher in my old high school. I enjoyed the teaching atmosphere but could not see myself in the classroom forever. School administration was a possibility, but the organization, leadership, and paperwork involved turned me off. A third alternative intrigued me, though. The new category of school counselor was just starting to emerge amid the social turmoil of the '60s. That role involved helping individuals and groups resolve differences, and that attracted me. No surprise!

Eventually, I took an interest in teaching others how to help people resolve conflicts in their lives, and I both taught and practiced marriage and family counseling for over thirty years. Retirement changed my focus but not my direction.

Currently, I am concentrating my efforts on showing people of all ages how they can help future generations to avoid the pitfalls of past ones by sharing stories and conclusions that only hindsight can provide. Helping others to find peace and happiness—sounds like a familiar theme in my life, doesn't it!

So where did that desire initiate? I have no idea. Both of my parents were like that, as is my older brother. So it seems like more of a continuation than a beginning. And where will it all end? I have no idea. Both of my daughters have very similar characteristics to mine, as their current occupations and passions exemplify.

The door just keeps revolving.

My hope is that descendants will view my life as connected in some way to theirs, to look at all of life as interconnected, to see that self-enhancement, mutual interests, and species survival are complementary concepts. Not only are families connected by bloodline generations but also by human characteristics. The dots are in place; we just need to connect them!

Regrets are part of every life and what "might have been" is often subject to environment and conditions. I came from a musical family. Many of my older brother's male classmates were both musical and athletic, so that seemed a no-brainer for him. I was not so fortunate in the musical venue, as the following story illustrates. My male classmates and closest friends were extremely athletic, but musical interest was virtually nonexistent. Only after high school did I begin to realize what I was missing, but by then my life was so full of career preparations and daily survival that I spared no time. The following story describes perhaps my greatest regret.

A Youthful Decision with Far-Reaching Consequences

When hidden internal desires clash with opposing internal pressures, how does one decide which path to take? I began to face that dilemma in fifth grade when some of us were given the option of beginning a musical instrument.

I was raised in a musical extended family where many played instruments and a few sang in church and community choirs. My mother and paternal grandmother both played piano, and my mother's older sister was quite accomplished at playing the theater organ for silent pictures. An older brother preceded my schooling by five years and continued the family tradition by joining both band and glee club in high school.

When my turn came, however, I really wasn't ready. Yes, I loved music and often begged my grandmother to play the piano so I could sing the latest pop hits of the 1940s, such as "Lavender Blue," "Cruising Down the River," "Far Away Places," "Ghost Riders in the

Sky," "My Happiness," "The Tennessee Waltz," "Lucky Old Sun," "A Tree in the Meadow," "Buttons and Bows," "The Anniversary Song," and "Some Enchanted Evening," among many others.

Sometimes my mother or grandmother even suggested the activity, and I was always thrilled to comply. But my singing was confined to the private comfort of home, where I always received much praise and support.

My inner circle peer group, however, was apathetic at best toward musical activities. Their main interest was athletics, also a strong interest of mine. All too often these two activities competed for my after-school time, as after-dinner time was usually reserved for homework.

Since I felt that learning an instrument was a family expectation, without objection I chose the tenor saxophone, at which my mother's older brother had become quite adept. Though I suspect that the school did not have available in its inventory such an instrument, anyway, I was told that I would first have to learn the clarinet.

My best friend, the school principal's son, decided he would try the clarinet, too, so that we could schedule our lessons together and help one another out. Good idea, but it didn't work. We both hated the clarinet; we both hated practicing, and we longed to be out on the ball field with friends. After a few weeks, we both quit.

I continued my hermit-like singing at my grandmother's home until my voice began to change, at which time, coincidentally, I became even more invested in athletics. In hindsight, it was a mistake that I came to regret. While my high school athletic career was satisfying, a broken leg in senior-year football never healed properly and curtailed any thoughts of college sports.

On the other hand, musical participation could have provided a lifetime of pleasure and an avenue to socialization that might have created friendships and opportunities that my reserved (and some would say "shy") personality never pursued.

What I especially would have liked were piano lessons, but they were not offered by the school and were too costly for my parents to provide privately. In addition, I perceived an unwritten cultural rule that piano lessons were for girls. I assumed that my friends would have considered any boy who took such lessons "feminine"—and I couldn't risk that!

I tried teaching myself a few times during my early teens, but had neither the knowledge nor the discipline needed for success. The call from the ball field was much too enticing.

The ability to make choices is something that all freedom-loving people cherish. But all choices have consequences, and social pressures can affect those choices. Readiness to combat childhood conformity and make enhancing choices is a product of individual development and emotional maturity, and varies with each child; but each choice can be a life-altering event!

In one way or another, at some point in time, each of us finds ways to escape reality. Sometimes our lives become so stressful that our minds just tune into outlandish fantasies or play tricks while we're asleep. At other times the opposite occurs—we may be so relaxed and content with life that we allow ourselves the luxury of consciously moving beyond reality into the spiritual realm of creation. The following story addresses this issue.

Night and Day—Home or Away

Scientific explanations aside, my night dreams seem to result from the desire of my brain to be active while the rest of my body wants to sleep. While this anatomical battle sometimes seems to have logical antecedents, perhaps resulting from events during waking hours, it can also be chaotic and unsettling, as seemingly irrelevant actions and events are brought into my "unconscious awareness," thereby making any attempts at accurate interpretation quite impossible. While I understand that night dreams can be intriguing, and sometimes frightening, they don't hold much relevance for me. While some experts tell us that we're constantly dreaming during sleep, rarely can I remember beyond a few seconds what I have dreamed about, as nearly all my dreams are benign and quickly forgotten.

But daydreams are different. My mind, and not just my brain, is fully alive and alert, while my body is still, but not asleep. Daydreaming is fun and incredibly useful. It is sometimes interpreted as an escape from reality (not necessarily a bad outcome), but I have also experienced it as a pathway to significance. Daydreaming has allowed me to be anything, go anywhere, and do anything without moving a step and without needing money. I can make my own reality, and do it invisibly! I have been a major league ballplayer, president of the United States, and a famous author—without ever leaving home.

I can create or end relationships, solve personal problems, enjoy fame or anonymity, envision world peace, or visit the Almighty—all without unpleasant consequences, and all within my control. I just let my spirit and imagination take over!

But, above all, my daydreams provide hope. I was once told, "Whatever our minds can conceive, our beings can achieve." If that's true, we will all someday experience true love and peace, because my mind has a clear image of what that would be like.

Yes, I am a dreamer, but I dream by day and with intention. In my dreams I have accomplished great things, because my mind only cherishes great things. Though those dreams haven't always turned out the way I envisioned, for me it's the journey that counts.

If I wish to describe an important aspect of my personality to descendants, there may be no better way than through this story. It is upbeat, hopeful, and positive. It takes a process that is often maligned and puts an entirely different spin on it, reframing it into a productive coping mechanism and providing an alternative model for life's vicissitudes.

It's tempting to circumvent stories that revisit pain, but if our intent is to help future generations avoid the severity of social pain, some of those stories are essential. Insensitivity, and lack of awareness of the cruelty felt by victims, has changed very little over the years, but the consequences have intensified. Before the advent of social media devices, rejection and ridicule were relatively isolated events; the pain was real, but the responses rarely involved the extremes of homicide or suicide. Instead, the victims "sucked it up" at the cost of their own self-esteem and social development. The following story depicts my response to what today might be termed "adult bullying."

The Irony of a Kiss

A kiss is such a positive experience. It can convey love, affection, appreciation and caring. But for me, at age fourteen, a kiss of death, for not kissing, would be a more apt description. For one nonkiss controlled my romantic life for years.

It began with a fall hayride during my freshman year in high school. It was my first date, and I hadn't even wanted it. But our class had come up with an activity that was supposed to provide fun and companionship. And since boys tended to be a bit shy, the girls decided to ask the boys for the date. There were twice as many girls as boys in our class; so getting skipped over was unlikely.

I liked the girl that asked me. We were good friends and talked a lot in school. But she also had a reputation for dating older boys, and I thought that older boys—well, you know.

All during the hayride I saw some couples going under blankets, and that made me most uncomfortable. I was afraid even to hold my date's hand, because the expectations and pressure to do more were enormous in my mind.

When the hayride was over, I walked her home. Her parents were not there, and she asked me to come inside. I made up some excuse to decline, so we just stood and talked for a few minutes. I don't know what we talked about. I didn't even know then. I was too busy panicking. I guessed I was supposed to kiss her, but I really was afraid to try, to somehow not do it right. I knew she was probably experienced in such matters, and I didn't want to show my lack of whatever it might be that I was lacking.

So I politely said good night and went home.

The next day was Sunday. Early in the afternoon, after church, the phone rang, and it was her nosey neighbor wanting to talk with my mother about church business. When I answered she said, "Is this you, David?"

"Yes."

"Don't you know that when you date a girl and walk her home that you're supposed to kiss her good night?" She spoke in a gossipy, arrogant voice. I had been exposed—that which I dreaded most was happening. I had feared rejection. Now I was getting ridicule, which was even worse.

I handed the phone to my mother and went into the bedroom and broke into tears. At that moment I said to myself that I would never have another date until I was at least out of college.

And I never did! In fact, the next date I had was at age twenty-four—ten years later—and this was the first girl I ever kissed, now a woman whom I had known as a casual summer friend since childhood. Even then I felt panicked, and if she had pulled back, I might never have dated her again. But six months later we married, and on February 24 of the year 2014 we celebrated our fifty-second wedding anniversary.

At age fourteen I believe I was considered by most peers to be friendly, nonaggressive, socially timid, and somewhat introverted. But I was also athletic, studious, obedient, and well liked by most adults. I was able to withstand normal teasing by peers but at the cost of self-confidence. Without those assets listed, and the outstanding support of my nuclear and extended family, I might have withered. Conditions have changed today; family support has deteriorated; academic standards have intensified; relationship skills have been ignored; athletic competition has been exaggerated. Greatness is externally measured, and the compassion of heart-to-heart connections has given way to "I gave at the office" mentality. If such conditions continue, future generations will suffer even greater consequences. They need to know the truth! They need to know how our stories and experiences have affected us!

In spite of having the most powerful brains on the planet, at times we humans make foolish decisions to pursue goals that could have ended our lives, but did not. What saves us? Deity intervention? A miracle of nature? Coincidence? Being in the right place at the right time? Just plain luck? Such speculation is the theme of the next story.

The Snow Shed that Vanished

The sun was shining brightly when we left Reno at the end of our Christmas vacation trip on a cold early January day in 1966. We really didn't want to leave, but grad school was calling me back to Portland, and a forty-four-dollar-a-week, temporary nursing-assistant job mandated my wife's return to the Multnomah County Hospital. We would head back east in June, so we had wanted to see as many of the western sites as we could afford.

I checked the weather report before we left and knew that a storm was brewing in the mountains that lay ahead of us, but I hoped that we could beat it. As we approached Susanville, California, in the foothills, the snow began to gently fall. The beautiful silvery flakes belied the treachery that was ahead of us, as we began the trek up the mountainside in our Rambler station wagon.

As we progressed, the flakes became larger, heavier, and thicker. There was little traffic, so the tire tracks of other vehicles were soon covered. My speed gradually slowed to 50, then 40, then 30 mph with few guardrails or utility poles to guide our travel. A few four-wheel drive vehicles, mostly jeeps and small trucks, passed us on our movement upward, but we later saw most of them off the road as the visibility became more and more intense.

Suddenly I realized I was catching up to a huge tractor-trailer that was barely moving, and I knew that slowing down was not a good option, as my snow tires might not be able to regain traction. I had to pass. Fortunately, the air became clear enough to see that the passing lane on this two-lane highway was open, so I continued my speed and successfully drove by. But now I faced another problem; I had to keep moving. If the visibility sudden worsened, and I stopped, I might now get rear-ended by this huge truck, which might not be able to see me. We had been traveling upward for nearly an hour, and I had no idea how far we had to go to get to the top and start downward.

Occasionally I could see that we were driving on the side of a mountain with no guardrails and a long drop over the side if I didn't stay on the road, and I couldn't always see where the road was, as all tracks were now totally wiped out. Our border collie in the back seat began panting heavily, obviously aware of our internal tension. Our windshield wipers were barely able to clear the snow, even at their fastest speed.

Suddenly and unexpectedly a wall of snow crashed down on the car, and for a moment I could see nothing but white, an avalanche no doubt; we were at the mercy of nature's winter power. But within seconds, ahead of us about twenty yards, we saw many bright lights inside a tunnel; somehow, we managed to make it to safety.

I wanted to stay there but knew we couldn't. With the huge truck behind us and only one other lane, going the other way, beside us, we had to keep moving. But surprisingly, when we left the tunnel and started down the other side of the mountain, the weather began to clear and ultimately turned to rain. Still, we were exhausted and in great need of rest. A couple of miles from the tunnel we came upon a restaurant and thankfully went inside, only to find many other travelers who were headed the other way but had stopped due to the "raging, impassable storm" on the other side of the mountain.

When we recounted our journey to the waitress, she was amazed that we had made it. We told her that we might not have, if the snow shed hadn't suddenly appeared to save us. She hesitated for a moment, then asked, "What snow shed?"

"The one a couple of miles back, at the top of the mountain," I explained.

"I've lived here all my life," she responded. "There's no snow shed up there. You must have been imagining it."

My wife and I looked at each other, and I'm sure the blood drained from both our faces. But we said no more about it for weeks thereafter.

Some adventurous travelers might have gone back to check it out, but we never did. We never wanted to. There are some things in life that it may be better just to accept. We have occasionally, though rarely, told this story to friends, but we have concluded nothing. Was it indeed our imagination? Was it nature's intervention? Was it some sort of creative or protective Intelligence? Or was the waitress mistaken about the presence of a snow shed?

We never questioned it. We just accepted our good fortune. But no doubt it had the effect of strengthening a lifelong resolve to use our lives effectively.

Do we see what we want to believe? Can we create what we want to exist? Or do we only believe what we physically can see, and what others can corroborate? We both saw the snow shed, but was it really there or did our minds create it? How much untapped power do we really have, and why did we have no desire to check it out? There is much in life that we do not understand. Perhaps someday our descendants will, if we but share our experiences with them, thus providing them the opportunity to integrate their findings with ours.

The famous quote "Sometimes a cigar is just a cigar" has been attributed to Freud and could well apply to my next story, which I wrote at a weeklong amateur writing workshop shortly after retirement. On the last day, we were asked to write a short article about our experience there and then to read it to the attendees from some of the other workshops. I decided on some frivolity—to write a story with no serious point other than to laugh at ourselves.

Writer's Cramp

The first day we arrived at the Campbell Folk School, it was suggested that we dine with different students at each meal, to become acquainted with those interested in different curricula. So I have done that, and it has opened my eyes to a remarkable phenomenon.

As I listen to conversations about quilting, woodturning, jewelry making, woodcarving, basket-weaving, knitting, pottery, and other such hands-on endeavors, there is a tangible product involved, one that can be seen, touched, smelled, and handled. The beauty of these wondrous projects, and the difficulties in creating them, is both admired and appreciated.

Then the subject turns to me, as my table-mates strain to read my nametag. "Writing," someone says, "Hmm, that's interesting. What do you write about?" After a short conversation about memoirs and essays, most of which bring blank stares and lifted eyebrows, comes the ultimate question.

"What do you do with those stories?""

"Maybe nothing," I respond.

"Then why do you write them?" I am asked.

I'm tempted to respond, "Well, when I got here, there was no one to take the class, so a few of us volunteered," but I don't.

Often I'm asked, "Are you a writer?"

"Yes" I proudly answer.

"What have you written?" (meaning, of course, "What have you published?")

"Oh, lots of things," I say, as if oblivious to the implication.

But I know where we're headed. It's just a matter of time until someone uses that dreaded word. I can delay the inevitable by answering the question "Where have you written?" with a deadpan "on my computer" response, but I know that such a retort will satisfy no one.

Eventually, here it comes. "Have you published anything?"

"No"

"Oh" (slight pause).

"Are you going to publish anything?"

"Probably not. But I might someday. Who knows?"

Why this obsession with publishing? I think. Can't I be a writer without having written for publication? I don't ask potters if they're potted. I don't ask broom-makers if they're going to be riding their brooms! I don't ask those in the classes on "stone work" if they're stoned. And I certainly don't ask those in the dyeing classes if they've dyed? So why are we asked where we've written?

Truth is, in our consumer-oriented, profit-making culture, doing something for the sheer pleasure and inner peace of doing it is hard to understand, unless, of course, it beautifies a home in some way, or is otherwise tangible. And if the item could possibly be sold (spelled p-r-o-f-i-t), it acquires even greater prominence.

For some, writing is a business; for some, it's a legacy; for some, it's therapeutic; for some, it's a challenge; for some, it's all of these.

Tomorrow, at our week-ending lunch, perhaps I should ask my table-mates "Have you sold your quilt yet?" "Do you have a buyer for your pottery?" "How much will your woodcarvings bring on the open market?" When will you start getting paid for your dulcimer talent?" But I won't, though it might be fun to watch their reactions.

Not all personal stories need be serious. I want future generations to know and understand all of me—my thoughtful side and my playful side. Life might be described as a realistic illusion, a paradox to be lived one day at a time. Our stories can provide models that could relieve some of the stress of daily living for our descendants.

Life is a connection between the past and the future. The past is the foundation of the present and the future is an outgrowth of both past and present. We handicap our human progress by not attending carefully to all three. The following two stories stem from my genealogical research and fill a gap in family history. I have chosen different styles of writing merely to show possible variations—the initial story is written as Dorliska might have penned it, while the second one is scripted as an objective reporter might have preferred.

My Name is Dorliska

My name is Dorliska Dean Vincent, and I lived from 1843 until 1924. Little did I know that when I wrote a diary in 1865, it would turn up in the hands of my great-grandson nearly 150 years later. So my story is being told through his understanding of events in my life.

I wrote that diary as a twenty-two-year-old mother of two boys, ages four and one. Married at age sixteen, I had already lost my first child to illness, in my first year of marriage. Sadly, such losses were to become a theme in my life.

All I ever wanted was a loving family to raise. My Wilber worked on a commercial sailing vessel, carrying all sorts of goods to and from many ports on the Great Lakes and St. Lawrence River. Wilber was three years older than me, and had shipped out on his first voyage in 1854 at the age of fourteen. We met five years later and married shortly thereafter. Ours was a wonderful marriage that lasted sixty-four years. Wilber was a kind, loving husband and father, and a wonderful provider. But his work took him away from me every year from April to November, during all the good weather, from the time of our marriage in 1859 until his retirement in 1896—thirty-seven years in the prime of our lives. And I became more and more lonely.

But a large family to raise—that would keep me busy and happy. Or so I thought!

I don't know why I picked 1865 to write that diary. I never wrote one before or after. It was an historic year. The Civil War was ending, though Lincoln's assassination dampened the euphoria. Still, we were so far from Washington and so close to Canada that events in Ottawa were often far more significant to our well-being.

But my own personal grief that year was almost more than I could bear. In April, my beloved mother-in-law, Polly, was stricken with pneumonia and died within a few weeks. And my other great love (besides Wilber, of course) was my four-year-old, Willy. He started school in September but became ill shortly thereafter with that dreaded scarlet fever. God took my little darling on December 5, and I was left with only Elmer, barely one year old.

Three years later I gave birth to Will, my angel's namesake, and the only one of my children that would leave me heirs. Elmer, age one in 1865, lived to age thirty-three. He married but had had no children yet when pneumonia took him in 1897, a year after Wilber retired.

In the meantime, when Will and Elmer became midteenagers and no longer needed my care, I still longed for children to be an antidote to my loneliness. Wilber was still gone on his job for most of the year, now making good money as a captain of a large sailing vessel. So we tried to have a second family in the early 1880s, when I was nearing forty. And we succeeded—for a while. We had two more children, only to lose them both to pneumonia within a year of their births.

By 1898 Wilber and I had had six children, and we had outlived five of them. Fortunately, Will survived us and was father to four children, one of whom was his last-born, Grovene, born in 1913, and mother of David, through whom I'm recounting these events.

When David would ask his mother, she would tell him that I was a stern, hard grandmother, not like her fun-loving maternal grandmother, who also had six children, all of whom outlived her and gave her children and grandchildren. That's what I would have liked, but it was not to be.

I buried five of my six children, none stillborn. I was able to bond with all of them for months or years, only to be left with sadness and grief at their young deaths. Perhaps I did become hardened, but I didn't start out that way. Over a lifetime, the pain just became too unbearable, so I defended my feelings with my grandchildren in the only way I knew how.

A Link to the Past

We are now celebrating the two hundredth anniversary of the War of 1812, the first and only major international war geographically affecting citizens of northern New York State following the War for Independence. There have been some minor skirmishes, of course, such as the 1838 Patriot's War, but any resemblance to a "real war" requires some imagination. Certainly there have been other foreign wars affecting citizens and families in this area through their personal participation in the military, but the War of 1812 deserves special recognition and significance as the second war for independence.

Our proximity to British Canada meant that our local ancestors not only fought to maintain national independence but also to protect their families and homes, as it put the war right on their doorsteps. It was further complicated by the fact that Canada had been a refuge for many Americans who opposed the Revolutionary War and wished to remain loyal to the British crown, but there was still much ambivalence on both sides.

My great-great-great-grandfather, Isaac Kendall, found himself in the midst of it all. He would probably have remembered bits and pieces of that first war for independence from the British, when his father fought with Seth Warner's Green Mountain Boys in Vermont. Isaac was born in Enosburg Falls, Vermont, a tiny community near the Canadian border, just as the first War for Independence was starting. His whereabouts and activities as a child and adolescent are a mystery but, according to Oakes' *Family and Genealogical History of Jefferson County*, volume 2, published in 1905, he left Vermont and migrated to Northern New York in 1795 at the age of twenty, with only a pair of oxen and a cart for transportation.

It's probable that Isaac settled somewhere in what is now St. Lawrence County, as a history of that county records that he was paid the sum of $500 (obviously a huge amount at that time) in 1805 to supervise the construction of the first bridge across the Oswegatchie River, perhaps near the present site of Gouverneur, New York. Oakes's historical account states that he made his living as a carpenter, so that would be consistent with his bridge-building efforts. The bridge lasted for nearly thirty years before being replaced, so he must have been quite competent at his trade.

His passion, however, was music, and history records that he wrote both the words and melodies to many original compositions, none of which have survived as far as we know. Since Isaac apparently spent much of his time in the wilderness, there must have been strange sounds for the bears, wolves, and coyotes to hear, as the melodic strains carried through the sparsely populated forests. Whether he sang the tunes or played them on some primitive instruments remains a mystery. As an aside, many of his descendants were quite musical as well, including a grandson who apparently received an honorary music award from Queen Victoria for playing at her court during the late nineteenth century.

So where was Isaac, and what was he doing, during the War of 1812? Given the history of his father's patriotism during the Revolution, it's unlikely that he was a British sympathizer. Still, there is no record of him serving in the US military, either. He would have been nearly forty years old at the outbreak of the war and could possibly have been a "spy" for the American soldiers. Considering the porous international border (the US-Canada border was not finalized with a treaty until 1818) and the trade and communication that must have taken place between British subjects to the north and American citizens to the south of the St. Lawrence River prior to 1812, it's likely that Isaac had access to information that could have benefited the American side.

In any case, Oakes's account says that Isaac was imprisoned in the tower at Kingston, Ontario, in 1813, accompanied by a soldier named Nathan Stetson. They quickly became friends and escaped prison together, using the door of an abandoned cabin as a raft to paddle across the foot of Lake Ontario to safety on the American shore, possibly at Cape Vincent.

It's unclear where his wife and children lived at the time, but several years later the homestead of at least two of his children was on Grindstone Island (opposite Clayton and today considered a part of Clayton). Clayton was barely a community in 1812 but was later acknowledged as Isaac's home. He lived until 1870, being nearly a century old at his death.

In 1813 Isaac's last son was born and named Aldridge Stetson (1813–90), obviously in honor of his imprisoned companion. Throughout his lifetime, that son was known as "Stet" and came to be regarded as a superb boat pilot on the St. Lawrence River, as was

Isaac's grandson, also named Aldridge, who lived into his nineties (1851–1947).

Another son of Stet, Eli Kendall (1848–98), also a noted river pilot, became the father of Harry (1886–1973), who fathered Harold (1909–2002), who was my father.

It may seem that I have a lot of information about this side of my family, but it is far surpassed by the holes and gaps. I feel fortunate that past genealogists like Oakes cared enough to compile these family memories, and without benefit of the vastly superior technology at our fingertips today.

Your descendants will desire stories about your life, knowing that you have had the ability to record them, either in oral or written form. Are you doing your part? Or will you become just another weak link in your genealogical chain, complaining that you have little information about your own ancestors, but irresponsibly or unwittingly providing little more than your birth and death dates for your own descendants who will crave to know the substance of your life—the stories in between those extremes. Soooo ... how many stories of your life are you recording for them?

Both of these stories were written as models for family and public consumption, but the second was also an article penned for *The Informer*, a news publication of the Jefferson County Genealogical Society of New York, and ends with a plea for members to concentrate on their obligations as future ancestors in addition to their research as present descendants.

For those who have owned and loved pets, the following story may be a tearjerker. For me it was catharsis, written as a tribute to the companionship and loyalty that Thena embodied. I wrote it only a few weeks following the death of this beloved Doberman, and though it is longer than most of my stories, I have been encouraged to share it with others. Perhaps those who have never owned or loved pets will shrug their shoulders, but others will identify and empathize with my account.

The Week I Played God

On February 1, 2006, I lost a friend. I've owned several dogs during my nearly seventy years of life, and they were all loved, valued, and probably spoiled. But (A)thena was truly special, and she died much too young, two weeks away from her ninth birthday.

Over the years most of my dogs have been border collies—energetic, smart, obedient animals who love to herd sheep or chase frisbees. Thena was my first Doberman, purchased and trained by me to be a demonstration dog for both obedience and protection in a dog-training business established by my daughter and me following my retirement as a college teacher.

In order to understand the last week of her life—which is the core of this story—a little background is essential. Our dog-training business was short-lived, and Thena soon became a gentle family pet, with all the sofa and bed privileges usually accorded to such. She loved people, and other dogs and cats, and the "play crouch" was a most familiar stance. She was also incredibly stoic and courageous, never starting a confrontation, but never backing down, either.

When people would approach her fenced-in yard, she would bark profusely, alerting her owners to a possible intrusion. Strangers would give her a wide berth, and often walk or run away, which only fueled her intensity for a favorite game of "keep away." Upon those rare occasions when her targets did not scare, but instead approached her at the fence, she gave them a second choice, as if to say "If you're not going to run away, then pet me." She was never aggressive. Fortunately, she never had to be. But I was always confident that she would protect me with her life, if need be.

One day in early June, 2005, following a day of "protective" work in the yard, she started limping. It seemed like perhaps a muscle pull or strain, so we assumed it would heal in a few days. When it didn't, we took her to the veterinarian, who gave us some medication but no cause for worry. However, several days later, nothing had changed and x-rays were suggested and taken in mid-July. The results were devastating, as the pictures revealed an aggressive cancerous mass (osteosarcoma) in her left hind leg near the hip joint, with some suspicious activity possible in the lungs.

With the doctor's help we discussed options, one of which was a three-hour drive to the veterinary hospital at Cornell University for leg amputation and follow-up treatment. All professional consultation pointed to immediate removal of the leg at the hip, which was accomplished on Friday, August 5. New x-rays did not reveal visible lung damage, though it was explained that it was probably there, but not large enough to show on x-rays yet.

When we took her home three days later, we were provided with a padded sling to help support her hind quarters until her remaining leg regained enough strength to do all the work itself. Discharge papers at Cornell mentioned that the staff all loved her and that she had "a heart of gold."

Essentially two choices were available for follow-up: chemotherapy treatments or holistic/homeopathic remedies. For us this was a no-brainer, as past family experiences with the former and possible side effects eliminated that option from our minds. Besides, my daughter had had a very positive outcome with Thena's littermate years before, when utilizing a more nontraditional veterinary clinic north of New York City. Either way, we were informed that she might not have more than four to six months of life left, anyway.

Thena's recovery from surgery was not rapid, but it was steady, and by September she was running smoothly on her three legs, and her quality of life was almost back to normal. Only rarely did she need help with a sling, usually getting into our SUV or climbing steep stairs. For most of the fall season, we were able to trade the flood of tears we had been shedding for the fun and laughter she had always provided.

But shortly after Thanksgiving, we began to see definite changes. Though we continued to give her the special food supplements and customized care to support her liver and immune system, which had been suggested through regular consultations with the holistic clinic, her energy was now more sporadic, as was her appetite.

New x-rays, taken on December 9, showed the first spot of cancer in her lungs. Four weeks later another set confirmed our suspicions of further deterioration. Not only had the original site increased significantly, but a new one had developed as well. Her breathing had become more labored as her lung capacity decreased, and some occasional coughing had developed. We knew then that our time with her was limited, but we were determined to keep her as comfortable as possible and to sustain a maximal quality of life.

Our hope was that one day or night, she would die in her sleep, thus avoiding that awful decision that pet owners often have to make and that we had made four times previously with other dogs we'd owned. But that was not to be.

In mid-January we discovered a nasty-looking growth under her upper lip above her teeth. It must have been there for days and could explain why she wasn't eating well. Another trip to the local veterinarian confirmed a mouth infection, possibly cancerous, and a round of antibiotics. By that time, we had also discovered that Thena responded well to a weekly shot of steroids, which seemed to greatly improve her quality of life for a few days each time.

Those "up" days, in which she showed more alertness, a stronger gait, more energy, and a better appetite were inevitably followed by greater "down" days, culminating in sad, red, draining eyes, lethargy, loss of appetite, and increased coughing, expelling massive amounts of phlegm and occasional blood. She never became incontinent, but her rare stools were black, stringy, and ugly-looking.

Wednesday, January 25, had been an especially bad day. As bedtime approached, and I helped her out into the yard for her last outing of the day, she headed straight for the furthest part of the fence, about thirty yards away from the house, where a few mounds of leaves and pine straw had been placed in areas where no grass would grow. She promptly nestled in and put her head down.

My immediate thought was that, like wild animals I'd heard about, she was instinctively preparing her deathbed. Then my mind raced to an earlier image, a discussion I'd had a few years earlier with a physician friend I was visiting, and who had a ten-year-old dog with both hind legs amputated. I recall questioning him about the wisdom of keeping the animal alive in that condition, considering an obviously diminished quality of life and the substantial extra care required. His response was branded in my mind: "I don't play God with my patients, and I don't play God with my dogs." In essence, he was telling me that his job was to prolong life, not to take it. But isn't that interfering with God's nature as well? Isn't amputation, in order to extend life a bit more, just another way of playing God? I wish I knew the answer to that dilemma.

But what I did see on that cold January evening was my beloved companion collapsing in the straw away from my side, her smooth skin exposed to the elements. Instinct might be preparing her to leave me, but I surely was not ready.

I called to her in a weak, compassionate voice: "Thena, c'mon girl." There was no response. I called again, a bit louder this time: "Thena, come." Still no movement. Now my insides were starting to react, and I began to sweat, in spite of the cold. Was this to be the end? I didn't want her dying out there, all alone, perhaps freezing to death by morning.

Once more I called, using the loud, stern voice she was accustomed to whenever I became annoyed with her. "Thena, get over here, *now!*" After some hesitation and as if being pulled in two directions—like me—she slowly arose and began to walk drudgingly toward me.

She stopped, head down, in front of me. My eyes filled with tears as I bent down, put my arms around her neck, and drew her close to my cheek. "C'mon, let's go inside."

As I stood up, now shivering in the cold, she looked up with an expression similar to that which I'd seen only once before, in the waiting room at Cornell when the attendant told me to take off her collar, a normal procedure before being taken to the back rooms for surgical preparation. Her look then was one of incredulity and panic, a sense of "What are you doing? I belong to you. You're not abandoning me, are you?"

That image came back to me now, though in a slightly different way. The difference was either calmness or tiredness on her part. I'm not sure. Perhaps it was even resignation. Probably all three.

But the communication I received that night was clear. "My time is near, and I tried to do what my spirit and soul told me. But you are my God, and you're not ready. So I'll let you decide." Slowly we walked together into the house. She never again attempted to leave my side.

The next few days were emotionally very difficult, as her activity continued to deteriorate. Even jumping up on her favorite sofa became difficult, and most of the time she would lie on a soft blanket we placed on top of the living room carpet. She never seemed to be in great pain or distress, just progressively weaker. Several times during the day and evening I would lie on the floor beside her and stroke her head and body, partly to reassure her by my presence and partly to prepare myself for the inevitable conclusion. Her body would often shiver and shake, and we kept her covered with a blanket. But she wasn't cold. We knew that. She ate little, but would drink water when we brought it to her. However, shortly thereafter she would begin coughing and expelling large amounts of phlegm.

Late each night I took her outside, providing support with her sling. Going both directions, she waited at the door while I prepared the sling to support her hind quarters. Back inside, I helped her up the stairs to our bedroom, and she scurried over to her bed, which had always been on the floor beside me. Covered with a blanket, she slept through the night. Occasionally, her labored breathing would awaken me, and I would think, "Maybe this is it." But it never was!

Back in the summer, when I had first learned about her cancer, and then endured the amputation, tears had come suddenly and frequently at the thought of losing her. But as the fall and winter progressed, tears subsided, even as the outcome became more obvious. But the floods returned late Saturday evening, January 28. On her last outing, the hind leg collapsed as she was attempting to urinate. I helped her up and supported her hind quarters as she completed the task. But her struggle and the futility of my efforts finally caught up with me. She seemed so weak and so sad!

Once back in the house, she moved quickly to her blanket and collapsed. I could control my emotions no longer, and the tears erupted, as I knelt down to hug her and stammered, "I don't want her to die, but I don't want her to suffer, either." My wife joined me in the despair, and for a moment we comforted one another, as we both endured once more the pain that had been accumulating for several months.

Suddenly my eyes focused on the living room bookcase that contained a shelf of small mementos and statues of dogs that we had accumulated over our forty-four years of marriage. My favorite had been a sand-cast of a Doberman in a play crouch. I grabbed it and carried it over to a spot on the kitchen counter where it would be more visible.

"This is the way I want to remember her. This is who she is," I blurted out. My wife nodded and was very supportive as always. But she also knew that I had to work this through myself, and gave me the necessary space to vent my pain. But as my emotional energy burned out, and some rationality returned, we both agreed that we needed to make that final decision. Since the next day was Sunday, it was decided that my wife would call our veterinarian on Monday and make the arrangements.

Many weeks earlier we had asked the vet to come to our house for the final shot, should that route become necessary. We wanted Thena to spend her final moments on her sofa rather than be taken to a sterile office. Tuesday was the vet's day off, but she had given us her cell phone number and a promise that she would come on that day if we wanted. We decided that Wednesday at 6:00 p.m. would be the best time, if Thena lasted till then and got no worse.

As if attuned to our decision, Thena would eat nothing after Sunday, and grew increasingly weaker. For the next three days, much of my time was spent on the floor with her, stroking her gently. She was always aware of my presence and occasionally responded with the usual Doberman habit of putting her long nose under my hand for more petting when I tired and momentarily stopped. I expected that her breathing would be noticeably more labored during those last three nights, but it actually seemed calmer. She would drink water, a little at a time, but a rumbling in her stomach would follow soon thereafter, as would coughing and phlegm expulsion. Her eyes were very cloudy and drained mucus almost continuously.

Wednesday dragged on too quickly, as we awaited and dreaded the doctor's arrival. I was surprisingly calm all day, spending most of the time attending to Thena's comfort and needs. I knew we were doing the right thing. She could not last much longer on her own, and all that her future promised was more discomfort and pain. Still, the thought of being without her ...

But I had to stop myself from such thoughts and to focus on positive memories. She had been an incredible animal, and I had had six months to thoroughly enjoy and admire her since her leg amputation. Then I remembered a videotape we had made when she was going through protection training seven years ago. I rummaged through our old tapes and found it. I played it several times, watching her bark profusely and struggle to "disarm" the perpetrator, straining at the leash, which I held tightly in both hands. I laughed as I watched, determined to remember her in that energized state.

When the veterinarian came into the house, shortly after 6:00 p.m., I replayed the tape for her, as we all prepared ourselves for the final shot. It was quick and painless, and while tears fell softly from my eyes, I gently stroked her body and head as it fell slowly to the pillow. Finally, I felt ready for the outcome. As I removed her collar, and the attendant quietly placed the blanket around her and carried her out to be cremated and returned, I could only conclude, from firsthand experience that playing God is not fun. I still wonder: Should I have been her intermediary god on earth, to take charge of her life and death issues? Or should I have left that task for the Ultimate God of the universe?

Even in her last days, amid the slow deterioration of her body, Thena had come to my aid by staying alive long enough for me to prepare for our separation. It had been indeed a mutual decision and agreement. My part for keeping her alive for that final week was to provide love, attention, and comfort, while she was already doing her part for me. The sadness of her death is still with me many weeks later, but I am comforted by the final paragraph of "A Dog's Prayer" by Beth Norman Harris: "And, beloved master, should the Great Master see fit to deprive me of my health or sight, do not turn me away from you. Rather hold me gently in your arms as skilled hands grant me the merciful boon of eternal rest … and I will leave you knowing with the last breath I drew, my fate was ever safest in your hands."

Thena, my friend, be patient and enjoy your rest. We will meet again at the Rainbow Bridge!

Perhaps nothing communicates our human essence more than how we envision and treat our living environments—nature, animals, and other humans. I can think of no better way for me to be remembered by descendants than through this story.

PART 3

Now It's Your Turn

Sharing Defines Love

I began this book with a positive vision for the future. I'm in awe of scientific achievement and technology, though much has unfortunately been used for harmful or frivolous purposes. Still, we have harnessed more of the universe in the past few decades than in thousands of years previously; and most recently Voyager I, with our permission, has even left our solar system, traveling into the vast black hole of obscurity, a feat unimaginable to most of us. Our acquisition of knowledge and our earthly accomplishments have been truly extraordinary, but with our successes have come elements of destruction. Perhaps our Creator feels the same way about Its creations—hopeful early returns but many subsequent disappointments.

We humans are in a race. Somewhere there is probably a finish line, but where it is and how to get there remains a mystery. We imagine and invent the answers and even pretend that we're in control, or in the process of gaining it. We might be, if we were all in a spirit of cooperation and unity, but we're not. Our capabilities seem limitless but we negate and cancel one another's progress with senseless competition and infighting. We have learned the art of creation but also the means to destroy virtually everything we've created; we have underestimated the value of cooperation and disregarded the concept of unity. We give lip service to the phrase "Two heads are better than one," then silently add "as long as your thoughts are not too different from mine."

Nowhere is this more evident than in the congressional hearings (October 30, 2013) about the Affordable Care Act, where each committee member either lavishes praise or drenches criticism, nearly always in accord with previous political party positions. It's as if no one can think for him/herself. Their behaviors merely intensify polarity and generate anger and disgust among voters, giving rise to increased demands for a viable third party, the entrance of which then guarantees that such a minority will control (but not win) the course of future elections—ironically and stupidly assuring a victory for the one of the two major party candidates to whom they are *most opposed.* Meanwhile, each of those major candidates pleads innocence and sincerity, citing a great desire to work with the opposition party but implying, "If only they will see that our party is right and agree to our point of view." Their strategy of "any means to an end" and "the end justifies the means" and "stick to our guns at all costs" usually eliminates any feasible inclusion of ethics and morals in their behaviors.

Recognized as national leaders, their actions filter down to the best and brightest of the next generation of frontrunners. For example, in late October 2013, New York City Police Commissioner Ray Kelly was shouted down even before delivering his scheduled speech at Brown University. He had planned to dialogue with opponents of his policies, but apparently all that some rivals wanted was to disrupt the proceedings, thus eliminating any possible learning or accord that might have taken place.

We still have time to change the ultimate outcome by consciously choosing a more unifying and loving process. According to *A Course in Miracles*, the definition of "love" is not passion, romance, or any of the other mindful and bodily attributes that we often invent. Rather, the synonym for love is "sharing," a simple word with broad and powerful implications for all relationships, of which family is still the most significant, however it's defined. My favorite definition of marriage exemplifies that exact sentiment: "When two become one and yet remain two."

That phrase covers both unity and individuality, and can be expanded to define a worthwhile goal for the entire family of human beings (i.e., "when we all become united and yet remain individuals"). Some would say that such an outcome is impossible, but, slightly paraphrasing Robert Kennedy's similar philosophy, "Most people see all the bad things happening and ask 'why'; I see all the good possibilities and ask 'why not.'" There is an enormous difference in these two approaches to problem solving.

Can we not share our lives and yet still remain individuals? Can we not communicate genuine respect and admiration for one another and suspend judgment, comparison, and harsh criticism as we share different ideas? Can we not value and accept the contributions, no matter how different from ours, of all people everywhere and seek to genuinely incorporate or blend each and every one into a united whole? What stands in our way, other than unproven belief systems and ideologies that we tenaciously clutch like a Linus blanket?

Principles of Destruction

Many are told by political party and social institution leaders that, while it may be acceptable to compromise on nonsubstantive issues, we should stand firm on matters of *principle*. How helpful is that, especially when most of us cannot even clearly define the word? Yet it's on matters of principle (hardcore beliefs?) where we are most reluctant to give ground; but isn't that precisely where giving ground is most needed? It's on matters of principle that we must find solutions that do not involve war.

Our forefathers chose three principles to put into the Declaration of Independence—life, liberty, and the pursuit of happiness. Does that not mean survival, freedom, and meaningful pleasure? Furthermore, that document states that governments are formed to protect and preserve those principles, which seems to imply the right to choose that which keeps us alive and makes us happy. Logic and common sense would add, "as long as our pursuit does not interfere with the rights of others engaged in that same activity." So it's the *pursuit* of our happiness—the process—that needs most attention. Yet we seem to focus on the endgame, the goals that we define as principles and then seek to impose on others through institutional demands for conformity.

What's really worth fighting for, other than survival (however we define it) and the freedom to choose? Is it worth the cost of destroying the peace in order to promote highly debatable principles around the world and within our own country and neighborhoods?

Most matters of principle stem from beliefs whose truths cannot be proven (i.e., all religions, abortion, gay marriage and rights, immigration issues, cultural traditions, etc.). As already discussed in chapter 8, our beliefs are based primarily on what we've been told and what we've absorbed without much thought. Much of this is pure propaganda, with very little evidence and almost no proof. Yet we send nations into battle to kill one another for the sake of protecting our own views or imposing our beliefs on others.

Most of our deep-seated beliefs have been (permanently?) programmed into us by our mentors. Where did the beliefs of those mentors come from? From their mentors, of course, who also absorbed their beliefs from their mentors, and so on. It's as if someone many generations ago started a rumor that seemed relevant and hopeful to solving a specific problem and then imposed it on a naïve or vulnerable population; from there it unsurprisingly expanded without much thought, though perhaps with much insistence, into succeeding generations. Isn't that how cultures are built? Isn't that how traditions develop? Are millions of deaths an acceptable price to pay for keeping our ancestral cultures and traditions? Are we *that* callous? Apparently so, according to history!

This unyielding propaganda was localized and not a major detriment to the entire world until we became a global economy with close political ties, easy worldwide travel, and instant communication. In the transition, we even survived two world wars, though with increasingly horrible weaponry and greater devastation. Then came weapons of mass destruction and the means to destroy us all. Are "drone battles and star wars" next in order to promote those rumors begun by our ancestors? Or might it be time to begin a new approach to life, one more pleasant and humane?

Are You Easily Offended?

Along with our stubborn obsessions with unproven beliefs has come the issue of political correctness. We have developed amazingly thin skins, and with it we've lost our sense of humor and our need for balance. We need to loosen up and lighten up! Perhaps we could adopt the age-old solution employed by little children when taunted on the playground: "Sticks and stones can break my bones, but words can never hurt me."

In contrast, we adults have become so easily offended that much national discussion has been driven underground, a process that permanently buries issues but does little to resolve them. Almost daily, news accounts abound of one or a few individuals suing some person or group because their feelings have been hurt by a word or phrase uttered within earshot.

Most recently, certain historical Halloween costumes have been socially prohibited or severely criticized, along with athletic team mascots, because a tiny minority decided to complain, though there may have been no obvious intent to dishonor or discredit anyone. While the principles of majority rule and minority rights are part of our national heritage, the recent trend seems to be toward minority *preferences* trumping alleged majority "wrongs." The recent debates concerning gay marriage and civil unions provide evidence of semantic encroachment—well beyond the issue of legal rights and lawful equality that most Americans seem to support wholeheartedly. Would it really change the world negatively if such word descriptions remained as they are, *or* if they were reversed? If conflict would be ended or unity created, let's call traditional marriages "civil unions" and let the word "marriage" relate only to gay unions. What difference do the words make? Why do mere words carry so much weight—with either group? Debates like this create more polarization, as each group stands its ground on *semantic* principles. The end result can lead only to an ugly retaliation by either group, as some of our most cherished freedoms of speech and expression continue to trickle away down this slippery slope of political correctness.

Moreover, we are providing opportunists with a pathway to wealth, fame, power, or advantage as they initiate frivolous lawsuits, for which they have no difficulty finding the help of trial attorneys who pocket much of the settlements. It's sad that "being offended" is getting to be a national addiction and providing the fuel for domestic unrest.

Occasionally, memoirs have been written by acquaintances that cast aspersions on ancestors of other families—and provide more opportunities for *being offended.* As I have researched my wife's and my own genealogy, I have come across ancestors who might be described by some as shameful family members or of questionable character, or worse! One distant relative was allegedly hanged in England for witchcraft; another was a clergyman who was apparently a "town drunk;" one great-great-grandfather was a church deacon who built a "still" in his backyard and sold alcohol to townsfolk who were not members of his church in order to pay his tithes, though alcoholic beverages were forbidden in his own church! I suspect there were others in our family backgrounds who had ethics, morals, and values that we would today question or condemn.

Am I ashamed of these people? Do I take it personally? Do I get offended when their exploits are mentioned? Not in the slightest! If anything, I chuckle at these stories, while honoring those brave ancestors who survived hardships in the best ways available to them. Who knows what I would have done under the conditions and circumstances that they endured! Their behaviors are no blight on me—unless I pretend to make them so. Even if the rumors, accusations, and exploits are totally false and unsubstantiated, so what?

The memories of others are precisely that--their memories—and subject to their interpretations. In such controversial cases, there is no truth! If others publish their opinions in memoirs, so what? All we have to do is reframe our thoughts from "Woe is me; my family's a victim of persecution" to "That says nothing about me" or "Look how far I've progressed from the choices my ancestor made." But the best way to counter these allegations is to write our own stories, citing our own memories, understandings, interpretations, and opinions.

Culture and Politics

Kaplan, in the introduction to his 1961 series of philosophical essays, warned of the assault on our freedoms that political correctness entails: "We are cultivating a cultural uniformity amidst unyielding political differences; the hope of the world, as I see it, lies in exactly the reverse: a political unity within which cultural and individual differences can flourish" (11).

In other words, the choice is between governing bodies that allow little cultural diversity vs. more flexible and harmonious institutions that encourage open discussions of widespread variations in cultural preferences. Certainly, the latter must have been the vision of our founders, who drafted the Constitution within a hodgepodge of ethnicity, traditions, and lifestyles. Has their dream of political flexibility and cultural respect turned into a nightmare of social animosity amid political rigidity? As accurate as Kaplan's assessment may have been over fifty years ago, it appears even more relevant today.

Are Love and Isolation Incompatible?

Most people still seem to believe that we owe our existence to some form of Creator and that a part of our Creator is likely within us, just as part of the parent is within the child. We call it "heredity," though some creationists might favor "spirituality." Neither diminishes the parent in any way; rather, it increases the value, joy, and potential of both parent and child.

As each new child (you and me) matures into a creator of unique ideas and thoughts, the benefits of this new knowledge can be passed on to other human creations—contemporaries and descendants alike. But this can only be accomplished if we intentionally share and respect that uniqueness.

The definition of love as the sharing of lives also suggests that love's antonym is not hate, but rather separation or isolation. Considering this possibility, love could not thrive in an atmosphere of seclusion, where people keep their deepest thoughts and ideas from one another, often for the purpose of avoiding conflict or embarrassment but consequently preserving a distorted and illusional version of love. All creation is thereby diminished and unable to benefit from one another's knowledge and insights (perhaps this withdrawal/separation/isolation is what really defines the hate that is so often considered the opposite of love!). Have we unintentionally promoted such separation and isolation by withholding our stories? Why would we behave so foolishly toward others except for fear of some loss?

Scarcity and Abundance

A Course in Miracles suggests, "Our sense of inadequacy, weakness and incompletion comes from the strong investment in the 'scarcity principle' that governs the whole world of illusions. From that point of view, we seek in others what we feel is wanting in ourselves. We 'love' another in order to get something for ourselves. That, in fact, is what passes for love in the dream world. There can be no greater mistake than that, for love is incapable of asking for anything" (xi).

Does this mean that real love is unconditional and should demand nothing in return? Jesus apparently thought so. Does this mean that sharing our stories with future generations constitutes real love, even though we may get little or nothing in return? Might we now create a new version of the Golden Rule: show love by sharing our lives (stories?) with others even though they may not share in return?

That principle of scarcity, that "there's not enough for all, and I may be left out, so I'd better fight for my portion," rules much of the animal world and probably fuels most of our personal, national, and even international policies and conflicts. Jesus, of course, emphasized the abundance, not the scarcity, in God's world and demonstrated it in his stories and actions.

As the earlier quote suggests, do we really love another for the purpose of getting that love returned? Do we demand it or expect it? Do we manipulate others in hopes that they will love us even though our own self-love may be absent? Do we do unto others in order to receive that which we lack and desire in return? Do we preach an altruistic Golden Rule but practice a selfish Golden Hoax?

Restoring Real Love

Sharing/loving involves both giving and receiving on the part of all. Without a giver, there is nothing to receive, and without a receiver, giving has no meaning. The two processes are totally dependent on one another. We give substance and perspective to our descendants through our stories, and they receive assistance from their ancestors (us) by examining those stories in light of their own circumstances. In the process they become the future ancestors and create new stories and new perspectives for their descendants, and humankind prospers as a result.

Without sharing, love is an empty word; without sharing there is only division, which rarely travels without its evil companion, "suspicion." According to *A Course in Miracles*, another name for lack of love (lack of sharing) is "sin." But removed from a religious context, might not sin be merely some behavior based on a mistaken understanding needing correction, rather than some evil atrocity deserving of God's punishment?

If nonsharing denotes the absence of love, might not the presence of sharing trigger the return of love? Love's capability may be inborn, but its actualization is a choice, and free will allows us to choose wisely or unwisely, to employ our spiritual unity or to follow our ego's isolationist tactics. Could sharing our essence with one another and with future generations be an initial step toward correcting mistakes and reconnecting at a deeper, perhaps more meaningful level?

Relationships and Social Media

Note that I have raised more questions than I have provided answers. This is intentional; I have no answers. Nevertheless, cursory observations certainly confirm that we humans have considerable difficulty in developing and maintaining relationships, not only with those closest to us but especially with those with whom we disagree culturally or appear to have little in common. Connecting mentally (through conversation) and physically (through bodily contact) seems to be less of a problem than connecting emotionally and spiritually.

The introduction and impact of social media on these relationships has been astounding. With instant communication, we can establish and maintain verbal contact with others virtually nonstop; with legal and social changes in acceptable moral standards, physical behaviors once labeled shocking and deplorable now incur shoulder-shrugging and even praise. Some of these changes are useful or long overdue but are not without dangerous side effects. Short text messages may communicate mental substance but are void of those nonverbal and paralinguistic features that convey up to 90 percent of the intangibles that determine relationships. Numerous reports indicate that our younger generations often spend several hours each day with computers and other such devices at the expense of learning how to build and maintain such relationships.

Part of the difficulty is likely an attitude that discourages relationship skill development and favors ego protection. Philosopher William James acknowledged that problem decades ago when he concluded that the greatest discovery of any generation is that a human being can alter his life by altering his attitude.

As explained in chapter 8, our attitudes are primarily a product of our experiences, and experiences can always be reframed. It may not be easy, but we can choose to perceive our world differently. How much do we love our descendants—our children and grandchildren for perhaps many generations—and even those unrelated to us except as fellow members of this planetary existence? How much do we really love them? That's an attitude question! Have our life experiences been so horrific that we now wish to show hate, even to unborn descendants, by refusing to share our life stories with them? We can rationalize our refusals and deny our own importance, but rationalization and denial is not justification!

Beyond attitude, skill development poses additional concerns, and though a full explanation of such development is beyond the scope of this book, I will call upon my own experience and professional training to mention a few of these skills. During my complementary careers as a therapist and counselor educator, I found the original work of Robert Carkhuff to be most useful in the development of these relationship skills, and I will briefly mention a few of them in the following sections. As stated earlier, giving and receiving are dependent on one another, and how we give our stories will influence their reception. An attitude of love and caring is an essential beginning, but the skills of relating must follow.

Attitudes and Skills

As emphasized in chapter 10, respect and empathy are perhaps the most vital components to any relationship but are often misunderstood and misused. Respect is frequently confused with tolerance and empathy with sympathy or pity; but tolerance and sympathy do little to sustain relationships. On the other hand, both respect and empathy are primarily skills that open up communication and encourage further sharing.

Respect is uplifting and promotes a feeling of equality, whereas tolerance can appear patronizing and condescending. Respect indicates that there is no difference in our value as human beings and thus makes no moral judgment about the beliefs or opinions others hold. Instead, differences are looked upon as opportunities to connect with, and learn from, one another. As with all relationship skills, our nonverbal and paralinguistic behaviors (see chapter 4) communicate far more than do the actual words we say.

Empathy conveys a recognizable attitude of intense effort to truly understand how another individual is feeling and interpreting life. In this world of extremes and variations in living conditions and circumstances, it is often quite impossible to accurately comprehend the emotions and situations experienced by others. But we can make a supreme commitment to attempt that understanding, and, if the effort is communicated and recognized, that's what counts most. Again, words only help when accompanied by congruent gestures and mannerisms. Underlying negative attitudes cannot be faked for long, and genuine caring quickly becomes obvious. If the communication is not genuine but is rather like an academic exercise or cerebral experiment, the relationship will be quickly sabotaged.

Other Considerations

Though gullibility is not uncommon in our quest for interpersonal trust, most of us have an intuitive ability to detect phoniness in our acquaintances. When we sense its presence, our defenses are immediately triggered and our trust is diminished. Any sharing that takes place thereafter is done cautiously and with very little substance, making it meaningless or intentionally vague and insignificant. Such social gamesmanship is a waste of time and energy.

If true love and friendship is indeed based on mutual sharing, the groundwork of genuineness and trust must first be laid. This, of course, is a process that takes time to build but also one that can be sabotaged in an instant, should trust be betrayed. Such betrayal is, of course, a prime cause of marital discord and family disintegration, while the amount of satisfying *time* spent with one another (even when few words are exchanged) both reflects and encourages unity.

While inconsistencies and incongruences are a normal part of most lives, they are often strengthened by a lack of attention to their causes. When we operate our lives on automatic pilot and unconscious behavior, when we allow our egos to control our decisions habitually and without conscious choice, we often make contradictory decisions that confuse others or that we later regret. When genuineness, mutual sharing, and trust have been the foundation of such a relationship, however, discrepant behavior can often be discussed and explained with fewer harmful consequences.

Our Flawed Institutions

While struggling with interpersonal relationships, we have enlisted the assistance of institutions of government, education, and theology to help us cope with these intricacies of family, spiritual, and social living. In the process, though, we have too often handed over control to power-driven egos that have abandoned or corrupted our good intentions and actually made things worse. We're all to blame—those who've made it happen, those who've watched it happen, those who've stood by and wondered what happened, those who've been oblivious to everything that's happened, and those who just don't care what's happened—and we're all accountable, to one another and to our descendants!

Assuming that these institutions are looking out for our best interests, we have been eager to expand their size and influence; in fact, many are self-serving and ultimately dangerous. They become not only too big to fail, but also too big to succeed! Trust and credibility have become major problems, and any questions about their activities can lead to defensive and evasive answers, as all attempt to escape accountability. We are in desperate need of leaders with the relationship skills mentioned above; those who can bring people of all parties and cultures together in a spirit of unity and truth rather than add to a dispiriting polarization.

Perhaps that should be the primary role of a national executive, one with little polarizing political allegiance but excellent relationship skills. The United States rarely possesses such figures in its governmental structure, though at times various presidents have tried to fulfill the role. Outcomes have varied immensely, sometimes due to personality, sometimes to policy. Most recently, Presidents Kennedy and Reagan have been more of the unifying types of leader, while Nixon and Obama have been more polarizing.

The founders of our governmental system created a truly phenomenal structure, an arrangement based on eliminating the problems associated with monarchy and dictatorship and incorporating the capabilities they envisioned with an enlightened and educated middle class. But they also understood the concepts of need and greed that have invaded the minds of humans since creation, and so built into their model a process of checks and balances and separation of powers that would prevent any one governmental body from becoming too dominant. This careful planning was to ensure the safety and freedom of the entire population.

What they apparently didn't expect was the arrival on the scene of the "career politician." To our founders, governmental service was a duty, a sacred obligation that a few must endure in order to protect the freedom and stability of the many. They feared the entrenchment and longevity of government officials that might slowly replace the monarchies from which they had just escaped. In addition, while lawyers were commonly involved in the constitutional debates, legislative deliberations, and administrative decisions, and therefore expected to be frequent candidates for political offices, most of them had to give up lucrative private practices in order to serve their constituents. It's likely that most could hardly wait to get back home!

Over the decades, however, continuous political office at the state and national levels has become one of life's greatest perks for many attorneys. Armed with reams of minutely detailed legal information and legislative bills that they themselves create but which even their colleagues often cannot comprehend, they befuddle and confuse a trusting public with self-serving laws and regulations that ensure their power and multiply their wealth. Under such conditions, corruption thrives!

Meanwhile, that literate but naïve and gullible public continues to ingest their rhetoric and reelect those who sound or look the best, regardless of their actual substance. Moreover, we allow ourselves to be distracted and preoccupied by our material creations and to pay little attention to our government and our freedoms, as spontaneous in-the-street interviews often reflect. This inattentiveness opens the door for lobbyists and special interest groups, who then bombard elected officials with campaign contributions and support in exchange for legislation and regulations favorable to their causes but not necessarily to the public good.

Our two-party system provides us with very limited choices, which only compounds the problems. As polls tend to imply, if we were given an additional choice to vote no, that might be the favored response of many.

What alternatives do we have, other than legislator term limits or a limit on the number of lawyers that can participate in governmental bodies? Trial lawyers especially are trained in conflict, not cooperation, and have been instrumental in promoting their own self-interests with their objections to any workable system of tort reform. Getting a conviction or exoneration is the goal, and the process involves doing

287

whatever is necessary, and creating or using whatever loopholes are available in the fine print to reach that goal—morality, ethics, and common decency be damned!

In our two-party system of governance, it might seem a logical step to elect and appoint such attorneys to legislative and administrative offices, but to what end? Are they likely to discard the processes that defined their former occupational lives, or are they more likely to continue behaving in familiar ways that led to their judicial success? With the increased polarization of the general public, which they both reflect and encourage, providing them rocket fuel, little change in their behavior is likely.

In the manner they have evolved, legislative debates tend to resemble courtroom squabbles but without an impartial judge or jury to preserve order and determine outcomes. When these bodies are smaller and the stakes lesser, the consequences are endurable, and local government (much closer to the people) can still work well in spite of it. But when those who thrive on conflict are put in charge of a big government getting bigger by the year, with virtually unlimited financial resources available through high taxation and senseless borrowing, and with little accountability to the people who elect them, the results are quite predictable, leading to the oft-quoted phrase, "Washington is broken." Though such legal behavior may have served our court justice system well, putting foxes in charge of the hen house may not be the best use of their talents or of the public interest!

Can we realistically expect such politicians to suddenly become cooperative and seek innovative solutions acceptable to all? Can we realistically expect them to adopt smaller budgets, to give power back to states and localities and to put themselves out of a job that allows them to make up their own rules and legislate for all others while often exempting and empowering themselves? In spite of their comments to the contrary, the one goal to which they can all agree is reelection, continuing their quest for additional power. And how is their reelection most assured? By more conflict, by sabotaging the opposition with half-truths, full lies, innuendoes, insinuations, character assassinations, and other allegations and accusations that alert the voting public to the alleged disasters that await it, should voters put the opponent into office. Moreover, they are allowed to lie to the public about their intentions and promises without suffering legal consequences. But if we citizens lie to them, we are subject to lengthy incarceration!

Who's to blame for the dismal ratings and atrocious results achieved by our representatives year after year? Who else? We keep them in office despite their miserable performances and allow them special privileges and benefits, often far in excess of what is reasonable to most of us. A recent poll suggested that more than half of voters want them all thrown out of office, including their own representatives. But will that happen? Or will we continue to promote those who are best at conflict and rhetoric—those who are most successful at damaging and destroying their opponents—and then later complain because our representatives can't cooperate and find solutions?

What if we were to confront each candidate with an insistence on *demonstrating* his or her present thoughts and past behaviors concerning compassion, kindness, love, respect, empathy, and problem-solving cooperation with others who think differently from them? I suspect that such demands would leave many of them speechless, a rarity indeed for a politician, but aren't those reasonable qualifications for government leaders?

In the absence of finding a viable party candidate using such criteria, what if we inserted our own nominee, based not on stubborn ideology but rather on the desire and ability to seek out-of-the-box, innovative, and pragmatic solutions to local, national, and international issues—and then held this new representative to those standards, subject to certain recall at the next election?

The voting public is responsible for the present brokenness of Washington, and all of us must accept culpability. We feed their greed! The buck stops not with those elected, but rather with those who elect! Political oratory notwithstanding, there is very little accountability among our elected leaders and their bureaucratic partners because we don't expect it, we don't demand it, and we don't get it! Why is that? Could it be that it serves a useful purpose for us? If our government leaders do not model accountability, then do we not all have a built-in excuse to do likewise in our own daily activities? As a culture, does the failure of our government let us "off the hook?" Are we using government failures to justify our own inadequacies?

Why have I emphasized our political deficiencies? Because they are obvious and observable, and what we see there as a model filters down to our social, theological, financial, and educational systems. The more power and credibility we give to an institution such as the government, the more we tend to give to our other institutions, and the more we hand them control of our lives and our freedoms. Both politicians and constituents readily acknowledge the waste, greed, corruption, fraud, and general abuse of power present at all levels of government and society. We acknowledge—and then we accept and go on!

As if by cunning intention, more services and entitlements are offered and dispersed to favored constituents, creating an insatiable addiction that demands more of the same. Historically, Americans mentally revolt against heavy taxation, so the various governmental entities must borrow in order to nourish the addictions, creating debts that must eventually collapse on the bodies of future generations.

To feed bailouts and entitlements and to keep some semblance of order while doing so, institutions must then increase their bureaucracies and therefore their sizes and powers, creating even greater needs for borrowing and unsustainable debts, ultimately focusing on devastating taxes for everyone (including the job creators)—the very item that propelled our founders' desire for a revolution! Our forefathers and early citizens were understandably afraid of big government and created a system of smaller governments closer to the people's daily lives, where regular working townsfolk could monitor their development. Sadly, much of the world's history would seem to confirm what our founders understood well—that greater centralization of power is incompatible with personal freedom.

The increasing centralization of our educational system has followed that of the government, with similar results but different players and focus. For all its good intentions, the new Common Core curricula will likely take the control of education further away from state and local communities and in the process stretch and shrink student minds so they will all fit the same mold. Those who can't or won't comply will simply fail and morsels thrown to them by those in control will sustain their lives but also reinforce their feelings of insignificance. Viewing their lives as unimportant and insignificant, few will ever write personal stories, and their existence will fade into oblivion. The governmental, economic, and educational elitists will thus gain more and more power, while the rest of us join the ranks of "wondering what happened." Is this compassionless process what we want for our future?

The decline of religious influence may appear to be an exception, but churches operate on much the same principle. Historically, theological institutions have been very powerful entities, psychologically controlling lives and eroding spiritual freedoms with propaganda such as sin, judgment, atonement, and others, as previously discussed. As other theological and philosophical alternatives have gained credibility, though, and church attendance has diminished, so have its financial status, the number of clergy, and its power to influence the masses. As church size has lessened, so has its clout!

In some nations where the line between government and religion remains blurred, rigid institutional control by an authoritarian church-dominated government is still maintained and expanded. In nations where such religion is voluntary, however, its influence has fallen considerably, though church doctrine still controls the minds of many parishioners who remain closed to other possibilities.

At this point, let me convey to readers that I have never belonged to a political party nor spent a dime in support of one; nor am I currently a dedicated church-goer, though I have a strong belief in a Creator, and while my job career was in education and mental health, I admit to being more of a maverick to what I've seen and experienced in both venues. Aside from the short stories I've provided in part 2, much of this book conveys attitudes, beliefs, and concepts (ABCs) I've acquired or developed over a lifetime of experience and observation.

Living together as a species is no less difficult than living together as a family. The consequences of failure can be devastating in either case but more far-reaching when species-survival is at stake. My comments herein are based on what seems "logical" and "wise" to me, yet I am aware that these two terms can arise from totally different assumptions about life and lead to quite different conclusions about issues. Therefore, I always try to keep an open mind; I hope you do too. Perhaps this is where philosophy comes back into play. (For a more thorough understanding of how I view life, I refer you to appendix C.)

Raising Consciousness

We in America set cultural standards of achievement and conduct, and establish arbitrary levels on which we then apply comparison labels, all in the name of economic and social progress. We next create insensitive and impersonal institutions to monitor and regulate these standards but, with few exceptions, ignore the fraud and corruption that results from their lack of accountability.

Life, of course, is much more complicated than philosophical words can express. Applying any one philosophical approach in entirety to the many demands of modern living might be admirable but also foolhardy and possibly even dangerous. Mixing and matching to one's own personality might be illuminating and enlightening but also burdensome.

We need not apologize for this somewhat chaotic approach to life, for it describes us all, and exemplifies the trial-and-error aspect of life described in a previous chapter. Thus, by imitation and default we tend to develop a cultural lifestyle first and then justify it by picking and choosing options which nicely fit that image, rather than carefully assessing the possible consequences of our options and then choosing a lifestyle based on those deliberations. Unfortunately, many of our life decisions are therefore poorly chosen at a young age and lead to self-defeating behaviors, either in the short term or long term. Perhaps, by giving our conduct a bit more conscious attention as adults, we could replace or modify some of these behaviors toward more social- and self-enhancing ones, and thereby communicate encouraging messages to our descendants.

The ultimate goal is both unity and diversity, a partial paradox but an attainable result, as the history of our country has demonstrated, with fifty self-governing states becoming one nation and yet remaining fifty sovereign states. The only caveat in carrying out our purpose and goals as individuals and communities is that we not thwart or prevent others from doing likewise and that we harm no one in the process—obvious limitations that our country and the world have yet to overcome.

Many would say that the peaceful combination of unity and diversity is an impossible goal for societies to fully attain, but how do we know? Has it ever really been tried, except perhaps on a small scale by a few saints, humanitarians, and isolated communities? As previously mentioned, scientists have pointed out (see chapter 10), the existence of ancient civilizations where warring behaviors were unfamiliar and unutilized, lending credibility to the theory that the use of physical conflict to settle our differences may be a learned activity alien to our nature.

In accomplishing our basic purpose and goals, it is imperative that we pay close attention to morality, ethics, scientific research, and democratic values. Herein lies much difficulty, as each of these terms may be defined subjectively and interpreted differently. Yet this is clearly an attitude and belief issue, resolvable by open discussion and reframing.

For example, many have said that morality and ethics are tied in with religious principles and point to ancient manuscripts that teach those principles. Yet some of the most moral and ethical people I know are atheists or agnostics. In contrast, some of the least moral and ethical people pretend to be religious stalwarts. In fact, both morality and ethics may have more to do with common sense than religion when it is understood that self-interest and mutual interest are one and the same (i.e., caring, compassion, and cooperation for and with others seems to incur a boomerang effect!) How we treat others influences how they treat us. Golden Rule, anyone?

Unfortunately, the trends for freedom, individuality, and unity are moving in the wrong direction. Where basic freedoms are still intact, they are being slowly eroded through imposed governmental and social regulations, on the one hand, and the voluntary though unplanned and often unrecognized surrender of our ABCs to institutional control, on the other. With an emphasis on materialism and conformity, and the accompanying neglect of self-examination and inner essence, we have by default abandoned our individuality in favor of propaganda and influence doled out by educational institutions, economic factions, and special interest groups. Finally, we have shattered our chances for unity by staunchly adopting political ideologies that polarize and divide.

Restoring the Melting Pot

Can we turn it around? Our history says so. For over two hundred years, in spite of great odds against us, the United States has served as a model of democracy for the rest of the world by internally demonstrating how and how well diversity and unity can work together. The history of human existence shows that cultural similarity is the glue that holds specific groups of people together. Yet our nation developed into a mighty force by abandoning this notion and inviting into our midst the often oppositional dregs of the world—the misfits, the poor, the daydreamers, the despised, the lazy adventurers, the uneducated, and rebels from all corners. Our ancestors spoke many different languages and respected a myriad of cultural traditions and religious activities. It worked because there was a unity of purpose— to establish a society based on freedom, open-mindedness, and peace where all citizens could pursue happiness and prosperity.

As we know, the process for getting there was neither peaceful nor tranquil, and occasional internal and external wars resulted. But we persisted and became the world's great "melting pot." Despite our vast differences, we are all Americans! But the fire under the pot has cooled, and the ingredients have begun to solidify into hardened morsels of ideology and multiculturalism. We need to reignite the fire; to once again show the world how to live peacefully and productively on a shrinking planet where nearly instant communication and travel now prevail alongside weapons of mass destruction possessed by many nations with countless agendas—a daunting task indeed!

A Model Still Worth Emulating?

How can we ask the world to put aside its petty arguments, its class warfare, its protective and aggressive agendas, its racial and ethnic disrespect, and its educational, theological, and cultural brainwashing if we can no longer internally model a more humane process ourselves? We are nothing more than hypocrites if we preach workable solutions but practice uncompromising ideologies. We must solve the trust issues within our own country before we can market such influence abroad. We must cease using protection from our international enemies as justification for disregarding attention to our internal enemies—ourselves!

The credibility of our own institutions is at an all-time low, beginning with all three branches of our federal government. Each branch is becoming less and less trustworthy and more and more suspect, with little accountability amid much waste, corruption, and fraud. Lies and half-truths have become the norm, and each branch interprets its constitutional authority so broadly as to begin infringing on the other two, all in the name of acquiring more power. We are in grave danger of losing those characteristics that once enthralled the world.

Churches are losing their moral power, and schools at all levels their community standing amid scandals and distrust of motives. Few institutional bodies have escaped unscathed, as greedy and power-hungry groups and individuals take advantage of opportunities afforded by the lack of public oversight and the naïve optimism of decent citizens who want to believe the best about those with whom they have entrusted their social, financial, occupational, theological, educational, and governmental lives.

Revisiting Our Greatness

Readers may wonder how parts of this book fit into my major theme of imploring people of all ages, in all circumstances and conditions, to write stories about their lives, so I will try to summarize the main points.

History books can provide only generalized data and are subject to the framing and interpretation of their authors. Such books are by nature biased in both content and analysis and can convey only abbreviated versions of life and culture, typically ignoring the contributions of people and events outside the mainstream of the dominant society. Specific villages, towns, hamlets, inner cities, and rural communities get very little coverage and acknowledgement and yet are fundamental pieces of planetary existence and development.

Without the stories of their inhabitants, our descendants will be missing significant slices of history upon which to build their lives.

Due to tradition, habit, opportunity, literacy, cultural programming, and lack of technology, few of our ancestors revealed personal stories. But times have changed, and these obstacles no longer remain—except the ones we have encrypted in our minds.

My goal is to motivate every person on earth, now and in the future, to leave behind stories of the life each has led. The greatest obstacle for all is the common view of personal insignificance and impotence, and the temptation and tendency to leave the transmission of our lives and culture to chance, or to the leaders, groups, and institutions that we have tacitly or consciously empowered.

Our founders realized that the human ego could not be trusted, individually or collectivity, and so set up a governmental system of checks and balances to counteract it. They also left to more local governments (individual states) all powers not exclusively needed for the protection of essential freedoms and rights of all citizens. Their experiences with monarchies and dictatorships pointed out the dangers of a powerful centralized government and demanded extreme caution.

Have we forgotten those lessons? In our concentration on material success and ambition, have we become oblivious to the danger of giving up our individual power? Are we falling prey to the prophecy sometimes attributed to the democratic process and contained in the sentence once attributed to former New York City mayor Ed Koch, "The voters have spoken; now they must be punished"? We cannot leave our history to those who might twist it toward their own selfish gains. That would be totally unfair and unhelpful to our descendants.

No one has lived the life of anyone else. No one has exclusive proof of how life should be lived. No one knows life except as she or he has lived and interpreted it. Nor should anyone assume that his or her honest thoughts and conclusions about life are wrong. Therefore, no one's life should be defined by phrases beginning, "I am just a ..." Everyone has value and purpose, and each of us has contributed input to the mysteries of life, most in ways we do not realize or understand.

We must continue to search for answers but also ask many more questions. There are no certainties (some even believe that life itself is an illusion), for certainty requires absolute proof, but evidence is not proof, and belief is not truth! Those who thrive on solving problems once and for all may find such thoughts depressing, but they needn't be. A bit of mental reframing is all that's required. According to Jesus, the teacher, life is a process to be lived more abundantly. We may differ in the interpretation of that process, but it is clearly a message of uplifting movement, not aggression, inactivity, or paralysis.

We can continue to pursue proof and truth in our own lives, while respecting and accepting the efforts of others to do the same. Scientific methods of inquiry may lead to some of the answers we seek, but science cannot answer all of our questions about life. Most may never be answered with certainty, but we can't even be certain of that!

Perhaps the most we can do presently is to consider issues and ponder questions about our attitudes, beliefs, and concepts as we've experienced life, absorbed ideas and internalized philosophies. Among these deliberations should be the debatable wisdom of relying on impersonal and soulless institutions to control or unduly influence what we think and express.

What remains is to document with life stories our ongoing thoughts and conclusions as they have affected our lives, including how we have come to believe as we do, and then to make provisions for safeguarding those stories for our descendants. Suggestions about what types of stories to tell and how to tell them have been detailed in preceding chapters.

Do We Need a New US Constitution?

Our forefathers drafted the Constitution at the end of the eighteenth century when the skies were for birds, not missiles; land transportation relied on horses, not automobiles; communication was by letter, not cell phone texting; shipping was done by sailing vessels, not powered freighters. In addition, land was plentiful; the number of potential states was small, with each one separate and autonomous; longevity was rare; and population was sparse. By comparison, the speed and complexity of life today is unfathomable.

Though the amount and degree of long-term change could not have been foreseen, that significant change would occur was obvious to those initial visionaries. So they developed a very flexible document, one with checks and balances, a division of power, and citizen rights that could be modified only by a long, drawn-out process. These precautions were, of course, a reaction to the monarchies and totalitarian governments that had plagued the world for centuries and from which most inhabitants or their ancestors had fled. Individual freedom was indeed a very sensitive issue and commanded the attention of every citizen.

While frequent references to the Constitution are still standard ploys of politicians in all parties, seldom are they more than ideological interpretations designed to back up positions already held. Oaths of office to follow the Constitution have become only pomp and ceremony, with the hand-on-Bible assurances soothing a citizenry that wants to believe the best about our leaders but is resigned to accept far less.

Ideally, the legislative branch makes the laws, the executive branch enforces the laws, and the judicial branch unbiasedly interprets the laws as envisioned by the framers. But 225 years later, only the most optimistic or delusional see more than a mockery of that intent. Currently, our legislators are rapidly becoming impotent, our executives tyrannical, and our judges partisan. Congress is a battleground where opponents justify their positions by fighting among themselves, calling one another names, and making absurd accusations, thus nullifying any decency that might otherwise exist. Administrators ignore laws they don't like and refuse to enforce them; then they make up or modify laws that fit their ideology and call them "regulations." Meanwhile, judges—with long-term or life-term positions—are beholden to whatever political ideology put them in office, and their legal opinions suggest dogma more than thoughtful reflection.

Since its inception, the Constitution has developed a heavenly aura, specific enough to permit governmental stability but vague enough to allow for needed modifications to an unknown future. Still, it was written for a very snail-paced culture and may not be appropriate for our rocket-paced society. Updating can only go so far; eventually technological systems must be totally scrapped to make way for massive changes. So it may be with governing! Politics has reached a point where the Constitution is being maneuvered, manipulated, and "used"—not followed. Where its vagueness and flexibility were once a plus, its ambiguity and elasticity have allowed it to become a political weapon for any person or any group that wishes to impose its will on an innocent or unsuspecting population. The Constitution is no longer the safety net as originally intended for a citizenry that feared tyranny; rather it has become a means to justify the actions of most any power-seeking group—conservative, liberal, or progressive.

We cannot depend on change from those who benefit from the present situation, for it is padding their minds and pocketbooks. The more that politicians fight for their own ideas of governing, the more they get elected or appointed to office by those who have been persuaded to support their positions. As individuals, we want peace and tranquility, but as a nation we have bought into Darwin's philosophy of "survival of the fittest." "Might" may not make "right," but it certainly does resolve the issue of dominance and control. We may be tired of wars that end in physical death and bloodshed, but we merely substitute wars of mental and psychological mutilation. We continue to elect those people who do it best—and of course we continue to get the same results!

So how do we commoners change things? Certainly not by violence. Any attempts to mount an insurrection would be crushed by the world's greatest military force, controlled by the executive branch and intended to uphold the status quo. We could continue to elect different representatives until we find the best combination of decent legislators, executives, and judges, but that would likely take decades of trial-and-error; most politicians look the same from the outside, making it initially very difficult to separate the uniters from the dividers. We could promote a permanent uprising of civil disobedience but at an enormous cost to our economic and social stability, considering the polarization that already exists.

Still, freedom from government tyranny may be as powerful a motive among some today as it was against the British in the 1770s. As I'm writing this section (mid-April 2014), there is a standoff in Nevada between a cattle rancher who believes his grazing rights are being trampled and the Bureau of Land Management (BLM) attempting to enforce the law. Guns have been drawn and threats made; reports indicate that many other citizens (and even militia) have actively supported the rancher. The BLM has temporarily withdrawn and apparently may pursue the matter in court. Regardless of the outcome, it may ultimately take force to remove the rancher from use of the land. What will happen then? Will even more citizens come to the aid of the rancher, in spite of his ill-advised and politically incorrect social remarks following the confrontations? Will armed forces intervene? Will we have a "wild west shootout"—a new mini-Civil War?

Bear in mind that the British also had the law on their side, because the law was designed by the Parliament and enforced by the king. But freedom was deemed to be worth fighting and dying for; so in spite of legal ramifications, the colonists rebelled, and we owe our independence and freedom from British governmental tyranny to their sacrifices. Could the same thing happen today? What might the results be?

Perhaps our best bet would be to work within the present system and begin the process of transformation to a new, more modern Constitution and to additionally prepare our descendants by writing personal stories about experiences associated with the old one. Involvement is the key! If you disagree with my suggestions, write about it. Tell your descendants and even contemporaries. Believe in yourself. You have never been a "just a," nor will you ever be one, and you and I are all wiser than our minds. As Thomas Paine once wrote about his Revolutionary War era, "These are the times that try men's souls." We are again being put to the test, and we need everyone's input if we are to rise to the occasion.

Perhaps our initial thrust in beginning this process of a peaceful transition could be to draft a small group of enlightened leaders with neutral or balanced ideologies and open minds (itself a daunting task) whose mission would be to set up a *process* of establishing a new Constitutional Convention, expanding participation to include a vast array of citizen conditions and situations—from the homeless to the wealthy, from new immigrants to centuries-old families, from illiterates to intellectuals, from atheists to religious zealots, and from varying ethnic groups. In order to be effective, every new participant might need to be *continuously* acceptable to *each* of the already chosen, and the entire group might be provided only the necessities of life and housed at a location like Camp David until completing a new document, unanimously supported, which would then be presented to the entire population at a special referendum. This entire process could take years or even decades to complete and would require much deliberation, dedication, cooperation, compromise and sacrifice. Could it be done? Why not? Our forefathers did it with far fewer resources, and it's lasted for over two centuries.

Original Sin or Innate Goodness?

Throughout my comments I have made several references to the idea of original sin. I consider this belief to be a crucial but erroneous component of our existence and one perhaps most responsible for pessimism and negativity in the Christian world. Regardless of intent, the word "original" connotes that the core of our beings is sinful—evil, wicked, and immoral. No matter how some may wish to soften the implication, with that thought as our programmed basis of perceiving the world, how can we not think poorly of ourselves and not be suspicious and wary of others? In addition, it provides an excuse for bad behavior for those looking for justification.

Worst of all, our perception of being born sinful creates doubt as to our worthiness, even though the story of Adam and Eve in the Garden of Eden has long been considered a symbolic myth by most mainstream Christians. Still, the belief that we are all born "sinners" is echoed weekly in pulpits worldwide. It is certainly a useful concept for enhancing the power of the church, though not so helpful in boosting the self-esteem of parishioners. Through the promotion and conviction of guilt, followed by the certainty of retribution in the absence of acceptable atonement, the church maintains its clout and influence by convincing all who will listen that God is a judge whose primary purpose is to use the gavel on each of us.

The antidote to sin is to be "saved" by following the teachings of the church, even though both individual clergy and different denominations may vary in their interpretations and prescriptions for a "moral" life. The goal of all religions would seem to be to create positive change in both thoughts and behaviors, to be more pious or obedient according to a predetermined assumption of God's wishes— as set down by ancient manuscripts or manufactured theories. Does it work? Obviously, for those who commit themselves to that particular belief system. Then why doesn't everyone conform?

The simple answer is that everyone does conform to a belief system, but the systems differ, from total atheism or agnosticism to total commitment to a specific creed. Unfortunately, too many become thoroughly entrenched in their beliefs and intolerant of those who differ, often spilling over into the political designation of "radical." They become so convinced of their correctness that they translate their beliefs into living principles from which they will not budge, nullifying possibilities of respectful solutions through compromise or transcendence. Skeptics and fundamentalists can be equally radical in their certainty, and thus equally irascible in their entrenched rhetoric. Principles (ideologies) persist, but principals (the masses) suffer!

This lack of flexibility creates stalemates that promote anger, blame, retaliation and continued conflict, as comparison, competition, judgment, and righteousness trump love, unity, humility, and cooperation. Could that really be what the Creator intends, that we fight over Its nature and message and that the ones with the most eloquent speeches or most powerful weapons win, while the losers die or slink away into obscurity?

The concept of original sin provides a convenient cause of our misdeeds ("I can't help it; I was born that way") and suggests that we use massive amounts of energy to overcome that innate sinfulness. It lets us "off the hook" at the same time it creates an enormous lifetime burden of fighting among ourselves and within ourselves, thus promoting even more self-doubt, guilt, and sin in the form of judgmental behavior and violence. The focus becomes that of personal rehabilitation (interpreted in many different ways), with love and service to our neighbors a distant second. But even that runner-up status is confusing because of the Christian premise that we are "saved" by grace and not by deeds! So why should we pay any attention at all to our neighbors' plights? And yet we do!

When we listen to our hearts and not our institutions and dogmas, we are amazingly generous people, as evidenced by huge voluntary donations of time, energy, and money amid reports of ordinary people suddenly faced with difficult health, accident, and environmental troubles! Our ego minds may be weak, but our hearts are strong! Are those hearts the result of religious teachings, or perhaps some sort of innate spiritual core? We need only to note once again that many of the most generous and caring people in this world are not Christians, and many are atheists and agnostics. This is not to indicate that religious beliefs aren't helpful in our planetary struggles, only that they are not necessary.

I began this section with a criticism of the doctrine of original sin. This concept has been useful in some regards, but looking at our core as *original divinity* can lead to the same goals, without the unpleasant side effects and unintended consequences. Why be pessimistic and self-degrading when optimism and self-respect will accomplish the same results?

The concept of original sin assures equality in the sight of God (i.e., we are all sinners). But wouldn't original "divinity" accomplish the same goal but leave us feeling good about ourselves rather than bad? After all, aren't we all made in the image of God, say Christians? Why must we assume that there was some kind of a fall from grace perpetrated by the first mythical couple and from which no one can escape? Such masochism! Such sadism!

Even if we were born divine, did we not sinfully rebel against our good nature, some might say? How else can we explain the violent state of the world for perhaps thousands of years?

Could it be that primitive minds were unable to cope with the rigors of social living, that in an effort to live with others who had different looks, ideas, and characteristics, humans made some bad decisions in their trial-and-error methods? Perhaps what we now call "sin" has arisen from mistakes related to survival, the worst mistake being the mental creation of an enemy, followed by the concept of war and the ultimate destruction of that enemy, lending credibility to the contention that violence is not part of our nature but has been learned and passed down through the generations. Humans long ago found that war works—at least sometimes, in some ways, for a little while, when we win!

Perhaps, as populations grew, different people, different cultures, latched on to different ideas to cope with issues of survival. Desires for protection and ease of living could have led to development of the human ego, which protects but also isolates, generating even more suspicion and distrust. Might not the development of this human ego explain much of the evil that we see in the world today just as well as the doctrine of original sin? It would certainly put more potential control of a different outcome in our hands, if our evil ways were seen as bad choices rather than predetermined wickedness.

Some might say that, if it had not been for our fall from grace perpetrated by our human beginners, God's world would have remained perfect; but due to that original sin, all humanity is thus damaged forever. The only antidote is to recognize our evil flaws and fight against our sinful nature. Really? Sounds more like a case for intentional self-destruction! No wonder our stress levels are out of control.

Could it just be that those earlier generations made some bad choices in their efforts to survive? Perhaps we now need to make some better choices—to truly love, share, respect, and cooperate rather than hate, isolate, tolerate, and compete. Maybe we could regain that original divinity that we lost sight of long ago but that is hidden somewhere in our core.

Conscious change is essential. Our minds are key. Primitive as they remain in relation to their potential, they have grown in such capacity over the centuries that we are now able to correct many of the unfortunate mistakes made by our ancestors. The views we have of our selves and others will determine our degrees of success.

We can continue to believe in the badness of all, or we can begin to consider the greatness of each. Both views have consequences.

Some Final Thoughts

It has been my intention in this book to stimulate readers' thought processes, not to persuade or preach—except for one issue, to influence and encourage every individual in every location, every culture, every age, and every stage of life to recognize his/her value and significance; and to use an awareness of that importance to share with future generations whatever you may have learned about yourself, about life in all its simplicities and complexities, and about a world that they can never know except through your stories, the stories of their ancestor—you!

Some of my thoughts and ideas about issues such as theology, education, philosophy, and government may have seemed provocative and challenging, perhaps even offensive to some. If so, I urge you to somehow record your beliefs and objections so that future generations will have the benefits of your wisdom. Like all other humans, I can make no claim to omniscience or omnipotence. But I have a voice, and it matters; and so does yours. Separately, we can do little; but collectively our wisdom is truly invincible.

ABOUT THE AUTHOR

Raised in a small tourist village in northern New York State, where he has returned in retirement, Dr. Kendall spent thirty years educating professional counselors. His life experiences amid studies in history, genealogy, and gerontology, coupled with his belief in the innate wisdom of every individual, have inspired this writing.

Especially significant was his maternal great-grandmother's diary, written when she was a young mother in 1865, which stimulated his thinking about how little most of us know about our ancestors, aside from mundane vital statistics. The diary generated many unanswered questions but also led to his interest in the flip side of genealogy—looking forward to what we can provide for our descendants, rather than backward to what we didn't get from our ancestors.

Through transmission of our stories, each of us has the opportunity to be teachers to future generations, including the yet-to-be-born. Autobiographies are unnecessary and burdensome to most, but short stories, anecdotes, and vignettes are within everyone's reach. Life stories, experiences, and conclusions are unique to each individual, and we cannot know which ones might be helpful to a given descendant. Our task is only to provide them.

Dr. Kendall is a 1959 graduate of Cornell University with a major in government and a specialization in international relations. Following ten years as a high school teacher and school counselor, he obtained his doctorate from the University of Pittsburgh and spent the next thirty years as a professor in the graduate school Department of Counselor Education at the State University of New York at Brockport, complementing his teaching with a part-time private practice in personal and family counseling.

Cynthia, his wife of fifty-two years, is a retired vocal music teacher, and together they raised two entrepreneurial daughters.

Appendix A

Richard Cory

Whenever Richard Cory went down town,
We people on the pavement looked at him:
He was a gentleman from sole to crown,
Clean favored, and imperially slim.

And he was always quietly arrayed,
And he was always human when he talked;
But still he fluttered pulses when he said,
"Good-morning," and he glittered when he walked.

And he was rich—yes, richer than a king—
And admirably schooled in every grace:
In fine, we thought that he was everything
To make us wish that we were in his place.

So on we worked, and waited for the light,
And went without the meat, and cursed the bread;
And Richard Cory, one calm summer night,
Went home and put a bullet through his head.

Edwin Arlington Robinson
(1869–1935)

APPENDIX B

Excerpts from the 1865 diary of
Dorliska Dean Vincent
Transcribed by her great-grandson,
Dr. David A. Kendall,
in 1996
from the original diary handed down by his mother,
Grovene Vincent Kendall

Dorliska Dean was born in 1843 on a small family farm about a mile east of St. Lawrence Corners in the county of Jefferson in northern New York State. Her parents, Elihu and Phoebe Huntley Dean, are buried in the cemetery there. Nothing further is known about the heritage of either parent. Her father died when she was less than a year old, at which time he was sixty. She had at least one slightly older sister, whom she refers to in the diary as Alvira, or Vi, or Mrs. George Cuppernull. At the time of her birth, she also had an adult sister, married to Abram Jewett, and living in the town of LeRay, a few miles away. It is speculated that their mother, Phoebe, remarried to a member of the Pierce family after Elihu's death, as she refers often in the diary to "Mother and Father Pierce." A young girl, Nancy (probably a teenager), is cited as often coming to help out, and was likely a half sister born later to her mother. My mother (Grovene) remembers hearing about Aunt Nancy Patterson, who married a man from Brownville, New York, and is buried there. They had no children.

In August 1859, Dorliska married Wilbur John Vincent of Clayton, New York (born in 1840, son of Jinks (Jenks) Vincent and grandson of Samuel W. Vincent, (whose name is on the plaque on the fence of the Clayton Cemetery as one of its original directors). They were married in the Depauville (a nearby hamlet) Methodist Church and later became members of the Clayton Methodist Church, holding many church offices until their deaths.

Their entire family story is one of triumph and tragedy. They were married for sixty-four years. Wilbur died in 1923 and Dorliska died a year later. In August 1919, their sixtieth anniversary was written up in a large article in the Watertown (NY) *Daily Times*. They had six children but only one who gave them any heirs. At the time of this diary's writing, Dorliska was only twenty-two years old but had already lost a daughter in infancy in 1860. A son, Willie, was born to them in 1861 and is mentioned prominently in this diary. Sadly, both Willie and Polly Stevens Vincent, Dorliska's mother-in-law, died of diseases during this fateful year. Another son, Elmer, also mentioned, was born in 1864 and was to die in 1897 of a strangulated bowel, according to his obituary. He had married Jeannette Dodge in 1886, but they had no children. My grandfather, Will Vincent, was to be born three years after this diary was written—in 1868. He had four children, of which my mother (Grovene) was the youngest, born in 1913. Dorliska and Wilbur were to have two more children, born in the early 1880s, but both died in infancy.

Wilbur shipped out on the Great Lakes as a "horse boy" on a three-masted sailing vessel at the age of fourteen. A few years later he became a second mate, and, still later, a first mate. In 1873 he gained his first command and captained several cargo sailing ships until his retirement in 1896. He and his wife were parted from April until late November each year, from the time of their wedding until his retirement, making her a very lonely woman much of the time. This loneliness is reflected in the diary, as is her steamboat trip to Chicago in June of 1865 to visit Wilbur. This entire year was pivotal to America, as it included the end of the Civil War and the assassination of President Lincoln. Yet few of such historical events are mentioned except in passing.

Much attention is given in the diary to weather. Weather is little more than a short conversation piece in our world today, but in 1865 it was often a matter of life and death for a sailor and always a matter of convenience and inconvenience for everyone in Clayton.

Social visitations were a prominent part of life in Clayton, as reflected in the diary. Present descendants can recognize many surnames of old families. Social support was an important part of daily survival, as bad weather, sickness, poor communication, and loneliness were enemies common to all.

At the time of the writing of this diary, Dorliska and Wilbur lived on State Street, near the corner of Beecher Street. The Clayton village map of 1864 clearly shows their home, along with the home next door of Wilbur's father, Jenks. They purchased the land when they married in 1859 but moved to their home on Riverside Drive ten years later, shortly after Wilbur received a promotion to first mate. They lived in that home (turning it into a summer tourist home) until their deaths—at which time it was inherited by their son, Will, a newspaper printer in Carthage, New York, who died suddenly in 1930 from years of breathing in toxic fumes. The house could not be maintained properly after his death and was sold in the midst of the

Depression years; it was torn down sometime around 1970. The site is almost directly behind the Thousand Island Museum and is now used for private parking.

To my knowledge, this is the only diary that Dorliska ever wrote. At least, it is the only one that has survived. It has been transcribed exactly as written in the original version, with no changes to punctuation, capitalization, spelling, grammar, etc. The size of the diary was only three by four inches, and each line contained only one to five words, some of which were barely readable. I have donated a fully transcribed copy of this diary to the Thousand Island Museum in hopes that readers can understand a bit more of the history of life in this region around the time of the Civil War, some 150 years ago. It is not very comprehensive. It is quite sketchy. Many more questions arise in our minds—questions we wish she had answered for us.

The following excerpts represent a sampling—a taste—of the life and essence of a young woman from a little rural village on our northern border. For inclusion in this appendix these excerpts were selected a bit randomly, while still attempting to provide some variations that would offer clues to ongoing thoughts and activities. On occasion she cited some poetry and nostalgia; at other times her entries were quite pragmatic and routine; periods of joy and thankfulness were often followed closely by sickness and death. Like much of life in every generation, it was a time of both sadness and gladness.

For ease of comprehension I have bolded the date at the beginning of each month. Some months have many entries; some have one or none. Each entry had a rationale, however. I eliminated Dorliska's trip to Chicago to visit Wilbur during the month of June; I cited almost no entries during the pleasant summer months of July, August, and September. But during February her beloved mother-in-law passed away; April noted Lincoln's assassination; the last three months of the year showed the slow demise of her four-year-old son and her reaction to his death. (Anyone visiting the Thousand Island area can view the entire diary at the Thousand Island Museum in Clayton, New York.)

Fast-forward a few hundred years, when many of our descendants will want similar information about our lives. We can anticipate their questions and take responsibility to write journals or our own personal histories and stories so they will know us in the way we would have liked to know Dorliska's generation.

Sunday, January 1, 1865
At home all day
good sleighing
and a happy
New Year

Wednesday, January 4
At home until
Evening then went
to Colons to
Ayotes party got
home at one
o'clock Mrs Hudson
here a sewing

Thursday, January 19
Pleasent in
The morning snow
ing in the afternoon
Mable Estes & Orin
Stephens and wife
in after noon
and Evening

Friday, January 20
At home all day
warm and pleasent
Father and Mother
Pierce here

Wednesday, January 25
Pleasent in
A M snowing and
Blowing in P M
Father and Mother
Vincent here to
dinner

Monday, January 30
Cold and Pleasant
at home washing
Mother Vincent
taken sick in
afternoon

Thursday, February 2
Warm and pleasent
at home all day
Alvira Cuppernall
here in the
afternoon Mrs John
Boyd in Evening

Saturday, February 4
Warm and raining
all day at home
Capt. Randle
and wife here
stays all night

It is sweet to
be remembered. When
we are far away
we are often led to
thin of those we left behind

Sunday, February 5
Pleasent at home
all day Willie very
sick Capt Randle
and wife here
and Dr Ellis Mrs
Andrews Mrs Hudson
her in afternoon

Thursday, February 9
Clear and pleasent
At home all day
Father and Mother
Pierce here stays
all night Mother
Vincent very low

Wednesday, February 15
pleasent all
day at home
house full all
day Mother Vincent
dies at 7 o'clock
in evening
Elmer sick

Friday, February 17
Clear and pleasent
all day Atends
Mother Vincents
funerel Father
and Mother Pierce
and Nancy here

Thursday, February 23
Warm and pleasant
at home all day
Mrs Hudson
Mrs Andrews &
Angeline Chesbro
here Giles Chesbro
comes home on
furlough

Friday, February 24
At home all day
Pleasant Dr. Cline
called on me
had a sore throat
Marelin Colon
here and
Mrs Chesbro

Tuesday, March 21
At home all day
warm and pleasent
Wilber goes to

321

Watertown in stage
Myron Gotham
and wife here
visiting had a
preasent of
photograph of
Myron and wife

Friday, March 24
Warm and pleasent
Went to Mr Buskirk
to see Jesse Buskirk
Just got out of
the Rebel Prison
found him sick
Mr. Eddy Mrs Wheeler
and Mrs Little thare
Mrs Wheeler called
on me in afternoon

Saturday, March 25
Mild and pleasent
called to Mrs Bell
vills Wilber gets
home from Water
town in afternoon

Remember well and
bare in mind that
a true friend is hard
to find and when

you find one just
and true change not
an old one for a new

Dorliska

Friday, March 31
All well at home
all day went
up to Buskirks
in the evening
to see Jesse found
him a very little
Better Marelin
Colon here to
tea Pleasant and
warm as summer

Tuesday, April 4
Pleasent at
home all day
Angeline Chesbro
her was taken
sick called Dr
Cline in Mrs
Chesbro here in
afternoon takes
Angeline home with
her Dr Cline here
to tea went to
Mrs Bellvills in

evening set out
onions and sowed
lettice in afternoon
raining at 10
in evening

Thursday, April 6
At home all day
raining a little
All well Wilber
down town brings
me home a new dress

Monday, April 10
Snowing and rain
Ing all day Wilber
started for Chacigo
i went to Mrs
Meoys in morning
and found her
a little better then
i went to Mr Leama
ns found him
sick Mrs Johnston
here in afternoon Willie
hurt his eye in
afternoon and sick
in evening

Friday, April 14
Pleasent Willie and

i very sick a call
from Dr Ellis in
morning Mrs Johnston
her to sit up with
me commenced weaning
Elmer

The Presiden shot
To day

Saturday, April 15
Pleasent in
morning raining
in afternoon
Father Pierce
and Alvira
here Dr Ellis her
in evening
found me wors
very sick all
night Mariah
William here
and sits up
with me all
night

Presadent Lincoln
Died at 9 1/2 oclock

Monday, April 17
Calm and Pleasent

323

as a summer day
The birds are warbling
their sweetest notes
it seams almost
to delight full to stay
in the house but oh how
i thank our heavenly
Father for the very
many blessings he
deeply bestows on
we unworthy children
i am feeling better to
day hoping soon to
be about again

Thursday, April 20
The wind is
Blowing furiously
and the rain
beats down in
torents and i am
very lonly Nancy
and I here alone
all day a company
of soldiers arrives
in town to
guard the lines
Received 2 papers
from husband

Friday, April 21
Raining all day
at home all day
very lonley and
oh Wilber if you
was always near
time would pass
off lightly but
without you the
days are long and
dreary Mrs Johnston
called in this
afternoon

Monday, April 24
Wind from the west
blowing hard all
day but Pleasent
went over to
Orin Stephens found
ther child died
Then went down
town all well
at home

Sunday, May 14
Raining a little
all day went up
to Mr Buskirks
in AM called to
Mrs Johnsons she

come home with
me and stayd
untill after tea
All well but lone
somehow I wish
you was her with
me how happy I should
be Wilber Jinks
told me he was
a going to be married

Tuesday, May 16
Cloudy in a m clear
in P M Jinks
went away to the
Cape Vincent and
got married I went
to George Cuppernulls
in A m in P M
went to Clarre Menno
in evening down
town Mrs Johnston
and I called to
Mrs Bows got home
in evening Abby
Buskirks here

Thursday, May 25
Pleasent and still
in morning went
to bord of the

propeller buckie
bond for Chigago
at 6 oclock in
morning in comepany
with Mrs randall
had a pleasant time

Tuesday, June 13
In chicago
unloading wood
raining hard
about all day
All well My Birth
Day

Friday, June 30
Pleasent and
warm got under
the exchange
elavator about
10 A M all well
on board at
6 in evening
started to
come home
on Ny central
rairrode
raining in
the morning

Wednesday, August 30

warm and bright
At home all day
All well and
I thank my
heavenly father
for his many
blessing and
for health which
is the richest
boon of heaven
willie down
to spend the
day with his
grandpa

Wednesday, September 6

Raining in
the morning
Pleasent the
rest of the day
at home all
day went up
to Mrs Johnson
to tea down
town in
the evening
Willie received
a horse his
pa sent him

Tuesday, October 10

Pleasent and
warm willie
taken sick
in morning
very sick all
day a call from
Dr Cline in
the evening
Mrs Johnson
stayd all
night with
me

Monday, October 16
Pleasent and cold
Mary Vincent and
Amy here Dr Cline
here in morning
Elis here in
afternoon willie
broke out with
scarlet fever
Elvira Cuppernull
here in afternoon
Mary stayd all
night and sat
up

Friday, October 27
wind a blowing

from the north
the snow a flying
and things look
dreary not a
leaf has left the
trees scarcely and
I am very disconsolat
thinking of an
absent one who
is crosing the
mad and dashing
wave Mariah and
I alone Mariah
went home about
noon

Sunday, October 29
Pleasent in
the morning wind
from west
cloudy in the
afternoon at
home and alone
all day writing
to my husband
the leavs are
falling from
the trees and
evry things tells
us that we

like summer
are Passing
away

Thursday, November 2
flying clouds
and windy
from the west
willie better but
Elmer very sick
Mrs bellvill calld
Mariah here
a while in
the evening
I waining and
watching for
a letter from
my dear husband
but it does
not come

Wednesday, November 8
Pleasent in
morning cloudy
in the evening
to mother
Pierces willie
very lame

Wednesday, November 15
very mild and

pleasant At Mas
all day Wilber
got home at
7 in the
evening all
well but willie
he stills grows
lamer very
glad to see his
papa

the afternoon
come home
willie in quite
good spirits
all enjoying
our selfs
in hopes
he would
soon be
better

Friday, November 17
warm and
pleasant wind
blowing hard
from the
west Jinks
here in afternoon
willie about the
same and I
thank my heavenly
father thus far
for sparing
my little
darling to me
thus far

Tuesday, November 21
Raining in
the morning
snowin in
the evening
willie about
the same
Sits in his
little chair
or lays in
his crib all
the time
but plays
with his play
things and
little brother

Sunday, November 19
raining in
the morning
pleasant in

Thursday, November 23
showery all
day all the

same as before
washed my
white clothes
willies birth
day

Wednesday, November 29
Pleasent all day
willie the same
altho me think
he fails slowly
Willber goes after
the doctor Ellis

Friday, December 1
Pleasent all day
willie the same
medicens works
well and he
seams some
better great
hopes of his
recoverys

Tuesday, December 5
Bright and pleasent
but my little
darlings spirit took
its flight to that
better land that
no travler everreturns

from taken wors at
½ past 4 breathed
his last at ½ past 5
he died like going to
sleep kissed me and
told me he loved me
to the last Ma and
vie and many other
friends come but
could not restore
to me my darling boy

Wednesday, December 6
Bright and pleasent
to others to this
houshold dark and
gloomy the funrel
at 1 oclock atended
by elder spencer
took my last
leaf of willie
he was beautiful
in death but he
is gon and i
am desolate

Thursday, December 7
Pleasent but
cold Ma went
home Mariah
Williams come

here to stay with
me went up
to Mrs Johnson
in the afternoon
it is Thanksgiving
giving but a
sad one to
me yet i am
thankful to
be spared to
seek pardon of
any sins that I
may meet willie
in heaven

Sunday, December 10
Pleasent at home
all day very lonely
but I do thank
god for his many
blessings though
i feel the loss
of my child much
though I know
that god doeth
all things well

Monday, December 11
Pleasent but
sloppy under
foot went up

to Georg Cuppernll
went to visit
willies grave

Wednesday, December 13
Pleasent and cold
Wilber helped George
again Mariah
come thare
about noon
went again to
visit willies
grave

Tuesday, December 19
Snowing and
blowing hard
all day Marelin
Colon here
rainy in afternoon
feeling very
bad all day
thinging of
my angell
baby

Sunday, December 24
Snowing very
hard all day
at home all
day and a

very lonely day
to me though
many are
enjoying it
in hope of a
mery christmus
but I am
thinking that since
last christmas
two very dear ones
have bin taken
from me

Monday, December 25
It is pleasent
out but very
sad is my heart
Thinking of my
little one who
has gon from
me never to return
frinds are around
me endevering
by their kind
voices to make
me mery Maryett
colon here and Marelin
vie and George and
Mary I go down
to the church

presens from frinds

Tuesday, December 26
Pleasent in the
morning went
up to George
Cuppernulls
stays all night
again I visit
my little boys
grave again I
grieve over the
providence
that has brought
this bereasment
about but know
that all must
be well God
gave and he has
taken away

Wednesday, December 27
(her final entry)
Raining very hard
in Am clears
off bright about
4 in P M come
home from Georges
at 4 oclock
Willber gon down
town and

I am alone
with my thoughts
and little
Elmer

Appendix C

How Do I View Life?

Throughout this writing I have given many clues about the meaning that life has for me. I have tried to do so in a manner that reflects both my personal fallibility and the respect I have for other viewpoints, however different they may be. Some may see many of my uncertainties as a lack of faith, but they would be mistaken. My basic beliefs about creation are nearly unshakable; but the purpose of our creation, the best means of thanking our Creator and the most effective pathways to carrying out our functions on earth are not yet fully known. I only know that we humans continue to demonstrate much ability and many talents and that much more is in the tank!

As noted many times in this book, I believe in the existence of a benevolent Creator and that each of us descends from that Creator in the same way that a child descends from the parents. (As with Jesus, our earthly human parents are merely conduits.) As such, we are also innately endowed with many of the same attributes as the Creator, including the capacity for love and free will, embedded in an intangible characteristic that could be labeled "spirit." There may be only one Creator, but there are many creations living together on this planet; already there are several billion at one time. That poses an extra problem—how to function without getting in each other's way!

So apparently we have been given another attribute to keep us from getting overwhelmed and lost, one whose primary function is self-preservation. Perhaps the most common term for that universal quality is "ego"—one of the words used by Freud to depict each person's identity. The ego is in charge of socialization, of relating to others, of assuring that our physical, mental, and emotional attributes remain intact and enhanced in the presence of others. The ego is a catalyst that drives and motivates our movements, makes decisions, and preserves our existence. The ego is *at* the controls of our life, but not necessarily *in* control of the outcome. Quite often it uses the autopilot or cruise control button and makes decisions without much thought, in a habitual or predetermined fashion.

The ego decides how and how much our inborn spirit will be used and is often conflicted by two intangible appendages that Freud described as the id and the superego—both concerned with self-enhancement, but the former indifferent to morals and ethics and the latter serving as a moral conscience. Much of the ego's life is devoted to resolving conflicts between these opposing forces that show up on a daily basis.

When the ego gets overwhelmed and depressed by this enormous responsibility, it can abandon its self-preservation goal and resort to extreme self-defeating behavior, as in homicide or suicide. But it can also call on its inborn spirit for help and can even reframe its mission by deciding to sacrifice itself in order to save others. Most of the time, however, the ego "plays it safe"—choosing to take small risks while wishing for big payoffs.

Of course, the Creator can override all decisions and all outcomes; when these overrides accompany events to our liking, we often call

334

them "miracles." Why these miracles occur when they do is pure speculation, though some scientific studies (and many anecdotal accounts) have suggested that prayer, especially the collective prayers of many, may have an effect. As children of the Creator we too may have the ability to perform miracles. Jesus may have been one of a few to access that ability, which may be part of the 90 percent of our mental capacity that most of us have yet to discover.

I have always struggled with the concept of a "soul"—a term common to some religious beliefs, but also confusing. Christians, for example, view the soul as some entity to be "saved," ostensibly to be returned to the Creator in some place called "heaven." Could the soul be where ego meets spirit, where earthly presence meets heavenly promise, where mortal survival meets divine infinity? Could the soul be our *essence*, developed by blending our inborn spirit and self-preservation characteristics as encased in the ego?

Could the soul be the result of individuals creating, organizing, combining, and exhibiting their behaviors, thoughts, and emotions over a lifetime? Is that our essence? Is that what we want to save? If so, how does it get saved, and where does it go? I cannot imagine a loving and benevolent Creator establishing for anyone a destination called "hell," so being saved from hell makes no sense to me. Because we humans have created much hell for ourselves on earth, many project damnation as a likely destination for those who offend our perceptions of God or disobey His assumed laws (or our manufactured ones?). But no form of eternal hell exists in my thinking. We make our own living hell and the only way to escape it is to die! We don't "go to hell" when we die; we merely leave the only hell there is! The Creator may give us an "Incomplete" in some phase of our existence, but it seems likely that the worst scenario is to be recycled until we "get it right." Thus, I view evil as entirely a man-made phenomenon.

If my reasoning has any merit (and it may not), with earthly death the ego has no more function and dissolves, while the (holy) spirit returns to its source, the Master Creator. The soul (if there even *is* such an entity) may then go to a final resting place (heaven?), or to another galaxy or universe (for another assignment?), or it may re-emerge in a different way through some sort of energy transformation (i.e., reincarnation?). A number of near-death and out-of-body experiences have reported enough variations to make most any outcome of earthly death possible. Since it appears that we are composed of energy, perhaps we cannot be destroyed, only modified. So why sweat it! Rather than fear death and avoid such discussion, we could be eagerly awaiting the next adventure (while continuing to make the most of this one), anxious to serve our Creator in an exciting new way. We may even create a new soul in our next life; in fact, the numerous formatting of a new soul or modifications of an old one may be our ultimate creative project.

In chapter 9, I discussed my thoughts on several basic philosophical ideas and will now attempt to blend them with my above-stated view of life.

I am first and foremost a pragmatist, interested in finding practical solutions to life issues. I don't pretend to know why we exist, only that we do, and that by accident or a superior Intelligence we have apparently been endowed with physical, mental, and spiritual capabilities and the power to choose how to use them. While it's possible that human species are accidents of some evolutionary inorganic space phenomenon, that likelihood seems improbable to me, though I must remain open to that option, should such truth ever be confirmed. For most pragmatists, "truth" is an ideal based on absolute proof that is unlikely to ever be found, though still worth pursuing since it brings us ever closer to our Source and/or solutions to issues of life.

In the meantime, my inner essence and outward observations convince me that all humans have an innate capacity for love and compassion, along with the capability to bond and band together to resolve all issues that might arise. Though we use relatively little of our innate abilities, we have been given all that we need! In the process of maturing and coping, however, we have developed egos based on fear and designed to protect us from one another, though the need for such protection is an illusion that people everywhere have turned into reality through our choices. These choices have sustained beliefs that conflicts and wars are normal and necessary for our survival and for the protection of our creations, be they moral, mortal, mechanical, or material.

We become so attached to those creations that soon they begin to control us and determine how we view our world. We then go to great lengths to protect and expand our creations, even to the point of enormous sacrifices of self and others, far beyond any reasonable assessment of the value of those creations. From there it is but a short journey to curtail or destroy the efforts of competing forces, "by hook or by crook."

According to Buddhists, we therefore create the evil that we see in our world by worshipping and defending those items to which we get attached. The answer, Buddhists say, is to renounce all attachments, to give up our obsession with these external illusions of life, to cease looking for happiness outside of our minds and bodies and to begin to concentrate on what really counts—acts of selflessness shown in our compassion and service to others.

Attachments do seem to be a problem in our culture, but only when they are jealously or zealously held. "Moderation in all things" is a cliché, but perhaps worth contemplating. As mentioned earlier, we humans seem to be all-or-nothing pendulum-swingers, a process that creates polarization and animosity. Our ABCs and corresponding behaviors, though, are choices over which we have control; we are the masters of our fate, and we reap what we sow.

Zen advocates going one step further in promoting positive actions by acknowledging what most of us recognize immediately. We talk too much! Oratory has too often replaced substance. We blame, distract, lie, confuse, and belabor with our words in efforts to protect and expand our attachments. Nowhere is this more evident than in the American political process. Unfortunately, the "bully pulpit" or "podium" not only dominates the governmental scene but also defines too many of our religious and educational institutions as well.

The purpose of life, as I see it, is to discover and use our endowed talents to the fullest, and to create a world of peace in which diversity can thrive amid an atmosphere of empathy and respect, covering all nations, all cultures, and all philosophies.

The Hindu emphasis is closest to my desire in this regard. Acceptance, not just tolerance, of religious diversity is a core principle. The concept of original sin is replaced with the belief that we create our own hell right here on earth. As with Buddhism, the pursuits of knowledge, enlightenment, and understanding are highlighted. Action, unity, and the mystery of existence are prominent themes, and there is a distinct lack of arrogance and righteousness. While life as we know it may end in earthly death, some form of existence continues, perhaps in another manner and another place. Whether a Universal Creator exists remains an unknown and, until some form of proof one way or the other is uncovered, we must assume that both are speculative but possible.

In general, ancient Chinese philosophy has many parallels to the Hindu point of view. As with most philosophies, variations exist in both location and interpretation, though core principles may be quite similar. Westerners must be careful not to confuse behaviors of the current Chinese government with the ancient philosophy that defines much of its culture and shows an appreciable respect for many different viewpoints on a given subject.

This approach mirrors my own in viewing humans as inherently good, while also noting that this goodness is vulnerable to conditions and circumstances that can overwhelm it and lead to misery and destruction. The development of the protective and comparative/competitive ego may be most responsible. In addition, educational, social, and governmental institutions—generated by the ego—foster values and thoughts that idealize material pleasures, the obsessive pursuit of which in turn undermines our endowed perfection. The prescriptive antidote to simplify our lives, limit our desires, abandon our excessive ambitions, and develop an attitude of gratefulness for what we have, is certainly worthy of attention in our fast-paced, stressful society. Virtue, morality, and social ethics are held in high esteem in Chinese culture, as is one's duty to family and community. These values vary considerably in America, though I fear the trend is in the other direction.

There is much to commend in this approach to life, which is closely allied to the principles that Jesus taught. (reference: *The Third Jesus*, by Deepak Chopra, 2008) Certainly, it can reduce the mental stress associated with the career- and status-climbing emphasis so evident in modern industrial nations. What's more, it induces a baseline of satisfaction with whatever life affords us. (Some might see this as self-limiting and undesirable, but it needn't be interpreted as decreasing our incentives. It can be reframed and reinterpreted to mean that life affords us whatever we work hard for and that we should be satisfied with the fruits of that labor rather than covet what our neighbor has.)

References

Ash, Mary Kay. 1981. *Mary Kay*. New York: Harper & Row.

_____. 1984. *Mark Kay on People Management*. New York: Warner Books.

_____. 1994. *Mary Kay: The Story of America's Most Dynamic Businesswoman*. New York: Wm. Morrow.

Braden, Gregg. 2009. *Fractal Time: The Secret of 2012 and a New World Age*. Carlsbad, CA: Hay House.

_____. 2011. *Deep Truth: Igniting the Memory of Our Origin, History, Destiny, and Fate*. Carlsbad, CA: Hay House.

Carkhuff, Robert R. 1969. *Helping & Human Relations, vol. 1: Selection and Training*. New York: Holt, Rinehart and Winston.

_____. 1969. *Helping & Human Relations, vol. 2: Practice and Research*. New York: Holt, Rinehart and Winston.

Chopra, Deepak. 2008. *The Third Jesus: The Christ We Cannot Ignore*. New York: Harmony Books.

Daniel, Lois. 1997. *How To Write Your Own Life Story: The Classic Guide for the Nonprofessional Writer.* 4th ed. Chicago: Chicago Review Press.

Dyer, Wayne W. 2004. *The Power of Intention: Learning to Co-create Your World Your Way.* Carlsbad, CA: Hay House.

————. 2006. *Inspiration: Your Ultimate Calling.* Carlsbad, CA: Hay House.

Foundation for Inner Peace. 1992. *A Course in Miracles* (2nd ed.) Mill Valley, CA: Foundation for Inner Peace.

Franco, Carol, and Kent Lineback. 2006 *The Legacy Guide: Capturing the Facts, Memories, and Meaning of Your Life.* New York: Tarcher/Penguin.

Frankl, Viktor. 1959. *Man's Search for Meaning.* Boston: Beacon Press.

Gilbert, G. M. 1947. *Nuremberg Diary.* New York: Farrar, Straus.

Goleman, Daniel. 1995. *Emotional Intelligence: Why It Can Matter More than IQ.* New York: Bantam Books.

Gould, William Blair. 1993. *Frankl: Life With Meaning.* Pacific Grove, CA: Brooks/Cole.

Haley, Alex. 1976. *Roots: The Saga of an American Family.* New York: Doubleday.

Hicks, Esther and Jerry. 2004. *Ask and It Is Given.* Carlsbad, CA: Hay House.

Jeffers, Susan. 1987. *Feel the Fear and Do It Anyway*. New York: Fawcett-Columbine.

Kaplan, Abraham. 1961. *The New World of Philosophy*. New York: Vintage Books.

Kendall, Robert D. 1995. *Communicating: A Pastor's Job*. St. Cloud, MN: Bobalu Publications.

Lipton, Bruce H., and Steve Bhaerman. 2009. *Spontaneous Evolution: Our Positive Future*. Carlsbad, CA: Hay House.

Maxwell, John C. 2003. *Thinking For a Change*. New York: Warner Business Books.

McTaggart, Lynne. 2007. *The Intention Experiment: Using Your Thoughts to Change Your Life and the World*. New York: Free Press.

Perls, Frederick. 1968. *Gestalt Therapy Verbatim*. LaFayette, CA: Real People Press.

Peterson, C., S. Maier, and M. E. P. Seligman. 1993. *Learned Helplessness: A Theory for the Age of Personal Control*. New York: Oxford.

Rosenbluth, Vera. 1990. *Keeping Family Stories Alive: A Creative Guide to Taping Your Family Life & Lore*. Point Roberts, WA: Hartley & Marks.

Rainer, Tristine. 1997. *Your Life as Story: Discovering the "New Autobiography" and Writing Memoir as Literature*. New York: Tarcher/Putnam.

Seligman, M. E. P. 1990. *Learned Optimism.* New York: Knopf.

_____. 1993. *What You Can Change & What You Can't: The Complete Guide to Successful Self-Improvement.* New York: Knopf.

Severy, Merle, ed. 1978. *Great Religions of the World.* Washington, DC: National Geographical Society.

Thomas, Frank P. 1984. *How to Write the Story of your Life.* Cincinnati: Writer's Digest Books.

Williamson, Marianne. 2008. *The Age of Miracles: Embracing the New Midlife.* Carlsbad, CA: Hay House.

Zaehner, R. C., ed. 1997. *Encyclopedia of the World's Religions.* New York: Barnes & Noble Books.